OUT OF THE OLD EARTH

Harry Heslop, 1934

HAROLD HESLOP
Out of the Old Earth

EDITED BY
ANDY CROFT & GRAEME RIGBY

BLOODAXE BOOKS

ISBN: 1 85224 152 7 hardback edition
        1 85224 153 5 paperback edition

First published 1994 by
Bloodaxe Books Ltd,
P.O. Box 1SN,
Newcastle upon Tyne NE99 1SN.

Bloodaxe Books Ltd acknowledges
the financial assistance of Northern Arts.

Cover printing by J. Thomson Colour Printers Ltd, Glasgow.

Printed in Great Britain by
The Alden Press, Osney Mead, Oxford.

Portrait of the artist as a young man.

Who Was Harry Heslop?

A few months before his death in 1986, the novelist Sid Chaplin came to Middlesbrough to read some of his wonderful stories of life in a Durham pit village before the War. As Sid talked about how he had started writing as a young miner in the late 1930s, he was asked who his early literary influences had been. Without hesitating he replied, 'D.H. Lawrence and Harold Heslop'.

Harry *who*? The quickest answer is to say: read this book. It is, after all, Harry Heslop's autobiography. But this isn't an ordinary autobiography. One of the first things you notice about this book is that it tells us almost nothing about Harry himself; he is one of its minor characters. Of his own childhood he tells us little, of his hopes and ambitions as a young man even less, and of his wife and children almost nothing at all. Harry hardly mentions his seven published books, says nothing about the very considerable critical and commercial success he enjoyed as a writer.

So why bother to read such an unhelpful autobiography? Many different readers will be moved by different parts of this book. The loving, damning picture of the mining village into which Harry was born at the turn of the century is extraordinarily rich and evocative writing – as good as anything by Sid Chaplin – the chapel and the pit, lay-preaching and socialism, 'clay ends' and 'grass ends', britching and mouse-pie, poss-tubs and poss-sticks, births and deaths. Although all but one of Harry's published novels were set in the Durham coalfield, with much of their action underground, he never wrote so well or in such careful and knowing detail about underground work as he does here. His account of his two years at the Central Labour College is unique; there are no comparable surviving accounts of an institution which helped shape the intellectual and political leadership of the trades union movement and the Labour Party for a generation. The sad testimony of his visit to the Soviet Union in 1930 stands apart from the many more famous books of enthusiasm written by celebrities making the pilgrimage to Moscow in the 1930s. And this working man's rather laconical view of that New Dawn underpins the story of his work for Intourist in the middle 1930s, seeing the great and the good on their way to Leningrad. Again, his eye-witness report on the Conference of International and Proletarian Writers in Kharkov in November 1930 is simply unique, a rich and irresistible picture of a society up-skittled by the terrible excitements and pressures of those years, writers and revolutionaries, prisoners and proletarians, giddy yet in deadly earnest, comradely and brutal all at the same time.

But we are still left with the question, 'who was Harry Heslop?' This introduction is an attempt to outline an 'alternative' life, to flesh out some of the bones of Harry's own story, to say some of the things which Harry was too modest and perhaps too sad, to say himself.

Harold Heslop was born on 1 October 1898 in the village of New Hunwick, near Bishop Auckland in County Durham, where his father William Heslop was overman at the local pit. His elder brother George started work in their colliery office at North Bitchburn, but Harry won a scholarship to King James I Grammar School in Bishop Auckland. When he was thirteen, his father was appointed manager of an ironstone mine at Boulby on the North Yorkshire coast. The nearest grammar school was at Guisborough, too far to walk, so at thirteen Harry began work underground at Boulby. Within a few months Isobel Heslop died bearing twins and his father remarried. Harry's younger brother Hector, clearly distressed by the death of their mother and the arrival of a stepmother, ran away from home. He was caught in Liverpool tearing seats out of a railway carriage, and certified by a doctor; he spent the rest of his life in a sanitorium in Sedgefield.

The family moved to Wylam and Harry to South Shields to live with a neighbour, Mrs Emily Gibson. For the next eleven years, with only a brief interruption towards the end of the First World War training with the 10th Royal Hussars, Harry worked at Harton colliery in South Shields. At sixteen he joined the Durham Miners Association and threw himself into the activities of the local Independent Labour Party.

He was soon elected Branch Secretary, busily inviting national speakers to visit South Shields. Among his surviving papers are refusals from Ramsay MacDonald, Sidney Webb, Philip Snowden, Charles Trevelyan and H.N. Brailsford; when Bertrand Russell agreed to speak in January 1922, he was told to look out for Harry on Newcastle station wearing a white (anti-war) rosette. In 1923 Harry was elected trades council delegate of his union lodge. These were revolutionary years, and tumultuous ones in the British coalfields. In 1919 the Miners Federation called for the withdrawal of British troops from the Soviet Union where they were supporting the Tsarist armies in the civil war there. The following year the Federation condemned the massacre by British troops at Amritsar, and called for the withdrawal of British troops from Ireland. In August Harry sent a telegram on behalf of his ILP branch to the King, protesting at the arrest of the mayor of Cork. In March 1920 the Miners' Federation tried to persuade the TUC general Council to consider a General Strike in support of the nationalisation of the mines. With the post-war economic recession, the cost of living was rising sharply, and the Miners' Federation submitted demands for wage increases, leading to the two week 'Datum Line' strike in October 1920 (described in Harry's novel, *The Gate of a Strange Field*). The following March the war-time controls on the coal industry were lifted by the Government, ending all existing terms of contract and permitting the coal-owners to introduce savage wage cuts, in some districts by as much as a half. On the same day a million miners were locked out by coal-owners and the Government declared a State of Emergency, sending the army into the coalfields. The Miners' Federation appealed to the 'Triple Alliance' (the transport and railway unions) for assistance, but were refused on 'Black Friday', 15 April. The coal-owners offered to end the lock-out on the basis of 'economic' wage levels; in a Federation ballot 70% voted to refuse these terms (77% in Durham). But by the beginning of July the levels of hardship were becoming unbearable and miners went back, defeated again (this lockout is also described in *The Gate of a Strange Field*). The average wage per shift was cut by a half to just 9s 6d and many miners' leaders were victimised. By December 1921 there were nearly two million unemployed in Britain – one in six of the total of insured workers; one in five miners were unemployed, and in some districts half the miners were without work.

In 1923 Harry applied for a Durham Miners Association Scholarship to study at the Central Labour College in Lon-

ABOVE: *Student days: Harry and Phyl on the right; Horace Morgan and Gwyneth (later Mrs Morgan); and Kaori Kinovhitsa.*

BELOW: *College students and staff, 1924-26: Harry on the ground, sitting right, next to Horace Morgan and Bert Williams; Phil Williams sitting inside left; Jack Lonsdale standing right, next but one to John McCutcheon; Alf Sparkes fourth from left in front row of sitters; Kaori Kinovhitsa second row, third from left.*

don. There were over a hundred candidates that year; after a preliminary exam forty were asked to sit another exam at the Miners' Hall, Durham, answering questions like 'Outline a case for the amalgamation of the county coalfield organisations in a single miners' union', 'What do you consider to be the most important reform necessary in the existing Compensation Law as it affects miners?' and 'How would you effectively deal with the non-union question?' Harry's answers earned him the highest marks and a place at the College. The Central Labour College had been formed by a breakaway group of students from Ruskin College in 1909, first in Oxford and then after 1911 in London's Earl's Court, under the aegis of the Plebs League and then of the National Council of Labour Colleges. Funded largely by the South Wales Miners Federation and the NUR until its closure in 1929, the College on Penywern Road provided an introduction to Marxist economics, politics and philosophy for young trade union activists. Through its doors passed many students who were later to distinguish themselves in British political life, including Nye Bevan (Labour Foreign Secretary), Ness Edwards (Labour Postmaster General), Morgan Phillips and A.L. Williams (both General Secretaries of the Labour Party), James Griffiths (Deputy Leader of the Labour Party), Bryn Roberts (General Secretary of the National Union of Corporation Workers, later NUPE), Frank Hodges and A.J. Cook (both General Secretaries of the Miners Federation of Great Britain) and Will Lawther (first President of the NUM). Fifteen of the Labour MPs elected in 1945 had been students at the Central Labour College (an estimated two-thirds had been either students or tutors for the NCLC). In Harry's year three students, Bert Williams, J. Sparkes and Phil Williams were later Labour MPs. While Harry was at the College he met Lewis Jones, another miner and a Communist from the Rhondda, also later a published novelist (*Cwmardy* and *We Live*).

Three things were to happen to Harry while he was at the College which were to change his life. First, Harry's grant from the DMA was approximately £90 a term (the average shift payment for a miner in 1924 was 10s 7^3/$_4$d, an annual income of just over £138 a year). With such wealth at his disposal he was soon smoking sixty cigarettes a day and ended up in Hammersmith Hospital with a diagnosed heart condition.

Second, while he was at the College Harry began work on a novel drawing on his experiences in the DMA. He sent it to

Harry as student, 1920s

Herbert Jenkins, a firm who had published a number of working-class writers like Patrick MacGill, James Welsh and Ethel Carnie Holdsworth. Jenkins rejected it, on the recommendation of three out of the five readers. But one of those who had liked the MS, a Mrs Rochelle Townsend, showed it to a friend of hers, Zina Vengerova-Minsky, who passed it to Ivan Maisky, then Secretary to the Soviet Legation in London. Maisky invited Harry to the Legation and offered to arrange for the novel to be published in the Soviet Union. In a translation by Zina, *Pod Vlastu Uglya* (eventually published in English as *Goaf*, but variously known for a while as *Under the Sway of Coal*, *The Wilderness of Toil* and *The Price of Coal*) was published with a preface by Maisky in September 1926 by Priboj of Leningrad:

> There is no more sinister death-trap in the earth than the goaf of the mine...The goaf is the home of a tremendous darkness – a darkness which is soundless as the uttermost depths of the sea. It is a most terrifying spectacle in a mine, and no miner, except when in the last extremities, will venture into the goaf for the distance of one yard. There is a superb dignity about the goaf. Nothing is more awe-inspiring, more fearful. It seems to stand at the edge of the coal with the gaping jaws of some immense hell, awaiting the intruder.

The novel describes the political struggles of Tom Drury, a young and militant miner and a member of the Minority Movement at 'Hunton' colliery in 'Shielding' in the county of 'Darlstone'. When he is elected Secretary of his union lodge, political rivalries are soon confused with personal ones and he leads a disastrous strike which leaves him facing criminal charges of incitement to riot, and 500 miners without work. At the end of the novel Tom is trapped after a roof-fall in the 'goaf' (the unsupported area behind the coal-face from which the coal has been extracted), contemplating the failure of all his hopes, the miners lost in the wilderness like the 'Children of Israel':

> Darkness, a sea of darkness, intense, horrible, a darkness that only a miner knows, that only a mine can produce, overwhelmed him. He was alone in the goaf. The lamp which he held in his hand was a useless thing, a mockery. The eyes search insistently for light and are fully conscious of the denial of light. But miners have to go on. Tom closed his eyes. Even then they did not rest. It was just the same as when he had them open. They still searched for the light. Closing them did not alleviate the pain of the darkness. The black pall seemed to become denser. It hurt him physically. When he opened his eyes they received no sensation of change. Open or closed, he saw nothing. All was black, without a star to lift the monotony of the heavy cloak.

Despite the novel's overwhelming sense of defeat, *Isvestia* liked it very much, enthusiastic about the picture of the 'mass struggle of the miners' and its concluding commitment to a socialist future. Within a few months it had sold over half a million copies.

Third, at the end of his first year at the College, Harry met a young ledger clark from Selfridges called Phyllis Varndell. She and her sister Dolly had been brought up in a strong Social Democratic Federation household, and they were often seen at the Saturday night dances at the College. The SDF was a revolutionary Marxist Party founded in 1883; in 1911 it became the British Socialist Party and in 1920 it dissolved itself along with other revolutionary groups to found the British Communist Party. Phyllis still recalls with pleasure the many family picnics, outings and dances organised by the local SDF; as a small girl she heard Sylvia Pankhurst at a Saturday night SDF dance at the Elephant and Castle. Years later Phyllis' mother would go leafleting for the Communist Party, though she never joined the Party. One of Phyllis's aunts was very friendly with a

Harry and Phyl's wedding, 27 March 1926

young and militant SDF member called Herbert Morrison, who often came to political meetings in her parents' kitchen; the affair never came to anything however, since her aunt said she wanted to marry a man who would 'get on' (Herbert Morrison, of course, went on to become Home Secretary). Phyllis' father Samuel was a caretaker and scene-shifter in the West End and a great one for the horses; every year he would go to Epsom and sleep under the hedgerows for the week. During the First World War Alice worked as a lorry-driver and Samuel served in the Army as a caterer, having swallowed a tablet of soap so that his weak heart would show up during his medical. Phyllis wanted to be a pupil teacher, but her parents separated when she was thirteen, and when her mother fell seriously ill, she left school to earn some money – just 15s a week. Harry and Phyl were married on 27 March 1926 at Brixton Registry Office and the reception was at Phyllis's mother's house, 24 Prince's Square, SE11, a stone's throw from the Oval. They lived there until the autumn, when Harry's time at the College came to an end.

Harry returned North to South Shields in October 1926, in time to see the miners defeated once again. The coal-owners wanted to impose a simultaneous wage cut (13% off the standard wage) and an extension of the working day, and when the Miners' Federation refused these new terms they found themselves again locked-out. After the failure of the General Strike in May (which Harry later described in *The Gate of a Strange Field*), the Miners' Federation struggled alone for six months. By then, however, poverty and starvation forced many men back to work and the coal-owners' terms (especially in Nottingham, where there was a breakaway 'Non Political' union). The Durham miners were the last to return to work at the end of November; even then in a county ballot, a majority were against returning to the longer hours and the shorter wages that were waiting for them. Phyllis still remembers the shock, when she joined Harry that month, of seeing the destitution to which the miners and their families had been reduced. When she arrived at Mrs Gibson's house she was offered a piece of pie – the only food in the whole house.

The management at Harton Colliery assumed Harry would take a clerical job at the office when he went back, but he refused, wanting to work underground with his old mates and eager to be involved in the life of the union. A few months

Harry and Phyl outside No.1 Gorse Avenue, Cleadon, South Shields, 1927

later Harry and Phyllis moved to 1 Gorse Avenue, Cleadon, South Shields. Harry threw himself into the DMA and into the Minority Movement there. The Minority Movement was founded in 1924 as a co-ordinating body for militant rank and file trade unionists with the declared aim of turning the British trades union movement away from 'class collaboration' and towards the 'overthrow of the capitalist system'. The first leadership of the Minority Movement were Tom Mann, Harry Pollitt and George Hardy, all members of the Communist Party. Harry wrote two penny pamphlets, *Who are Your Masters?* and *Who Are Your Masters Now?* – attacks on the anti-trade union sentiments of local newspapers owned by the Northern Press. He began writing for the *Miner*, a weekly penny paper published by the Miners' Federation until it closed in 1930. And within a few weeks of returning to South Shields Harry was leading NCLC classes in Marxism and Economics. At the end of 1926 a new Durham and District College was established with a winter programme of 18 classes in Marxism and Economics. In December they organised a day school at the DMA offices at Red Hills in Durham with J.F. Horrabin and John McCutcheon (who had gone with Harry from Durham to the Central Labour College and who was also to enjoy literary success in later life with *Troubled Seams* and *A Wearside Mining Story*). The following March there was an all-Durham NCLC conference addressed by Ellen Wilkinson (MP for Middlesbrough East) and J.P.M. Millar (General Secretary of the NCLC) with representatives attending from 129 local organisations. That Easter there were weekend schools at Wingate, Shotton and Wheatley Hill (led by Mark Starr, author of the celebrated *A Worker Looks at History*), Willington (led by Will Lawther), at Sunderland and at Newcastle led by Harry. Among the Labour Party candidates in the Municipal Elections in Wallsend in 1927 nine were NCLC students, while Harry, nominated by his union lodge, unsuccessfully contested the Shields Ward.

By November 1927 however the report of the activities of Division 9 of the NCLC admitted that the longer hours now worked by the miners in Durham were seriously affecting attendance at their classes. Worse, 'many of the more active spirits of the Durham College have had to leave the area owing to the position of the coalfield'. That month 900 men were made redundant at Harton colliery, including Harry. There were over a quarter of a million unemployed miners in Britain.

Harry and Phyllis moved back down to London in Easter 1928 to stay with her mother while he looked for work. He may have been a famous writer in the Soviet Union with a bank account in Leningrad full of roubles, but in London he was an unemployed miner (as there were of course no pits in London, he was classified as a 'general labourer'). He worked for six weeks at David Greig's bacon factory, shifting meat. Then he got a job as a general labourer at Waygood Otis Lifts; within a couple of months however he was hit by an overhead electrical cable; when he returned to work four weeks later, he found himself without a job. Then he worked for a few weeks sweeping up in an engineering factory. But for the next four years Harry was unemployed, receiving just 23s a week. So while Phyllis got a clerical job to pay the rent (which was one guinea a week), Harry sat down to begin writing in earnest.

Although he was contributing to *Plebs* (the monthly magazine of the NCLC), Harry was clearly disillusioned with the anti-Communism and anti-Sovietism of some of the NCLC intellectuals. He wrote a vituperative attack on Raymond Postgate, a mock obituary of one of the 'giants' of the NCLC. Postgate had left the Communist Party, Harry said, to 'retain his pure-white revolutionary soul', an opportunist and a turn-coat who now denied the gains of the Bolshevik Revolution and the achievements of the Soviet Union. Worse, for Harry, Postgate had recently minimised the contribution of Engels in a *Plebs* article and accused Marx of being incoherent. 'Marx not coherent! Not detailed! Not explicit! Not...My God! Surely the bones of this giant will continue to smell for many ages.' Not surprisingly *Plebs* declined to publish this piece, which duly appeared in 1928 in the *Communist*.

By now, Harry was writing for the Communist *Labour Monthly*, and reviewing for the *Worker*. This was the weekly paper of the Minority Movement until its demise in 1932, and edited by Bob Ellis, a Communist Party member whom Harry had met when they were students at the Labour College. Soon Harry was spending three days a week helping Bob Ellis produce the paper. Meanwhile he was working on a play about a mining village in Durham; althought the Haymarket Theatre showed some interest in the play, it was never performed. Harry had more luck with his next attempt, a novel about the General Strike. On 3 September 1928 he signed a contract with Brentano's. The next April *The Gate of a Strange Field* was published in a 7s. 6d. edition, dedicated to Phyllis. This was immediately followed by Soviet and American editions (in the US the novel was published by Appleton's).

It is the story of Joe Tarrant, leaving school at fourteen to work at Hunton Colliery in Shielding. He is elected Secretary of his union lodge and becomes entangled in its personal and political rivalries. Losing his belief in the Labour Party, and increasingly hostile to both the ILP and the NCLC, Joe's faith is restored in London in May 1926 where he witnesses the calling of the General Strike. 'Joe felt thrilled as never before. The spirit of the unseen world rose up before him to bid him be of good cheer. Hope began to penetrate into the deeps he knew so well. Now the Labour Movement would justify itself. The gauntlet was cast into the face of reaction. Let the worst come.' He returns to Darlstone to throw himself into the struggle there, to discover the betrayal of the miners by the TUC General Council in abandoning the General Strike after only nine days. 'Once again the miners were deserted, left upon the plains of industrial conflict, watching a band of leaders fleeing from the wind of their own rhetoric...Tot Johnson did the usual thing. He got drunk to celebrate a great defeat.' Joe has lost his faith, and now he loses his mistress; at the close of the novel he very nearly loses his life when the pit floods and he is trapped underground, watching the dark waters rise:

> The news of the disaster would be over the face of the earth by now. The newspaper people would be working at high pressure, telling the world the story. He could visualise the headlines. And the leading articles! Journalists would be flocking to Shielding. They would discover the old place. The irony of it all was the fact that it could have been prevented. And the women! And the children! The sufferers and bearers of the mines! The feet of women, children, men would all converge upon Hunton Colliery until a monstrous crowd had gathered. Over all would reign sorrow, the most abundant weed in the wilderness of the North. The parsons would be there too. He shuddered at the hypocrisy of the world. It could all have been prevented. The unseen waters would have remained unseen...But the cupidity of man, the stupidity of the rulers...

'This is an unusually moving novel,' announced the *Manchester Guardian*. 'His story is compelling, not only as a record of an individual life in the hardest circumstances, but as a revelation, at once critical and sympathetic, of the mining industry since the war, and of the human heroism, suffering and weakness involved'; the *Daily Herald* said the novel belonged to 'the finest class of realism in its plain and moving picture of life in the Northern coalfields'; while the *Northern Mail* regretted that the novel had not been available for the recent, much publicised visit of the Prince of Wales to Durham.

The month after the novel was published, there was a General Election. Harry Pollitt, recently elected General Secretary of the British Communist Party, decided to stand against Ramsay MacDonald in his safe Labour seat of Seaham Harbour, to 'raise the banner of independent working-class struggle against the three capitalist parties and to carry forward under the battle cry of class against class the revolutionary fight both inside and outside Parliament'. Pollitt wrote to Harry, asking him to help. Harry had been a member of the Communist Party, but (as he explained in a letter to Raji Palme Dutt later that year) 'owing to the extraordinary difficulty I have experienced in the matter of finance – I have been unemployed since 1927 – I could not possibly afford time and money to Party work…in these recent years I have been compelled to weigh every half-penny with extreme care.' Nevertheless Harry still accepted the invitation and found himself in the middle of a bitterly fought campaign, travelling round the constituency with Pollitt in a baby Austin, while MacDonald was driven in his Rolls Royce. MacDonald received 35,000 votes, Pollitt just 1,451 and MacDonald was invited by the King to form a Government.

Meanwhile Harry needed to follow the success of *The Gate of a Strange Field*. He finished his next novel *Martha Darke* in May 1930, published that September as *Journey Beyond* by Harold Shaylor. Shaylor had been an editor at Brentano's and when that firm collapsed he took with him some of the best of Brentano's list to launch his own firm. *Journey Beyond* was of course immediately published in the Soviet Union (translated by Lydia Slominsky, translator of *The Gate of a Strange Field*, and wife of Zina Vengerova-Minsky's nephew).

Martha Darke is the daughter of a miner from Hunton in Shielding. She enters service in London, where she marries a young bookshop assistant called Russell. When Russell loses his job Martha is forced to char. Russell catches pneumonia tramping London in search of work, their little daughter dies, and Martha is caught stealing to pay for the funeral. She comes out of prison, intending to go on the streets, and Russell, feeling his whole life a failure, decides to kill himself. As he stands hesitating on the Embankment he meets an old work-mate who tells him of the possibility of a job, a non-union labouring job available because the company has been sacking trade union activists. The novel clearly draws on Harry's own experience of unemployment in London (Russell works briefly in a bacon factory and then in an engineering plant, where he is badly hurt in an accident). Here is Russell signing on again:

> He left the place shuddering at the unreality of it all. Labour Exchanges are places where false and true are mixed. Charity is always grossly unreal. Indefinable unreality, of course, corroding in the end, destroying always, always. The clerks were anything but real. They lived in a world of their own, lived on this unliving mass of down-and-outs and condescended to gaze over the absurdity of the wide counters at poor humanity. The iron entered into Russell Brent's soul. He knew why he had come to this, but he was not satisfied with the 'why'. It impeded the process of his thought. Behind it all was Martha, and the baby. They had to be defended, kept in decency, clothed, loved. At the same time, they menaced the peace of his mind. They brought to him a question which he proceeded to hurl into the teeth of Fate, for Fate to answer. It was an unscrutable dread that menaced his life, a damnable, horrible burden. And he blamed it. But Why? Why? Why?... Unemployment had returned. One must get used to it. In the beginning it hurt venomously. As time passed, he became used to it. All fetters must be borne. It is of little use cursing. All the better for the bearer if he wears them with a little tenderness ... He was now securely gripped in the tentacles of unemployment. The wheel of society had thrown him off.

Harry sent a copy of the novel to the miners leader A.J. Cook, who immediately wrote back to congratulate Harry, saying 'I enjoyed every minute of it.' However it was to be several months before Harry read this letter, for by the time *Journey Beyond* was published, Harry was on his way to the Soviet Union.

The International Bureau for Revolutionary Literature was established in 1925 in Moscow to help co-ordinate the hitherto haphazard contacts between progressive writers. Bob Ellis was the only British delegate to the First Conference of Proletarian and Revolutionary Writers, held in 1927. For the second conference, held in Kharkov in November 1930, Bob Ellis was accompanied by his assistant at the *Worker*, by now well-known to millions of Soviet readers. Harry's fourth novel, *Red Earth*, a utopian picture of a successful Revolution in Britain in 1941, was already translated into Russian, and was to appear the following year (it was never published in Britain).

Harry describes his visit to the Soviet Union and the Conference at some length in this book. What he doesn't give us, however, is his speech. It was on the last day of the Conference. The stars of the occasion, Alexander Fadayev, Louis Aragon and Ludwig Renn had all finished speaking when the chair announced that Comrade Heslop from England would now address the conference. A Red Army Officer escorted Harry to the platform to thunderous applause as the band played two lines of the Internationale. He began by surveying the state of working-class writing in Britain. 'Proletarian art in Britain is in a very backward condition,' he admitted, 'and is in fact hardly begun.' Of his own work he said little, except to protest that the manuscript of *The Gate of a Strange Field* had been cut by a quarter in order to conform to the standard novel length, coincidentally cutting most of the anti-capitalist references.

> Modern British bourgeois literature has sunk to a depth that is truly astonishing. It has reached a level of rottenness that can only be described as positively nauseating. It is the literature of dead people. It betokens the final phase of dying capitalism...I believe that during the coming period, we, in Britain, will be able to express on the artistic arena the political struggle of the workers in a manner that will effectively hasten the attainment of our socialist goal. The British delegation will certainly strive with all its might in this direction.

As he sat down the whole conference rose to sing the Internationale once again. He was setting himself an impossible task, of course, single-handedly to create a literature about the experiences of working people, and in so doing to change the course of English Literature. Though no one could say Harry didn't try.

When he returned to Britain in 1931 Harry brought some topaz beads and two fur coats for Phyllis. The coats were soon cut up for cot blankets for their first child, Maril, born in 1933. Harry also brought with him the idea for his next novel, a psychological thriller. *The Crime of Peter Ropner* was eventually published in February 1934 by the Fortune Press, run by Harold Shaylor after the failure of his own firm. The novel opens with Peter Ropner on board a steamer returning to London from a business trip to pre-revolutionary Russia. His wife has taken a lover in his absence and rather than face her husband, has killed herself. Peter sets out to find her lover and throws him into the Thames; he is tried for murder and sentenced to death, though this is commuted to life imprisonment. When Ropner is eventually released from prison he discovers that the lover somehow survived the assault and is now living under a false name. Since he cannot be charged with the same murder twice, Peter determines to do the job properly this time...

'A mystery story in a thousand,' said one reviewer, 'a powerful and unusual story with an unexpected ending,' said another. For another it was an 'enthralling novel' of 'undying fascination'. Dorothy Sayers in the *Sunday Times* praised the novel as 'strong meat'; 'it is as well that we murder-fans should occasionally be reminded that in real life a murder is not a pretty piece of pattern-making, but an ugly mess of lust, greed, violence and spiritual disintegration.'

In the October of 1934 the Fortune Press published *Pod Vlastu Uglya*, now called *Goaf*. Published so soon after the pit disaster at Gresford when 264 miners were killed, the novel immediately caught the public's attention. 'A remarkable book,' said the *Sunday Sun*; the *Manchester Guardian* declared that 'no one can read it without a fuller appreciation of the men who risk their lives to warm the earth'; the *Daily Herald* thought it should be illegal for mine-owners *not* to read *Goaf*. Harry was certainly doing his best to keep the promise he had made at Kharkov in 1930.

The excitement of that conference was clearly still with him in a note he wrote in 1935:

> We took ourselves seriously in Kharkov. We blazed a trail, too... Kharkov was landmark in the history of world literature...1930 has other memories. How we hurried from Dnieprostoi to Dom Soyusov where we watched the depressing scene of eight brilliant men answering for their crimes against Soviet justice. Could drama scale the heights it reached early that morning when Vyshinsky pronounced sentence of death upon five of those wretched men? What was the highest spot of 1930 for me? Why, the return to London. From the eager, bustling activity of the USSR to the barren wastes of England, wastes lying ready for the weeds of fascism. The contrast was too startling...

Harry's enthusiasm for the building of Socialism in the Soviet Union was still clearly undiminished by what he had seen there. If anything it was greater. Sometime in 1934, Ivan Maisky, now Soviet Ambassador to London, helped find him a job at Arcos, the Russian trading mission in London. He was a keen subscriber to the Moscow-based *International Literature* (conceived at the Kharkov conference), which in 1932 carried a long critical appreciation of his work. The following year they published a letter from Harry complaining about the state of English fiction, all 'two-penny horrors' and 'literary back-scratchers'. A story, 'Ten Thousand Men' also appeared in *International Literature* in 1933, about a failed strike at, of course, Hunton in Shielding, featuring characters from *Goaf*, and ending with a vision of the necessity of hope:

> 'You cannot isolate yourselves in struggle. Your fight is wider and deeper than any Federation Board. You've got to make it a larger question, a county question, a national question. You've got to line everybody up, class against class, until capitalism is swept away from the earth. That is the only way...Don't you see, over there, in the USSR, they are building Socialism! Don't you understand that? We have got to help. We've got to line up some day.'

When *Goaf* was published he sent a copy to Sergei Dinamov, editor of *International Literature*; in June 1935 Harry was writing to complain that his name had been removed from the magazine's list of permanent contributors; Dinamov asked him to write a piece on the Liverpool novelist James Hanley; Harry sent Dinamov the proofs of his next novel, *The Blue Shale*, and in 1939 *International Literature* featured an extract from a historical novel about the struggles to establish trades unionism in the Durham coalfield. In November 1933 Lydia Slominsky wrote to Harry; she had been commissioned to translate Kipling for publication in the Soviet Union – could Harry send her copies of Kipling's two *Jungle Books*?

The Blue Shale was rejected by Gollancz in November 1934, and then by Jonathan Cape the following January, before he signed a contract with Wishart Books in April 1935 (receiving his first advance, of £25). He asked Ivan Maisky, a continuing admirer of Harry's writings, if he could dedicate the novel to him, but Maisky was unsure of the possible political implications of this, so when the novel appeared as *Last Cage Down* in November 1935 it was dedicated to Emily Gibson.

Last Cage Down returns to familiar Heslop territory. It is set in the mining village of 'Franton' in 'Darlstone', and its principal character, James Cameron, combines the physical courage, the oratorical power and the political militancy of both Joe Tarrant from *The Gate of a Strange Field* and Tom Drury in *Goaf*:

Miners are a peculiar breed of men. They live in such dramatic and close association with each other, huddled like sheep against a swaying wall, warming themselves at the fires of their own companionship, that they instinctively feel the necessity for a leader. They choose him from their own ranks, and having chosen, they obey him implicitly until he stumbles. Cameron went into the earth with his comrades and toiled with them, leading them in the battle-line so to speak. Few could beat him at the game of hewing. He stripped his great body of most of his garments, felt the points of his pick, sat down on his cracket, and slew the coal-face with correct blows. He could 'kirve' and 'knick' with the best men in Darlstone, and he could fill a tub on even time. He loved the glory of his toil, for there is glory in the toil of a miner. It is so tremendously skilful. The whole being of a man must be in tune with the silver rock before him and the frowning strata about him. He must know when to kirve, when to knick, when to smash down the 'caunch'. He must make this dead coal speak, speak with the many tongues of coal, weep as a woman weeps when she mourns. If he is skilful he will make the coal leap voluntarily from its fastness with a shriek of joy; but woe betide the miner who lets it hurl itself from the face in silent anger at the destroyer of its peace of aeons, for it is loath to leave its fastness, and when it does it is angry.

Like the miners' leaders in the earlier novels, Cameron is a popular lodge secretary, and like them he leads the union into a disastrous strike. Where *Last Cage Down* is different, is the way in which Cameron's leadership is effectively replaced by the end of the novel by that of the Communist Joe Frost. This is Frost talking in the Miners' Hall about the 'land of the workers', the Soviet Union, in particular about the building of the Dnieper Dam, 'a monument set up to the names of Lenin and Joseph Stalin':

But James Cameron did not see the vision that Frost and his auditors were seeing. They saw a host of men and women pouring out their simple toil upon a gigantic construction, which, when completed, was going to change the entire nature of the Ukraine. They saw men and women performing a useful job of work without the weary haggling after so many extra farthings a shift. They scrambled about the huge structures of steel and concrete watching men trampling great masses of concrete into the mould, building socialism with simple tools – feet, hands, concrete and steel. They were damning back the Dnieper of the ages, raising the river to drown an obstruction which had prevented the growth of the country, mounting a steel and concrete collar over the illimitable power of water to create electricity in abundance, for Donbas, for collective farms, for grain elevators, for every conceivable thing...'Comrades ...it was wonderful...it was stupendous and magnificent...'

The picture of Phyl and Maril used on the cover of Woman Today *in 1936.*

Comparisons were made with Zola, Lawrence, Tressell and A.J. Cronin. 'A grim, honest picture of mining life, said the *TLS*, 'told with compelling and convincing energy'; Ethel Mannin in the *New Leader* declared that it must be read by all those 'not yet awake to the necessity – and urgent necessity at that – for the overthrow of the economic system'; 'a fine story finely told,' wrote Compton Mackenzie in the *Daily Mail*, 'if the ultimate catastrophe be not a superb piece of writing I do not know what descriptive writing is.' (But critical acclaim is one thing, and sales are another; at the end of 1937 the novel had not sold enough to even meet the advance royalties Harry had received, so he still owed Lawrence and Wishart £10 2s 6d...

Harry was clearly moving back towards the Communist Party at this time. He sent a copy of *Last Cage Down* to his old friend Harry Pollitt, who wrote back saying 'I am sure I will enjoy it as much as I did your previous one'. He also sent one to Raji Palme Dutt, editor of *Labour Monthly* adding that 'no one who aspires to write these days can survey the political scene without appreciating the correctness of the diagnosis which you and your comrades of the Communist Party have made in the last decade. Perhaps one day I will be courageous enough to join you...' Dutt was very enthusiastic about the novel, 'a big advance' on *The Gate of a Strange Field*, confident that Harry would soon re-join the party. He almost certainly did re-join the Communist Party in the late 1930s or early 1940s.

Harry's closeness to the Party may be seen when in 1936 he was invited to attend Tom Mann's 80th birthday party (the speakers were Pollitt, J.C. Little of the AEU and Allan Findlay from the TUC General Council). That year the Communist Party women's magazine *Woman Today* carried a picture of Phyllis and Maril on its cover. *Woman Today* was edited by Vera West, the Swiss wife of the Marxist literary critic Alick West. The Heslops were good friends with the Wests in these years, and would often visit them at their 'posh modern flat' in Clapham. The following year Alick West published a study of Harry's work in his book *Crisis and Criticism*. Arguing that 'the aesthetic value of literature depends on the relation of the writer to the productive activity of society', and that 'the condition of good work is the power to feel this activity and to see the world in terms of it', West favourably compared *The Gate of a Strange Field* with James Joyce's *Ulysses*. While recognising the difference in the 'relative gift of language',

West argued that *Ulysses* represented a literature in decline, a novel 'that does not organise social energy', merely irritating it 'because it gives no aim it can work for'. By comparison *The Gate of a Strange Field* contained a 'new social vision, of the individual as part of productive society, and of productive society as a part of nature'. In Harry's writing, West wrote, life has 'a warm, bodily reality which Joyce, cut off from the social experience that makes life such, cannot create'.

Meanwhile Harry and Bob Ellis were hard at work on a book about the abdication crisis. On 10 December 1936 Edward VIII renounced his throne; on 15 December Harry and Bob signed a contract with George Routledge and Sons to deliver 30-40,000 words by Friday 18 December (on an advance of £25). *The Abdication of Edward VIII* (by 'Lincoln J. White') was published in early 1937, soon selling over forty thousand copies.

That year Harry contributed to the *Left Review* pamphlet, *Authors Take Sides on the Spanish War:*

> The *only* answer to the Fascist attack on culture and on Spain which a writer ought to give is: Down with the the Fascist Monsters. With the blood of the people of Spain is being written a chapter of human history which will remain imperishable through time. I join with my comrades of the pen with the Spanish people in their war on Mussolini, Hitler, Franco and their allies.

The next few years were Harry's most prolific. They were also his least successful, full of rejections and disappointments. His next novel, *The Gibbet in the Slake*, was a historical novel, about the Durham miners leader Will Jobling (the last man in Britain to be gibbeted). Edgell Rickword at Lawrence and Wishart (Wishart merged that year with the Communist Party publishers Martin Lawrence) rejected it in May 1936; so did Peter Davies that December. It was never published. In 1935 John Lane considered publishing T*he Gate of a Strange Field* in Penguin, but finally rejected it. Provoked by the inaccuracies in a radio talk about mining by the writer F.C. Boden, Harry unsuccessfully offered the BBC four radio scripts about the Hartley Colliery disaster of 1862, the mining engineer Michael Faraday and mining ventilation. In March 1936 he sent film treatments of *The Gate of a Strange Field*, *The Crime of Peter Ropner* and *Goaf* to Alexander Korda, who rejected them. He sent the synopsis of *Goaf* to Gaumont-British Picture Corporation/Gainsborough Pictures who also turned it down. His next book, *The Old Vestreyman* was a biography of the mining

Harry Heslop:
a photograph taken in
later years.

engineer James Mather. It was finished by June 1937 and sub-sequently rejected by Ivor Nicholson and Watson, and George Allen and Unwin; in 1938 he tried, unsuccessfully, to interest the *Sunday Sun* and the *Manchester Evening News* in serialising the book. Undeterred, he wrote his next novel, a comic picture of small town life in the North East, *Alderman Green Resigns* under the pseudonym 'Wallace Grange'. In 1937 Secker and Warburg were sufficiently interested to ask him to re-write it, (they were unhappy with Harry's use of North-East dialect), but they rejected the new version the following May. Both the US publishers Viking and John Lehmann at the Hogarth Press rejected his next novel, *They Came to a Valley*.

Harry and Bob Ellis then began work on a sequel to the abdication book, a detailed indictment of the British ruling class and its wealth, privileges and power (Sidney Webb obtained permission for them to work in the British Museum, where of course they took turns sitting at the desk that Marx had used). The book, *Monarchy & Co*, was rejected in July 1938 by George Allen and Unwin, by Viking in February 1939, and by Gollancz (on the advice of John Strachey) and Secker and Warburg (who wanted to publish the book but were afraid it might have an adverse effect on their fortunes). In September 1938 Michael Foot accepted a story for *Tribune*, but Foot left the paper soon afterwards and the story never appeared. During 1930 Harry began collecting essays by Engels from the *Pall Mall Gazette* on the Franco-Prussian War. Lawrence and Wishart were interested on turning the collection into a book with an introductory essay by Harry. But though the book was finished, another war intervened and the book was never published.

By this time Harry had left Arcos and was working at the National Insurance head office at Kew. When the office was shut in 1939 the staff were dispersed and Harry found himself working at the Walworth Road Exchange where he had drawn his dole a decade earlier (and about which he had written in *Journey Beyond*). They now had two children, as Phyllis had been asked to look after a baby whose mother had died in labour. This was only supposed to be for a month, but when War was declared Maril was evacuated with her school; the arrival of baby Michael meant that the family could be evacuated together. So in May 1940 Phyllis and the two children travelled to Taunton, where her cousin lived. Two months later their house on Prince's Square suffered a direct hit in the Blitz, and Harry joined his family in Somerset. For the rest of the war his job was to cycle around Taunton and the surrounding countryside, rounding up people for their medicals. Phyllis's mother, meanwhile was living in Paris, where she was interned by the Nazis; six months later she was repatriated and joined Harry, Phyllis and the children in their new home.

In 1945 Harry started work as an advertising agent for Woollaways, a local building firm who specialised in concrete houses (which Harry detested). When they asked him to become a travelling salesman he refused, so in 1948 he found himself out of work again. At the end of that summer he began working for the Ordnance Survey in Taunton; when the office transferred to Exeter he refused to move, and so was unemployed – as so often before – for the last three years of his official working life.

Harry, of course, was far from idle during these years. In 1946 he sent a play called *Front Page Splash* to London Unity Theatre, and to Michael Redgrave; he began rewriting the book about James Mather; he submitted a radio script to the BBC about Sir Goldsworthy Gurney (a Cornish doctor and mining engineer and a great influence on Michael Faraday). That year too he wrote a film treatment of his 1936 novel about Will Jobling, now called *To Reach the Slake*, for Ealing Studios; although they were interested for a time, it was never made into a film. Then in 1946 a novel he had begun ten years earlier as *They Came to a Valley* was published under the title *The Earth Beneath* by T.V. Boardman and Co (with an advance of £50!), and dedicated to Maril.

The Earth Beneath remains Harry's greatest single achievement, a rich and scholarly history of work and family life in a small Durham pit village in the nineteenth century, about poaching and preaching, Methodism and Socialism, about the miners' struggles underground with the coal and on the surface with the coal-owners. It begins with the migration into the new coalfield of farmers evicted from the North Yorkshire dales in the 1840s. We see them sink a new pit and build a new chapel, and we listen as they do to the new talk about miners banding together in trade unions. The climax of the novel is a re-creation of the disaster at Hartley Colliery in 1862, when 199 men and boys were trapped underground without air:

> It was in the singing that they achieved most comfort, for then they could all join in and each express a yearning and a long-drawn hope for deliverance now that deliverance from their deplorable inhumation had receded so distantly. The fear of doom had penetrated to the children, and even they forgot their fate so much as to send their shrill treble voices into the gallery to mingle with the firmer notes of the men.
>
> They sang a great deal, because it gave them hope to live and lent them all a peculiar courage to die. About them all were spread the dark untextured wings of death. Their singing was silenced when a man began to pray, for now, when a man prayed he spoke from the deeps of his own conviction. The startling simplicity of the request – that they be saved – sent their hopes soaring, and then when deliverance did not come they would sink and men would choke and children would sob. The fact that they should all die, that one hundred and ninety-nine should perish! The idea of their joint and common death was not only repugnant, it was monstrous.
>
> Simon Akers knew that the end was fast approaching. He could feel it. The inexorable approach of death was something which could not be escaped. He tottered among them, and he did not walk alone. Death went with him touching man and boy here and there. The weakest had all died. The rest were dying. Everywhere was death. He tried to call out but the words stayed in his throat. He fell upon his knees and crawled amongst them, shuddering as he felt the dead. He stopped crawling and lay still. A moan escaped his lips. He collapsed like a stunned bullock. He was the last.

'Almost Tolstoyan' declared *Cavalcade*; 'in this brilliantly limned social canvas Harold Heslop presents a penetrating and evocative picture of the Durham coal mines in the days of nineteenth century expansion…one of the outstanding social pieces of recent decades.' *The Times* liked the 'enthralling' description of the mining disaster. The novel was also reviewed by Vernon Noble on the BBC North Region's *Northern Bookshelf*; the feature included an interview with Harry (on a record cut in Bristol). *The Earth Beneath* was translated into Italian (published by Delnicke in December 1948, for which Harry received £19 2s 6d). There was talk of a French edition (Librarie Stock were interested) and even a Romanian edition. Constantine Simonov, President of the Foreign Commission of the Union of Soviet writers sent a telegram at the end of 1946 wishing Harry 'Best wishes for Warmest New Year Greetings'. The US National Library for the Blind transcribed *The Earth Beneath* into Braille in 1948. The novel sold 6730 copies in Britain and 2189 overseas, earning Harry a total of £402.

In October 1947 *The Earth Beneath* was published in the US by John Day (with an advance of 500 dollars). Although some American reviewers clearly had some difficulty with the book (one thought it was set in Wales!), it was very well received in the US. The *New York Times* said the novel had earned Harry 'the right to take his place as a narrative artist of rare quality …Mr Heslop has created tragic writing of a high order.' '*The Earth Beneath* is a story of incredible poverty, gruelling labour, the daily companionship of danger, existence in a country where each day's work spread a hideous blight over country that had once been beautiful,' observed the *Herald Tribune*, 'Mr Heslop writes movingly, and with authority, and his book has the simplicity, staunch dignity, and warmth of the men and women whose way of life he chronicles.' The novelist Pearl S. Buck (whose husband was President of John Day) wrote to congratulate Harry on 'your very fine novel', 'it is one of the best novels I have read'. It was even entered for the MGM movie contest (on the strength of the recent success of *How Green was My Valley*).

Harry had made it at last. Or had he? In July 1947 Boardman rejected *To Reach the Slake*; the following year John Day also rejected it. He was still trying to find a publisher for *Monarchy and Co*, rejected in October 1947 by John Day. Harry was at work on a new novel *The Holy Earth* (a supernatural, re-incarnation romance about two GIs travelling back in time to the Monmouth Rebellion); this was rejected by John Day in February 1948 and in April by Boardman. Harry then started a historical book about Burke, Wesley and Dr Johnson, though this was never finished. His last novel, *To Manage this Age*, about the Bomb, was never published. Even the *Coal Magazine* returned a story in 1947, 'Imageless Metal' (on the grounds that it contained too much death and disaster for the readers...)

On 1 January 1947, a few weeks after the publication of *The Earth Beneath*, the mines were nationalised. Harry's old mate Will Lawther was now President of the NUM; Phil Williams, who had gone from Crook with Harry to the Labour College, was now a Labour MP, William Whitely was Government Chief Whip, and Bill Blyton was in the House of Lords. Harry meanwhile was still working in the Labour Exchange in Taunton. He was active again in the Labour Party – chair of Taunton Constituency Labour Party and of the Branch in Milverton where they now lived, editor of the *West Somerset Clarion* (a monthly Labour Party sheet known as 'the best little paper in the country'), delegate to annual conference and chair of the Somerset Federation of Labour Parties. He twice fought the Trinity ward in Taunton, the second time achieving a record Labour vote of 1183, though not enough to be elected to the council.

It is not clear when Harry left the Communist Party. During the War he was a member of the Russia Today Society, and he was writing regularly to the Foreign Commission of the Union of Soviet Writers in Moscow where his letters were published. Harry wrote to his American publisher in 1947, anxious that his 'red connections' might prevent *The Earth Beneath* from being published in the US. But in 1946 he was invited to contest Gateshead for the Labour Party; he refused since the family were now well settled in Taunton. In a 1950 letter Harry thanked Victor Collins (Labour MP for Taunton from 1945 to 1950) for having 'picked me out of King Street, Covent Garden, number 16' (Communist Party headquarters). Harry spoke for Collins over 50 times between 1945 and 1950. But Harry was increasingly unhappy with Collins' uncritical acceptance of the drift of the Labour Party to the Right; Harry was opposed to the British possession of nuclear weapons and bitterly attacked the role of Britain and the US in Korea in 1950. Surviving copies of letters to Collins accuse him of abandoning

ABOVE: *Victor Collins (Labour MP for Taunton) speaking at the Empire Hall, Taunton; sitting behind him is Herbert Morrison, next to Harry.*

BELOW: *Shot of the audience at the same event while Harry was speaking.*

Socialism, of being corrupted by Westminster, and of tolerating no criticism within the local party – 'you have imbibed the ethics of the capitalist,' accused Harry. In 1950 Harry was part of an unsuccessful manoeuvre to de-select Collins. As a result Harry lost the nomination to fight Frome in the 1950 General Election, he was removed from the editorship of the *Clarion*, and from the Divisional Labour Party. By 1951 Harry was reduced to pleading to be allowed to remain a member of the Labour Party, trying to convince the local Labour Party that he had 'only one party card in his pocket'…

He was successful, and the breach with Collins was mended. In 1952 Harry was elected Secretary of the Constituency Party, a post he held for the next twelve years. In the 1955 General Election he fought North Devon for the Labour Party (one of his opponents, also unsucessful on that occasion, was Jeremy Thorpe). In 1974 he was made a life member of the Labour Party.

Meanwhile he was still writing. And still being rejected. He unsuccessfully submitted a radio talk about Walter Bagehot to Desmond Hawkins at the BBC in 1951. He wrote a radio play, *Two Men Came to Haswell*, about Michael Faraday in June 1951 (Sid Chaplin recommended this to the BBC). Two years later Harry's next novel *The Cry of Dust*, about a Labour MP from a mining area who becomes corrupted by Westminster, was rejected by both John Day and Boardman. During 1953 Harry was trying unsuccessfully to interest John Day in a book about George Gissing.

The following year he turned to writing TV scripts; the BBC rejected his first attempt in 1956; the same year Associated Rediffusion rejected a TV adaptation of *Two Men Came to Haswell*. Harry even collaborated with his old mate Bob Ellis (now working, much to Harry's dismay, on the *Daily Express*) on a TV play, though this too was rejected. He submitted several manuscripts for a Granada 'TV play contest' in 1958, including one about Dostoevsky; all were rejected. In 1961 he submitted a play to an Associated TV Play Contest; it was rejected.

By the late 1960s Harry appears to have abandoned imaginative writing altogether. Instead he was working on a long study of Marx (of which six different versions survive). But his luck was no better. *The Class Nature of English Society* was rejected by Routledge in 1966; *Karl Marx: An Essay* was rejected successively by Routledge, Allen and Unwin and the Oxford University Press in 1970. At one stage Harry was even hoping

Family group for the 1955 General Election contest of North Devon.

to publish the book himself. This autobiography, which he called *From Tyne to Tone*, was his last book, apparently finished by 1971. And of course, Harry could not find a publisher for it. The manuscript ends, after a final flourish denouncing Attlee, Morrison, Bevan and Gaitskill for betraying Socialism, on a note of peaceful resignation. He had his family, Phyllis, Maril and Mike and his four grandchildren. And if no one was listening any more to what Harry had to say, he could at least talk to himself:

> And here I sit and watch the years ebb away in silence and in peace. Should I wish to walk abroad I can wander to the edges of the Exmoor Forest, find a convenient stone upon which to sit and there speak to myself of the things that might have been…

Harry died in Tone Valley Hospital Taunton, at the age of 85 after a long illness on 10 November 1983. Thirty-seven years had passed since his last book was published, though he left a mass of unpublished novels, plays, short stories, poems and essays (including one on Cybernetics). With so many rejections, so many disappointements, so much bad luck, it is not surprising that Harry was reticent about his writing at the end. His published books were long since out of print and forgotten.

Who was interested in Harry Heslop the writer? Who, after all, was Harry Heslop?

Although Harry was an extraordinary and exceptional man, there is a sense in which his life can be read as a representative one, which speaks of the political experience of a generation of working-class men and women, their hopes and fears, achievements and disappointments, betrayals and defeats. His story begins with the high hopes of the Syndicalist industrial struggles of the early years of the century, takes us through the mass unemployment of the Depression, from the idealism of the ILP through the betrayals of the first two Labour Governments to Marxism, Communism, admiration for the Soviet Union and 'Uncle Joe', and it ends with the disappointments of the post-War settlement and the revelations about Stalin. His is the story too of how for a few years the doors of the London literary establishment were opened for working-class writers and how firmly they were shut again after the War.

Almost alone, Harry Heslop created the mining-novel in Britain, and won respect for it. He had taken the novel underground and challenged the reading public to follow him. And they had. He proved it was possible to write about life in a pit village without either the sentimentality of George Orwell or the scorn of D.H. Lawrence. Other miners like Lewis Jones, Walter Brierley, Len Doherty – and of course, Sid Chaplin – were later to build on his achievements. His books may not have brought about a revolution, but they certainly contributed to a growing popular commitment to take the mines into public ownership.

For half a century miners and their families seemed the best and most representative section of the British people. The working conditions of miners were the most dangerous, their work the most necessary, their trade unionism the most loyal and their class conciousness the sharpest. And the cultural expression of that life – an industrial, provincial, collective and working culture – allowed working people to see their own lives represented in fiction. For a few years Harry Heslop took those lives into the heart of British literary culture, just as the miners who were his contemporaries at the Labour College took their political hopes into government. Harry's writings represent the best of what working people were capable of; what, given the chance, British society could have been. If a self-taught miner could write, and write so well, ordinary people could take control of their own lives, their own industry, their own government...

Today there are no pits left in the Durham coalfield; the miners are no longer the 'praetorian guard' of the Labour Movement, defeated, divided and facing the privatisation of the industry. The Soviet Union has collapsed and what remains of the Soviet Communist Party is in disarray. The British Communist Party dissolved itself in 1991. All that Harry believed in and worked for is reviled, ridiculed, betrayed, defeated. All that survives from a long life of intellectual and political effort is his writing. Read this autobiography and wonder – at the world he re-creates. And the world we have lost.

ANDY CROFT

A NOTE ON THE TEXT

The original manuscript of *From Tyne to Tone* is longer by approximately a fifth. We have made a few minor textual corrections, and deleted some repetitions. We also made the decision to cut the last two chapters completely: they are much less vivid than the rest of the book and cover Harry's later years too quickly and too thinly. An unedited copy of Harold Heslop's autobiography is kept by Durham County Council's Arts, Libraries and Museums Department. The copy is held in the Local Studies Collection at Durham City Library, and is available for reference use during advertised opening hours. The only one of Harry's novels still in print is *Last Cage Down*, published by Lawrence and Wishart. We wish to thank Phyllis Heslop and Maril Wrigg for their encouragement and help in answering so many questions and for making available Harry's papers.

OPPOSITE: *A cartoon of Harry done at the Kharkov Conference in 1929 by a Soviet artist.*

Chapter One

In all the urgency of his industrial creations Man rarely essayed so mean and contemptible a habitation of souls worse than New Hunwick. It lay upon the once beautiful face of south-west Durham like a festering wound. Across the fields, Old Hunwick still hugged the church and held aloof, but that was no condemnation of the village, for in actuality there was little that might distinguish it from any of the other places where coal-measures were wrought and scabbed the face of nature.

One thing those early miners did not do and that was expose the pit head as the main feature of the village. Rough Lea Colliery was hidden further down the slope of the valley, near to the railway that ran from Durham to Bishop Auckland. Between the village and the pithead stood an ancient farm house, ringed with poplars. The coal-measures had been breached by a drift which tunnelled towards the village some distance from the farm. The drift leaned into a gentle gradient, as if reluctant to disturb the face of an ancient husbandry that was old before the Bolden Buke was fullly compiled. Beyond the wood that skirted the road from the village to the pithead the old Hall still housed in its ruins the families of the men who stroked the surrounding fields into production, regardless of the fact that the excrescences of Rough Lea and Sunnybrow collieries flowed relentlessly over its ancient tillages. The hall was screened by a tall brick wall which ran all the way from near the drift mouth up to the village, where it turned at right angles and continued to the ancient gateway. On the other side of the wall stood a plantation of beeches, which held aloft a kingdom of rooks.

The one abiding presence which tamed industrial man in all his assaults upon its earth was the lovely Wear, which continued to pass its slow-moving waters without regard to the destruction done along its banks. The stretch from Newfield to Sunnybrow was almost untouched. Unfortunately, Newfield did spill much of its garbage along the far bank, and darkened and soured that length of the river in which the Romans had swam and from which they had taken brown trout. Up above Newfield lay Binchester, a Roman camp still undisturbed by archeaologists, quiet farming land in the possession of the Eden family.

The church stood on the edge of Old Hunwick, at the turn of the road that dropped down to the railway station. Without belfry or tower, it had long lost its fight for the souls of Hunwick Methodist folk as well as of those who felt no need for God. It looked to the passer-by damp with its tears oozing from its own forlorn frustration. Higher up in the old village the Green lay unmolested, enclosed by ancient cottages, good little places in which dwelt many of the friends of my parents. There was that quiet of all old places that lingers above their ancient foundations when they have been allowed to attain their own dissolution in their own time.

All was destined to be a simple industry in and around my birthplace. The little pit at Rough Lea produced more than one commodity, coal. That which it did not sell from the screens it 'cooked' in immense beehive coke-ovens. When these contraptions were set ablaze they tore the darkness out of the moonless nights, and flung the surrounding countryside into a ruddy glow which hung aloft as a sulphurous visitation. That was not all. Most of the smaller seams were encradled in a blue shale of unusual purity, and this, after weathering, was milled into a clay from which exquisite toilet ware and granite-hard fireclay bricks were manufactured. Rough Lea toilet ware found markets all over the world. The bricks were used to line the smelting furnaces at Cargo Fleet and Jarrow.

The amenities granted to New Hunwick were a place to light a fire in order to cook and bake, a communal tap, and, here along the streets, a shed which housed a suitably fashioned platform which men designated as 'the nessy'. This lamentable structure strutted from its foul, open box into a wide receptacle where the contents of 'the nessy' were raked and covered with ashes from the kitchen fires. When the bin-like receptacle was filled the company carter happened along in his own time and cleared the sorry mess into his coal cart and hauled it on to some ploughed field when the farmer agreed, or took it to some pit. The fearsome structures were built close to the backdoors of the houses. In the summer months the flies became a horrific invasion. Flypapers descended in numbers from the kitchen rafters. The struggles of the trapped flies set up a continuous hum which always interested me.

Few of the houses had more than two bedrooms. All had a kitchen, and some a 'front room'. In the kitchen all the chores were performed, despite the fact that most held a double bed always occupied by the father and mother of the family. Here the miners reproduced themselves. Here the progeny crawled and dunged until they were picked up and sent off to school.

The women suckled their children until they were almost three years old. They offered a gratuitous love to their children in the form of an open admission to an almost uncovered breast. When the baptism of the child was over and the old crone who had 'helped the doctor' at the birth had completed her stint of attendance, the nappies were all collected, washed and ironed, and folded away against the advent of the next child. All the children crawled and ran bare-bottomed and skirted, male as well as female, until they had learned the control of their bowels, and until they did so it was much less trouble to remove excrement from the floor or the body of a child than to wash napkins. The boys were not 'britched' until their bowels were in safe keeping, nor were the girls put into bloomers. The child that showed a marked disinclination to rectify his urinary behaviour was given a mouse pie to eat, an infallible remedy for bed-wetting. The mouse after being caught was skinned. The flesh was taken from the bones, and the resulting mass was cooked after the fashion of a sausage roll, and this the child was cajoled to eat. The infallible remedy for uncontrolled anal emission was to burn the discharged mess on the kitchen fire.

The inordinate length of time of suckling a child at the breast was a form of birth control. How efficacious this might have been, or how successful, it is impossible to say. Strangely enough, the time between the births of the first five of my parents' children was in each case twenty-seven months.

The mining folk had to exist in these primitive conditions. Life was shaved to the bone. Wages were meagre. Every member of the group depended upon the masters agreeing to their labouring in or about the mine. A female child was a misfortune which continued until it was old enough to 'go out to place'. The entire family lived entirely on the earnings of the father, who received no help from any source until 'the lads were able to go into the pit'. The colliery bred its own workers.

It all added up to a simple existence, simple, serious and deadly.

The village possessed few buildings that stood in any relation to the church in size or importance. There were 'three places of worship', the Wesleyan Methodist, the Primitive Methodist and the New Connexion Churches. For any special non-religious occasion, such as a concert or a political meeting, the Temperance Hall was used. This was a grim structure, mainly of galvanized iron which stood under the rookery. Liquid refreshment could be obtained at the Wheatsheaf Inn, where Jack Richardson rehearsed his brass band, the Helmington Inn, both situated at the Lane Ends, and the Mason Arms at the top of the village, just opposite the Primitive Methodist Chapel, that is on the road to Crook.

Near the Mason Arms stood the ball alley, an imposing structure if its utter vulgarity was any measure of its aesthetic purpose. It towered to a great height, and was just a buttressed wall, faced smoothly on its playing surface with cement. It stood athwart a playing pitch of compounded clay upon which the two kinds of quoits – clay ends and grass ends – could be played. On this cemented wall face was played the game of handball. Such a game had fallen into disuse before the first world war. It bore a similarity to the game of 'fives', as described in *Tom Brown's Schooldays*. A bold line was marked across the width of the alley some thirty inches from the ground. This declared space had not to be entered while the ball was in play. If it did so the opponent received a point and was the one to strike the ball into fresh play. The ball was played with the bare hands, and was driven back against the wall by the players in turn. The one who allowed the ball to go out of play conceded the point to his opponent.

Many tense and fascinating games were played on that alley. The heyday was the visit of the Mordue Brothers, two men who played for wagers and did exhibitions up and down the county. One of the brothers was Jackie Mordue. He was attached to the Sunderland Football Club, and towards the end of his playing career formed one of a famous trio of footballers with Charles Buchan and Frank Cuggy. For a small man, Jack had a hefty manner when dealing with the hard rubber ball on a handball alley. When a big game was in progress the players wore costumes which were highly decorated cotton bloomers, specially knitted stockings and light shoes. In a long game the hands of the players became swollen, sometimes extraordinarily swollen. The men raged at their game. My mother's brother Job was a local adept at the game. He, too, was a footballer of some note, but in the amateur world of the sport. I liked to watch him play, for I somehow felt that I had some share in the glory of his game. I grieved when he lost a point. He was a big boned, fair haired, good looking man, a great coal hewer in his own right, a bottom shooter of immense renown, and a gentle man.

A quoit match was always an occasion set apart for the delectation of grown men. It was always played on clay ends. The hob was embedded in the centre of a clay area. The distance between the two ends was some twenty-one feet. Each hob was driven into the clay and only some three or four inches left exposed. The purpose of the game was to ring the hob. Each end offered a maximum of two points to the successful thrower. The aim of the player was to prevent his opponent from scoring the points, and the main effort of the first thrower was to lip the hob, that is to throw so that his quoit rested forward from the throw *on* the hob. It always amazed me when watching a match to observe the accuracy with which the iron ring was thrown. It was an exercise undergone by strong men of unerring mind and judgement, and immense muscular power. Magnificent were the duels that were fought in those days. Champions declared themselves, and champions hurled their challenges to the rest of the world from the small ads columns of the *Northern Echo* and the *Newcastle Evening Chronicle*.

Grass ends was different. This was a game for old men and boys. The aim was to ring the quoit, but one was satisfied to get his quoit nearer to the hob than one's opponent. Disputes about the distance from the hob was settled by the referee who employed the length of his arm from elbow to finger end, the width of four fingers, an extra finger or a matchstick. Measurement was always empirical in and around the mines.

They played other games in the mining areas, games which I have rarely seen duplicated elsewhere. There was tipcat, a prodigious exercise. The cat was a short piece of wood pointed at each end. The four sides were numbered I, II, III and X. A sharp blow on the point with a stick threw the cat upwards, and then it was struck forward again. The distances of each throw were measured by the stick, and in the time-honoured way. The winner was the one who covered the greater distance. Curiously enough, this game was not confined to children. I have seen grown men gamble heavily on the cat. Another game was that of knurr and spell, an ingenious game, and possibly the one calling for the greatest skill of all. The knurr was actually a ball of wood, mainly ash, fashioned by nothing more than a sharp pen knife. This ball was placed into the cup of the spell which was tensed against a powerful spring. The players each held a club, an instrument fashioned from a stouter piece of ash which was planed to a smooth 'face', and attached to a long stick. The player took his stance, released the spring with a touch from the club, and struck the ball while it was in the air. Distance was the deciding factor in this game, and this was measured by a chosen length of stick, and the finer measurements in the old way of palm and finger.

Most of the miners were uninterested in religion. There was enough chapel and church space to accommodate them all had they wished. Few accepted the duty laid upon them by any place of worship. The majority of males played a languid waiting game from midday on Saturday until bedtime on Sunday. There was little else they could do. A journey to Bishop Auckland on Saturday evening was the most ambitious journey for most men. If there was some pitch and toss being played in some quiet lane many would wander hither and thither to gamble what little they had in their pockets, or merely to watch and advise if they were empty. As wages were paid fortnightly the intervening weekend was as barren as a ditch. They left their women folk, fully aproned, to gossip across the spaces between the rows of houses, unmindful of the stenches from the open middens, and to shout their remarks without regard to charity. The children, who attended the Little School until they were transferred to the Big School near the church, took the weekends into their keeping and were happy in some large, undefinable way. Their lives until they went into the pit or to place were rested over the weekends.

Both Hunwicks were screened from the colliery and the towering shale tip and both constituted a village that was withdrawn from the scene of its own industry. Rough Lea was a place where mining was carried out in singularly simple forms. The tubs of coal were dragged out of the mine in long trains, or sets, each tub coupled to its neighbour with a three link coupling, by a main and tail haulage system. This was a simple reversible act of haulage. The main hauling rope was wound on to a drum by the steam engine and as a result the set of tubs and the tail rope was drawn to the surface. The tail rope, which was manipulated on the contra-reversing drum on the engine passed over a return wheel deep in the pit. By reversing the process, the empty set of tubs and the main rope were dragged back into the mine by the tail rope. The train full of tubs was received on to the pit head. There each tub was weighed in the presence of the checkweighman and ascribed to the number of the token which had been hung inside the tub by the coal hewer. The tubs, as they were treated, were tipped on to a slide which led to the screening apparatus, and passed on to a siding where the empty set was assembled.

On the pit heap all was bustle accompanied by the groaning of machinery. Everything was dull with dust. Men shouted and swore in the gloaming as others went stolidly about the business of the day. The blacksmith hammered pony shoes into shape and sharpened innumerable picks for the next shift of coal hewers. The screens groaned and thumped as the coal was separated into big and small, 'roundie and dust'. The rejected stuff was channelled to an endless bank of pans which carried it to a high hopper. Here waited the oven loaders with their fantastic wagons into which it was loaded so that it could be transported to the precise coke-oven which was being prepared for its three-day tryst with fire. Labour raged throughout the week from six in the morning until five in the afternoon, except on Saturday when it ended at one o'clock.

About the pit-top lay acres of waste land, the chief feature of which was the colliery pond, timber lay about in disorderly heaps contrasting with well-stacked formations of good timber, all jostled by the other appurtenances of the mine, rails, baulks, tarred brattice cloth, drums of oil, shattered tubs and empty trucks. Away from all this happy playground for children crawled a street of colliery houses, which halted almost under the screens. Between the houses and the pit head ran the railway sidings, a thin path separating coal trucks from the small kitchen gardens. And over all belched the smoke and steam, and into it screamed all the noise of coal production.

I was born in the fourth house down from the Hunwick end of the street, the second child of my parents. I believe that my birth was difficult. My mother, Isabel Heslop, née Whitfield, had borne my father a son twenty-seven months previously. My father was a little man. I always remember him as being completely bald. Legend begat that when he did have hair it was profuse and ginger. He was a studious man who was determined to make some headway in the mining industry. By the time I was born he had obtained both certificates of competency, one of which was signed by a gentleman called White, and the other by Herbert Henry Asquith. The certificates had been framed and hung upon the chimney breast of the front room. Being possessed of such *cartes d'identité* he had every reason to hope that one day he might become a more important official than a deputy.

The manager of the entire complex was a small, rotund, bald-headed man called Michael Heslop. He and my grandfather Heslop were sons of brothers who had wandered into the district after their father's land somewhere in the North Yorkshire dales had been enclosed some time about the passing of the Reform Bill of 1832. How that family of peasants took root among the mining proletariat is a story that has been long forgotten.

Religion bothered the Heslop family all the days of its existence. My father's father, George Heslop, was the possessor of a remarkable tenor voice, a fact vouched for to me by many of his contemporaries. All that it ever got for him was the post of choir master at the Primitive Methodist Chapel. When my grandfather died, in 1935, the gold watch and albert which had been presented to my grandfather when he retired from the post in 1906, was handed over to me. I have it still. My father was a lay preacher on the Bishop Auckland circuit. He took his religion seriously. He could pick a quarrel on a politico-theological point whenever he chose to do so. I cannot recall hearing him preach, but I must have been present when he was occupying the pulpit, for attendance at chapel was mandatory in our family. I am convinced that he was sufficiently instructed in simple theology to make a contribution to simple pulpit oratory. He was a politician in his own way, which was emotional. In the beginning he did lean towards the then burgeoning socialist way of thinking. He read with care *The Labour Leader* and *The Clarion*, but being an astute man he did not make his political opinions publicly obvious in his early life. Towards the end of his life he became a member of the Blaydon Conservative Association. But, by then, it was too late.

In those low seams in south west Durham, and I speak of their height being measured in inches, it was necessary to 'make height' along the 'going ways' by either taking down a slice of the roof or taking up a similar slice from the floor of the seam. In the measures of which I speak the blue shale which enfolded the seams had considerable industrial potentialities. The shale, or 'seggar clay', as the miners called it, was fairly easily excavated. It was transported to the surface and built into massive heaps, or tips, where it was left to weather and crumble over immense acres of arable land. The mountains of the shale may have gone from Rough Lea by now, but it is of no moment.

Life in Rough Lea was no different from life in Hunwick. It was just a matter of sustaining life at its lowest point of comfort. No other kind of life was ever intended to exist there. Work was wrought in two daily shifts of hewers and one shift of transport workers. The first shift of hewers commenced at 4 a.m., and ended at 11 a.m., while the second commenced at 9 a.m. and ended at 4 p.m. The overlap at 9 to 11 enabled the men to travel the long distances underground and make the change-over. The association of men below ground was known as 'marrows'. The term is unique in the north east. It is more than a synonym for 'mate'. It meant that the man with whom one shared a working place, or 'cavil' shared as marrows down to the last penny earned. Both shifts of marrows were served by one shift of putters and transport workers, who commenced at 6 a.m. and finished at 4 p.m.

Rough Lea was owned by the North Bitchburn Coal Company Limited. It was more or less a family affair in which the more fortunate of the Heslops played fairly important roles. How they won their ways into the high places I have been unable to discover. I believe that religion, or the lack of religion, was responsible, for none of them belonged to the Primitive Methodist faction. It may have been that they were possessed of brains, but of that I have doubts, for Michael Heslop once told me that when he had a problem in the pit he always went to my grandfather for advice. I have a feeling that there must have been some schism in the past.

I once visited my grandfather some years before he died and I was chatting with him when Harry Thompson came in with a few brown trout wrapped in a rhubarb leaf. He suggested that I should carry them to Michael. To this I agreed. Michael by then had left Hunwick and had settled himself and his family in a beautiful old house that had once belonged to the owner of Quarry Burn brewery some couple of miles on the

Crook side of Hunwick. I walked to the little hamlet which had housed most of my mother's family for many decades. Michael met me at the door and invited me in. He and his family were charming. I still think that the errand was contrived by the three old men.

After dinner Michael told me that my grandfather was the best mining engineer in the family. This surprised me. He went on to tell me that he could always depend upon him in an emergency. 'Your grandfather', he said, 'knew pit work better than any man I ever knew. He was of the pit.' Later he asked me if I had ever done any timber drawing. I told him that I had been present when timber was drawn but only in a minor capacity. 'What's your seams like?' he asked. 'Six feet?' I nodded. 'Any man can draw a jud in a six foot seam,' he said. 'Your grandfather could draw one faultlessly in a two foot seam.' He waited until I understood. 'There never were three better men than your grandfather, Harry Thompson and Jack Coates,' he almost whispered.

I knew that he was reminiscing to himself and so I waited. 'Did you know…did anybody ever tell you…they were almost finished drawing when the fall came and a great stone pinned Harry down across his hips.' I saw him smile, almost lovingly. 'Harry beseeched them to leave him and get themselves clear, but they both stopped. They tore at that stone and got Harry free.' He paused again. 'They should've had a medal,' he went on. 'All three just got clear of the fall when she came. Nearest thing we had in Roughy to a triple tragedy. Both Harry's hips were dislocated.'

Timber drawing in those days was an act of great daring. Its purpose was to ease the strains upon the more important contiguous parts of the mine. Before commencing the job of felling the standing timber all that could be salvaged had to be carried clear of the anticipated extent of the fall, things like four feet long iron rails, sleepers, unset timber, forgotten instruments of production, tram wheels, anything that might be brought into further use. This completed the drawers moved to the far end of the pre-determined fall and commenced their onslaught on the roof supports, those across the tubway were of single props with a headtree, other supports, those across the tubway were a single plank of wood stretched across and supported at each end with a prop, a 'pair of gears' as such are called. Slowly, carefully the supports would be removed – any obdurate prop was merely cut in two by a hollow blow of an axe – and the superincumbent area would be enlarged. Even the shattered timber was recovered, for little could be wasted in a mine.

As the area became enlarged as a result of the roof supports being removed the earth began to whimper and then to protest. The men engaged on this task had to be able to distinguish the many voices of the roof. In the deep seams it never ceases to protest. It is most dangerous when it vociferates. Wherever it occurs there is no more awe-inspiring a task than that of timber drawing. With the continuation of felling all things assaulted moved into loud protest. This demanded a hearing, a listening and an understanding such as that demanded and experienced by the critic listening to an orchestral concert. How often, when sitting in a concert hall, have I watched the appreciative listeners *drinking* and savouring the sounds of the symphony and suddenly found myself transported into the deeps and crouching alongside those magnificent interpreters of the voices of the earth as it was moving to its impending fall, watching them *tasting* with the deepest pleasure every sound being uttered by the crunching mass as it was moving to the ultimate point of its own crashing crescendo. How attentively did those ancient miners listen for every note in the great orchestration, and calmly evaluate every sound emitted by the massive, moving, resistless, crunching power of stone as it approached the moment of its own obliterating consummation.

I have watched as I have helped at this task of easing the earth of its own pain, and I have felt humbled as I have recognised the exquisite skill and judgement and patience of those men whose duty it was to contrive a limited catastrophe. All the time they were in the presence of an awful doom, and yet they worked with grave nonchalance. At times they would whisper for silence. The word would sibilate along the passage and we would all stand hushed. A swift blow of the axe would be followed by the fall of a pair of gears. These we would scramble away. At each individual felling the fall would impend over the enlarging area of non-support. Tensely we would wait upon the final whisper: 'She's coming!' We would feel the loud boom as it sank into the entrails of the earth beneath our feet, and without hurry we would slink into a safety where we could identify the more ominous growlings ·bove us. The terror of a now loudly expostulating roof would continue until time almost failed of its gratuity. The swift move back out of danger and then the crash of the fall of the roof as it submitted itself to a chaos and pandemonium beyond estimation. And there we would leave the disruption to continue in its own time to find its own peace, knowing as we did that the upper world, so formidable in its aloneness, resented this disembowelling and would repair it.

It was as if the upper earth had gone into a deep labour in order to produce a catastrophe, but when all was over it became obvious that only the upper folds of the rock had been aborted. The fall, in most cases, was confined to the edges of the standing coal, and its further advance along the gallery was restricted by the roof supports in its path. It was always curious to note that when the fall had overlain itself in its entire mass just how dangerous the roof had become before it was felled. And, yet, any man could cast a contemptuous glance at the fall when he passed by.

Coal is a tenacious mineral when it stands within its nativity. The earth weighs upon it with the enormity of the aeons, pressing relentlessly until the excavations are unable to forbid the consummation of marriage of the floor and the roof. The pressures remain incessant and formidable. The nether world protests vociferously against all the agonies it is compelled to endure. It avows continuouly its deep disapproval. One listens and one is momentarily afraid. The seams of coal, dipping in their eternal obeisances to the rising sun, gleam in all the light which men shine upon them. And all that is actually happening is that coal is being mined.

It was into this world that I was born.

It was in this shadow-existence that I was to become a man, and to behave after the manner of men who had begotten me. I was not trapped. I was immured, as were all my contemporaries, in a mining world that we could not and would not change, but whose destiny it was to pass away.

Chapter Two

My mother's maiden name was Isabel Whitfield. She was the third daughter born to Ralph Whitfield and Ann Dunwoody. Both originated in Higher Weardale, of peasant stock. Ralph laboured on the fells. Ann, a big-boned wayward lass lived her own life until she met Ralph. Although she claimed a birthplace somewhere in the Pennine area, I have a conviction that she originated in some Westmoreland village. She was pregnant with Ralph's third child when they decided to make honest folk of themselves. In all, she bore Ralph six sons and three daughters, and she reared them all but one son and one daughter.

At the time when they were wedded, Ralph was employed as a navvy on the construction of the Waskerley reservoir high on the foot of the range, which was to provide the greater part of Durham county with the softest water known to northern man, so soft that it would lather at the touch of soap from the cold tap. It also granted unconquerable teeth decay to generations of 'Geordies'.

Ralph was encouraged by his father's eldest brother to refuse to go to the hirings and to take up navvying with him about the area. The tragedy that drove Ralph from the dale for the rest of his life occured during the excavation of the reservoir on a day set aside for blasting. Some unfortunate giant challenged Nicholas Whitfield to a wrestling contest. Reluctant to engage himself in a contest which he knew would end unhappily, he was goaded to accept the challenge.

The episode has passed out of the memory of the folk, but in those days sixty years ago I heard it discussed in my grandfather's kitchen. Nicholas angled for and secured a positive hold on his opponent and, so the tale went, told him to fall 'else he would break his back.' Which he did after he had swallowed his opponent's furious rebuke for making the suggestion. The deed done, he laid the giant on the grass and fled the scene. They found Nicholas' body a day or two later. He had committed suicide by swallowing two cartridges of dynamite.

My maternal grandparents lodged some time in Wolsingham, whither they had gone in order to escape the scandal. For some years they made their home in that delectable village. When my mother was born there they moved into the Hunwick area, where my grandfather went below ground to earn his living as a coal hewer. He remained as a hewer of coal in those low seams until he was seventy-three years of age. They found a home in Quarry Burn, and there they remained until they died.

After my mother there was one more child, a son born to the couple, whom they named Ralph. In all there were five sons, Henry, Stephen, Joseph, Job and Ralph, and two daughters, my mother and aunt Sarah. Except Stephen, all the sons went to work in the mines. Stephen migrated to Jarrow, where he earned a living as a salesman and collector of insurance. They were all tall, well-built men, mighty of muscle, and ingenious as hewers of coal. Sarah married a bricklayer of considerable skill, Stephen Coulson. She bore him a long family, most of which died of pulmonary tuberculosis. The 1914-18 war ended the lives of two of the boys. Sarah was twenty years older than my mother. She was very frail, and in the end the same disease destroyed her.

My mother never really got over being the spoiled daughter of a family of men. Over all the years prior to her marriage with my father they all did their best to pamper and spoil her. When she did marry she proved herself to be an untutored house-wife. Her maiden years were replete with pleasure, which she found in the nearby towns of Bishop Auckland and Crook. Hers was a strange alliance with my father. I am sure that it must have been a great trial for her until she realised that she had to make do with making do, as they have it in that part of the world. Religion was a thing apart for most of the Whitfields. Grandfather attended the Primitive Methodist Chapel, not because he was religious, but, as I remain convinced, just to get away from Ann. He never offered a grace at meal, never spoke a prayer from his kitchen floor, never breathed one in his bed-room. Outside the chapel prayer played no part in his life. How good or bad a hewer he was I am unable to say. After retiring from the mine as one of the first recipients of the Old Age Pension Act of Mr Lloyd George's he disintegrated with alarming rapidity. I followed his coffin through the deep snow of the January of 1913, some five months before we buried my mother. The Great War was little more than a year away from history.

Ann Whitfield was the most unreligious woman I have ever met. Her every spoken thought held a sexual urge. She was simply a peasant bawd in her own right. For her a dirty story or a two-edged insinuation was the joy of life, that which she treasured to the gates of her senility. I remember her face, an unkissed, unloved parchment made by the years. I remember her better when she walked abroad in black alpaca, decorated bonnet and umbrella and strong leather boots, a tall, angular person endowed with great physical strength. She rarely spoke foul language. She did not behave riotously. Under her stark exterior she hid a furious contempt of the life she had been required to live. None of her sons treasured her. She and all her sons but Henry were content to grace a church or chapel when they had to follow a coffin there. None of them were at any time generous to us, the children of their sister. Perhaps it was their conviction that they had contributed enough to their sister's pleasure.

They did not visit our home, and we did not offer to enter any of theirs! Birthdays and festival days were not observed after the simple manner of the poor. None of us ever received a coin from any of our relations. The giving and receiving of alms were unknown in our families.

I believe that my grandmother loved her daughter. She came to her aid in times of sickness, and she did all those domestic chores for her which she ought to have done for herself, such as simple sewing, the making of shirts and underclothing, mending and repairing, doing the family wash when my mother was abed with child. In return she asked nothing, nothing, not even a simple chore. Poor soul!

Washing the clothes was a task that required great strength in its execution in the north east. When a couple set up house there were three domestic requisites that had to be obtained for they could not be borrowed more than once, and these were a poss-tub, a poss-stick and a mangle. Today their place has been usurped by the washing machine. The poss-stick was a curiously shaped instrument made of ash. It was cut from one piece of wood. The shank of the contraption was reduced to about three inches in diameter, and was about two feet in length, and protruded, unbroken, from the rest of the clump of wood from which it was fashioned. This part of the stick was the 'posser', and was machined along a length of some ten or twelve inches at a diameter of some ten inches. Cross incisions milled to a depth of seven inches and an inch wide gave the tool the appearance of a four clawed beater. A handle inserted at the narrow end of the stick enabled the user to raise the stick and then bring it down sharply upon the clothes lying in the deep soapy water in the tub. It was quite a different instrument to the Yorkhire 'Dolly'. When the clothes which had been previously soaped and scrubbed – the 'whites' were boiled on the kitchen fire before being tipped into the tub – they were put in the tub and then beaten. It was a woman's job! She pounded the inoffensive clutter in the tub until she could do it no more, and then she eased her aching bones by seizing the 'possed' clothes and put them through the mangle, a huge machine of cast iron with rollers ten inches in diameter and almost a yard long. A woman's work to be sure. In all my life I did not see a man lend a hand, for it was work that was beneath male dignity.

Washing day was a non-event in the home. The family ate scraps. The children snatched what food they could find. The work was laborious and tiring. And yet there were women who 'went out to wash', that is to supplement the family income by doing the wash for other women. I recall that the woman who came to our house for this purpose received two shillings for her services.

Drying the wash was a business that occupied the rest of the week until Friday night. Lines were stretched across the back lanes and the clothes were pegged to these and held aloft by long poles. At the end of the day the lines were brought into the kitchen and stretched across the room and the damp clothes hung up to complete the process of drying. Once dried, a day or so later, the clothes were then devoutly mangled and brought back to the kitchen to be aired. Such clothes as those which had to be ironed were set apart for that domestic ministration, and in due time they were hung up on the lines. Friday being the day set apart for baking the bread, the fire was brought to a raging heat, from which the hanging clothes received the finished treatment, and by the time the bread 'was laid' before the kitchen fire the clothes could be taken down and 'put away'.

My mother was too frail to partake arduously in this heavy work of the Durham miners' wives, but somehow she struggled on and bore her children. After her death I once talked to my paternal grandfather about her. He assured me that she had 'the Whitfield complaint,' and that she could not have lived a great many years. She was not, he said, a strong specimen of the women of the coalfield.

I was born in Rough Lea on the first day of October in the year 1898. My mother gave birth to her third child, a son, late in the December of 1900. This child was furnished with the name of Hector. All, or most all, of the unfortunate males of that generation received Boer War appellations, like 'Redvers', 'Baden', 'Buller', 'Powell', some men received 'Kitchener' or 'Roberts'. The girls did not escape, and were commissioned to carry through their lives such names as 'Pretoria', 'Kimberley', even 'Mafeking'! All this apart, the arrival of the new baby liberated me from my conscription to the yard of our miserable little home. I was allowed to play beyond the 'nessy'.

At the top of the street in the area beyond the colliery gate all the lime, sand and bricks necessary for building or repairing the structures above and below ground were deposited in great mounds. All this clutter formed a delectable and not forbidden playground for all the children in the hamlet. A small gauge railway for the tubs ran from the bankhead to the yard so that the materials required in the mine could be loaded and then shunted to form part of a suitable train of tubs. There is more actual building done in a mine than might be imagined. Arches have been constructed against the most menacing roofs that would have done credit to the builders of great cities. A strange world, indeed. It was more than a world of play. Couples went a-courting among the debris of that strange, unexciting world.

As I grew older this world opened for me its many dirty windows, and in some dim way I understood much that was happening. Away from the simple joys and mishaps of that stores area I ventured as I was allowed, or taken, into that part of the world where the coke ovens were made to rage in all the wonders and beatitudes of their fantastic processes. It was fascinating to watch the wagons emerging from the hopper filled with coal and being pushed down the slope to gain speed before the trammer leaped upon it to make a safe journey over the roaring ovens. It was just a matter of exploiting the gradients on both outward and inward journeys. The lift from the end of the lower gradient was made by mechanical means. The truck possessed a wide mouth, from which the sides narrowed sharply to an aperture at the base which was small enough to allow the contents, small coal and coal dust, to drop into a cold oven through its upper vent. The task of the trammer was to stop his vehicle precisely above this vent. This done he pulled the lever and allowed the contents to escape. He then closed the slot of his truck and manoeuvred his machine to that point at the end of the line of ovens where he could join the gradient which would take him back to the hopper.

Each of the ovens possessed a rather large vent, like a small doorway, at the side, through which the coke would be removed. From the top of the 'doorway' depended a well adjusted wheel, or rake bolt, which was unhooked and laid aside until it was time to 'fell' the oven. The process was quite simple. Prior to the loading of the oven, the 'doorway' was built up with blocks of concrete, or similar material, but in such a manner that air vents were left at places between the blocks. Special 'oven-shutters' went the rounds closing the ovens for the next turn-over of coke. When a rank of ovens were made ready for coking they were ignited, but in what way I was never able to discover. Once on fire, nature had its will on the rejected spillage from the mine. For three days and three nights the oven blazed so riotously as to violate the atmosphere over a considerable area. At the height of the conflagration the flames leaped great distances into the air. The heat was unbearable. To stand and watch was to become mesmerised. The world appeared to have become offered in sacrifice to the production that depended upon coke and which is no longer remembered.

It was a wonderful experience watching the oven men 'killing' an oven. Beyond the perforated wall across the door was a white hot mass that squirmed and heaved in dreadful beligerency. The killers waited for the moment when they could begin operations. Stripped naked to the waist line of their trousers, they attacked first the walled doorway, wielding their sledgehammers with a remarkable fluency of strokes, attacking individually in short bursts then leaping out of the clutch of the tremendous heat. After a few bursts the rampart was breached, and the debris cast out of the way with the aid of long handled shovels. Then followed the 'drowning' of the coke. The water came from the colliery pond, pumped under the necessary amount of pressure. Each oven had its own 'tap', a large affair to which was attached the end of a large hose which ended in a smaller nozzle which powered a flow of water into the heart of the fiery mass. As soon as the water hit the mass of coke everything was blotted out by a scalding steam from which everybody present on the rank sought refuge in the nearby cold ovens. Like an animal held at bay the coke passed into hissing protestation.

As soon as the hissing, screaming and scorching had died down the feller and his mate hung the bolt on its hook, passed the rake on to the wheel and began to *feel* the coke. The purpose of the feverish manipulation of the rake was to find some break in the coke for the rake head so that the 'coke' could be broken from the mass and pulled out of the oven. As the water continued to play on the coke it helped in shattering the congealed mass into manageable fragments.

Of all the laborious jobs I have come into contact with this was the most fearsome and painful. Once the contents of the ovens were brought into control the rest was labour. Soon the rake was manipulated freely and effectively and was bringing huge slabs of gleaming silver out of the fiery lair. The job of the assistant was to heave the hot stuff into a huge barrow with an enormous fork, and then trundle the barrow up the ramp over the space between the oven platform and the ten ton truck standing near it. This barrow was amazingly tall and presented various difficulties before its essential purpose could be realised. First, it was a task loading the hot coke into it, secondly it was difficult to balance it over the ramp, and thirdly a matter of some ability to tip the contents into the truck. The simple technology of those bygone days presumed the presentation of superhuman strength in conjunction with enormous agility without the possessor being fully mindful of them.

Nothing was so beautiful for me as those silver slabs of coke being withdrawn from the screaming ovens and wheeled into the trucks. To watch the act was to glory in the beauty of endeavour and to be mindful of the travesty of its fate. It gleamed with the radiance of bright silver, too beautiful almost to touch. As it cooled and took on the further majesty of polished silver it seemed to solidify into something reaching out beyond grandeur, to purposeful human labour. Today there is no coke like that which the north eastern collieries produced for the metallurgic industries, for such delicate loveliness has lapsed into an unremembered past.

As children we played many fascinating games about those dreadful ovens. We roasted potatoes and ate them down to their scorched blackness. We kept clear of the tramps who made the ovens their homes. We carried crickets home on our clothes. Their cheerful chirpings, when they were successfully lodged in some crevice in the fireplace, were always a trouble and an unhappiness to the housewives who had to live with them all day. They concocted strange brews with which to get rid of the pests, and they whipped us children for bringing them home.

I often recall with secret pleasure those early evil days. The passing of the years sweetens the distant pleasings. After all, they were years that added stature to a simple boy. There was that little locomotive that panted and struggled about the environs of the industrial complex. Were it here today it might be a treasured museum piece. The year would be 1905, and it might have been forty, nay fifty years old. That would have taken it near to the George Stephenson era. What a task! What a doom! To push and pull thousands of tons of coal, thousands of tons of coke, massive quantities of timber, bricks, seggar clay, and beautiful earthenware into and out of that deplorably dirty area of production.

That locomotive had a brother, or a forerunner. I did not discover it, but I was convinced that it had been left there for me. It was a much simpler engine, one that had outlived the days of its usefulness, one that had been taken to some remote valley between two enormous mounds of blue shale and left there, forgotten. As the shale tips had increased great lumps of shale rolled down from the tops when the waggons were tipped and had gathered about the locomotive, gradually obliterating it. For some reason the tipping had stopped, and when I found it I gathered it into the keeping of my childish imagination, all to myself. I made it my very own secret. Whenever I could slip away from the notice of my increasingly harassed mother I clambered over those mounds and hour after hour shared its forgotten aloneness. It was the most wonderful privilege of my young days to clamber up the iron steps into the cab. That deserted cab, with all its simple furnishings became the centre of my very own kingdom of shale. The simple mechanisms had been left intact. The water gauge still functioned, and the fire-door opened and shut. The starting handle I could not move no matter how I tried. The whistle had long been dead. The windows were intact, and through them I peered into a vast world that existed far beyond the shale rubble that lay decomposing in the air. How many thousands of miles we journeyed into the kingdom of a child's imagination it would be difficult to assess.

What became of my locomotive I do not know. I did not outgrow my passion for it. When I went to school I still found time to visit my immobile engine. When my father was promoted and we moved to High Grange I went to say goodbye, and there I left it to all the ravages of time, shale tipping and rust.

All over those early years my mother provided the family comfort and my father reproved his children after the manner of the sons of the north country. Their's was a unity without love. It was always his duty and his pleasure to thrash us, and as the years passed his thrashings became more and more explosive. Often they were without the savour of mercy, and then my mother intervened. There was that sorry day when he discovered that my eldest brother had played truant from school. That thrashing was so compulsive that my mother had to throw herself upon her child to prevent further ill being done. None of us played truant after that. That good hiding became a family remembrance. Being a most perceptive man, my father was capable of recognising other men's evils; being a deeply religious man he was capable of inflicting merciless punishment. His appreciation of wrong doing was meticulous. There was that occasion when, as a small child, I became restless in chapel on a torrid afternoon during an interminable sermon. My father informed me when we got outside that he would thrash me when we got home. I walked home with him in a fever of apprehension. When we reached home he told me to go into the front room and take my trousers down.

'What has he done?' my mother asked, fearfully. She was then far gone with her fourth child

'He's been a bad lad in chapel,' he informed her.

'Don't be too rough with him, Bill,' she pleaded. 'He's only a bairn.'

'He's got to learn,' he said.

He followed me into the front room, taking the strap with him. Every family possessed a strap, a thong of leather with many ends. Without a word he began whipping me across my bare buttocks. From then, until my mother interfered it was my shrieks and his blows.

'Why can't you have a little mercy, Bill?' she challenged.

'He's got to learn how to behave,' he said.

And yet he could be kind, sometimes considerate. After his

own fashion he loved his children. He certainly could be kind to other men's children. He kept a packet of sweets locked in the top left hand drawer of the kitchen press, and these he would distribute to the children, always little girls, who came in from our neighbours. He would distribute them in the presence of his own bairns and not offer them one each. He recognised no evil in his act. He believed in the absolute rightness of all that he did. At times he was as rigid as Jacob, at others he was as merciless as a centurion. He never learned to be gentle until he became possessed of three step-daughters

Perhaps it was his daughter, Rhoda, who made him kind and considerate to other little girls. Rhoda was a frail beautiful child who stumbled into this world shortly after my thrashing. The doctor seemed to be ever entering our home to administer to her frail but demanding needs. Somehow she got within a few weeks of her first birthday when she was accidently scalded. When we got home from school we found distress rampaging through the little home. The child died that night.

The sounds of my mothers grief ring across the decades to my writing table. We three boys were asleep in the one bed when the commotion occurred. We got out of bed and ran into the other bedroom, and there we saw our mother in all her pitiful, pleading distress. A neighbour woman came upstairs and ushered us back into bed. Then she went to spread calm upon a woman lost in a tempest of emotion and guilt.

The next morning we found our little sister lying strangely still among a new whiteness over the front room table. Father had gone to work, leaving mother in her terrible grief. The neighbours were kind after their own simple fashions. Most of them had trod the paths that led to a Gethsemane of grief, but none after so obliterating a tragedy. The coroner issued a certificate without holding an inquest. Two or three days later they carried the child to the churchyard.

In those days the matter of the burial of the dead, Methodist fashion, was quite impressive. The night before, the two bidders, fully attired in their best clothes, came to view the corpse and take their instructions. Thereafter, when the sun was set, they set out to knock on the doors of the houses in the village and bid the householders to attend the funeral. The subsequent performance followed simple lines. In response to the knock and when the door was opened the bidder said:

'You are welcome bid to attend the funeral of Rhoda Heslop,

which will take place tomorrow from the house of William and Isabel Heslop, number four Rough Lea. Gather at two and lift at half-past.' To which the person at the door would say a quiet 'Thank You', and close the door.

The neighbours and friends gathered at our house at the appointed time, the men standing in the roadway to gossip and the women going into the house to view the corpse. My mother stood by the little coffin sobbing her heart away. Outside, the two women in charge of the refreshments, carried out a chair and placed it on the near side of the roadway. Inside the house, Hodgon Fletcher, the undertaker, closed the coffin, which was then carried out and placed on the chair. Mourners and friends gathered close. A man gave out the first verse of a hymn. After a wavering start the tune was found and the hymn was sung. This over, the coffin was slung in two rolled up table cloths, which four young women took hold at the ends, lifted their little burden and headed the cortège towards Hunwick church-yard.

The dead disposed of, the gathering broke up. Most of the people went to their homes. Neighbours and near relations returned to the house and partook of a meal.

It is difficult even now to forget the anguish of my mother after the last mourner had gone from the bereaved home.

Chapter Three

My brother George and I were obliged to attend chapel three times every sabbath, whatever the weather, and without let or hindrance. Real illness was the only excuse for non attendance. When we moved from Rough Lea to High Grange on the appointment of my father to an official capacity in North Bitchburn Colliery, the stringency of chapel attendance was not relaxed although the distance from our new home to Hunwick chapel was considerably increased. The morning service was devoted to Sunday School, and the other two meetings to the rampaging in the pulpit which continued on each occasion well into the second hour. The final hymn of the evening service was not the last meeting of the day. There was always the prayer meeting.

George and I were not introduced to the prayer meeting until after we had got settled into our new home. We both found it interesting to watch the congregation pass out of the chapel and go about its own several businesses, and to experience the fading of the hymn into an unaccompanied chant as the preacher closed the 'great book' and placed the hymn book gently on top of it, crept out of the pulpit, down the four steps, holding on to the newel post as he passed into the carpeted area in which stood the communion table.

For me, a young child, it was always an experience tinged with awe. All those who had chosen 'to stay behind' sank upon their knees and waited for the preacher to utter the injunction: 'Let us pray'. They all waited until John Heslop, the organist, had closed the organ and taken his departure from the organ loft, crept down the stairs and joined the little band of supplicators. Invariably, it was Sandy Metcalf, the choir master, who broke into the first lamentation, prefaced by a statement of general approval of what the preacher had said 'from Thy holy book, Lord'. Hazlitt has it in one of his essays that 'the popular preacher made less frequent mention of heaven than of hell'. Now that I come to recall them, those prayers were complemental to the sermon and the stresses that had been laid upon the beseechings and namings of the punishments that had been defined. It was the opportunity for those simple worshippers to lay their implorings at the foot of the throne. Whenever an apposite point was made in a prayer loud 'Amens' and 'Hossanahs' escaped from the dedicated bowels of those faithful. My grandfather generally followed Sandy, and after him my father would raise his own voice. Grandfather prayed passionately, ravenously, exposing his own goodnesses and his own good behaviour as acts worthy of condemnation rather than condonement. 'Thy book, Oh Lord' was always dressed in inverted commas and deeply underlined and sprinkled with star dust. Simple words were offered in complex sentences. Incoherence was always overlooked by a loud 'Hear him, Lord'. My father prayed gently, subjectively, and not straight into the ear of the Lord God, for he was sure that He would recognise the finest of his thoughts, the gentleness of his impeachments and the softness of his approvals as coming straight out of the pages of the *Hibbert Journal*. He did not offer himself as a theologian, but as one who had accepted guidance and anticipated encouragement. But the high spot was grandmother Heslop.

St Paul has it most succinctly that 'a woman keep silence in the churches, for it is not permitted unto them to speak' because 'it is a shame to speak in the church.' Had St Paul known my grandmother he might not have included that stricture in his law, for not only did she speak in church, she applauded and denounced whenever she thought she ought to do so. And she did it with a well directed ejaculation. Woe to any preacher who 'tampered with the Word' in her presence. She reserved her denunciations, her condemnations and her approvals for the prayer meeting. She did not rant; nor did she rave. She pleaded and supplicated and she whispered. I can see her now, a little, frail woman, a leaf on the bough of Methodism, not five feet high, not seven stones in weight, a thin, time-worn little creature, dressed in black, buttons to the ears, and bonnetted like a flower, a bonnet like a black halo with a thin white spray that danced to every movement of her head.

She was a border woman who had moved south with her family from a nestling hamlet tucked somewhere among the Cheviots to the Tyneside and then to Newcastle. Often did I sit sharing her lonely company and listening to her tales of her early life. Her speech in conversation was as soft and limpid as a clear stream. It was that of high Northumberland wherein the sibilant stress nursed the consonants into sweet accompaniment with the softly uttered vowels, at all times musical. 'Dinna rive your meat, laddie,' she would adjure me. 'Give it aal a fine chew wi' your teeth. Niver fratch wi' your teeth. Chew, laddie, chew an' grow into a fine man.' So lovely a cadence, pure and radiant, as when the violin rises in the melody and sweetens the playing into soft gentling of tone. I never heard speech like her's until I listened to Tom Burt, the first working man to be elected to parliament.

She told me her tales of her early days, 'when we lassies what worked at Haggie's rope works, had to cross the Tyne by the steppy stones.' She told me of the great comet that 'meant to sca'd the sea dry, if the Lord had let it.' Often she breathed a comforting mass for the souls 'o' them canny men an' bairns that perished in Hartley pit.' She was not always gentle, but even when she spoke in anger it was marvellous to listen to her. Her frail body had borne my grandfather eleven bairns, eight daughters and three sons, 'arl o' whom but two, a frail laddie and a poor wee lassie, I reared.' Grandfather was dead and buried when she confessed to me: 'I always felt sorry for my man, your grandfather. He was a proud and forgiving man in all things, but there was one thing that allus grieved him, and what he niver got over. He was a grandfather to a vast load o' children that were the bairns of other men's sons.' She shook her head over her memories. 'A great punishment that, laddie,' she whispered to me. 'I often sits an' wonders why.'

Today, some forty years after her death, I think I am beginning to understand her. She was, undoubtedly, of a tempestuous nature, yet she was a little old dear who had a passion for flowers, especially nasturtiums, which she grew from a tub standing in the backyard of her home. 'They're so good,' she said to me as I watched her tend them, 'If I just dropped them on the cement they would still find root. They're so thankful for life.' And sparrows. She was kin to every one that chirped in her yard, on speaking terms with them all.

But in the prayer meeting she was not even afraid of the Lord. She always had something to reveal to Him, often cajoled him. Sometimes she came near to chiding Him for his failure to noticing. When she prayed it was *through* her big white handkerchief, which she held over her face. She always rebuked the preacher when she felt that he needed rebuke. Once she scandalised the little group when she cried out as if in grievous pain: 'Lord! Lord! Save our preacher! Suffer him not to walk in the way of the transgressor of Thy word!' Sometimes her voice rose into a thin scream, like a bow drawn casually over the highest reach of the E string. On this occasion the little group of philistines almost broke up in disorder. It was the time of the *New Theology* of R.J. Campbell. She almost despaired of her church. There was that moment when she spoke directly to God about the offending cleric after he had joined the Church of England. 'Lord! Let him not travel the same road as Newman! Bring him to Thy footstool and let him ask forgiveness!' It was all so strange and personal. Prayer, her prayer, was always a deeply personal experience. Delivered with grace and regret, it was ever a beseechment for her, or somebody else's, forgiveness. She did not pound the form against which she knelt. She cried out in deep woe. She offered her tribute, and granted her tribulation, for all that had happened during the past week. Indeed, she carried all she had to offer right up to the top step of the throne, and there she bent both knees as she placed it, peremptorily albeit, right into the lap of the Lord God of Hosts. And when she had bowed herself out of the Presence, all that was left for the Preacher was to close the prayer meeting.

After the prayer meeting we all descended the hill into the village and entered the old couple's dwelling. By the time both men had got their pipes alight Michael Heslop would walk in unannounced and the veil would be drawn across the temple, and the three men would talk of mines and the ways of mines. Grandmother would sit in her rocking chair and nudge herself into her dreams, forgetful of the wrongs done in the pulpit and of wrongs righted in the prayer meeting.

As a child I found it amazingly interesting to listen to those men discussing the strange world into which I had been born, and to which I was not a complete stranger. Each man would smoke his briar pipe. They all smoked a thick twist at three pence halfpenny an ounce. Each would lop off a piece with his pocket knife and, without closing the knife or putting it down, would rub the tobacco into a fairly fine condition before inserting it in the bowl of the pipe. What fascinated me most was the ability of each man to spit across the hearth into the heart of the fire. None of them ever stirred from his chair in order to do so. Michael Heslop was the best spitter of the three, and I should think, the best spitter in the coalfield. He could and did spit clean through the space of the handle of the kettle as it stood on the hob. His was a perfect aim, through his almost closed teeth, and his was the perfect accomplishment. My father was less gifted in the art, if art it was, but he was by no means unaccomplished. Grandfather was a quieter smoker and spat less frequently.

In those days smoking was permitted in the mines in south west Durham, for they were not bone dry. As a matter of fact pumping was the main subordinate occupation in the production of coal in that area. Being so wet, the coal dust was more coagulated and less volatile. Explosions in that part of the county were rare occurrences, nevertheless there was an instinctive fear abroad throughout the county that stemmed from the presence of large accumulations of coal dust. Away back on June 25th, 1845, Michael Faraday, drawing on his experiences in Haswell Colliery the year before, had declared at a public lecture in London that 'explosions are not simply the effects arising from the mixture of gases, but from the combustion of the coal-dust and the coal-gas which the first explosion made', but this had not yet seeped into the minds of mining technicians. Time was still on the side of Faraday.

All coal mines and, indeed, all ironstone mines, produce the deadly firedamp. The ignition of an accumulation of this gas produces a flash of fire, which, under given circumstances, flies forward against the incoming fresh air. Any coal dust lying in the track of the fire is raised into a cloud and feeds the gathering force of the conflagration. Momentarily a massive explosion sweeps forward along the intake with unimaginable force. Nothing under the earth within the compass of man's explorations is so destructive as a coal-gas explosion.

I have witnessed a pocket of firedamp deliberately exploded in order to 'get it out of the way'. This was in the Boulby ironstone mine. I actually saw Dick Atkinson, the deputy, crawl into the place with a lighted candle fixed to a long pole. The result of the ignition of the gas was negative. It was just a loud bang and a sheet of flame. There was no combustible – as the miners call it – lying about to sustain the explosion.

When Michael Heslop called on a Sunday evening to chat with my grandparents they did not discuss religion. When the men started to talk she invariably flung her white linen apron over her face and rocked herself in her chair. At times she would whisper her pity whenever the discussion turned on accident or tragedy. Within her vast illiteracy crouched a knowing and understanding creature, who brimmed with pity and who drew into her memory much that passed that of the others as of little importance. Religion bothered every one of them. Over the years that have passed and carried them all into oblivion I have often pondered on why they were all such willing burden-bearers of the Lord God. My grandmother not only offered pity and comfort to all sufferers, she granted tentative absolution to the smallest sinners. My grandfather was the great decision maker in the world of the suffering and cheerlessness in which he lived, but his was more abstract, more reflective. He found the note on which to begin the hymn at every funeral in the village. He never stormed the pulpit, and very rarely did he address the Sunday School.

My father was a lay preacher on the plan of the Bishop Auckland circuit. His services were sought over a large area, even into upper Weardale and as far afield as Teesdale. An argumentative man at all times, he could cause an uproar at 'Quarter Day' of the circuit, and at the half-yearly meeting of the Co-operative Society. It was strange that he never understood that his outrageous acts at such meetings, and his declamations from the many pulpits, would be received with scant pleasure by the men who employed him. He devoured the *Hibbert Journal* to the end of his life. I have often wondered if he was ever impressed by any of the theologians he found between those green covers. Personally, I always found them singularly pretentious, although sensibly tensioned, upon the assumption rather than the fact, and I am painfully mindful of a criticism by Marx of Hegel's ability to turn his predicates into subjects and elevate a chance historical act into a test for ultimate reality. Being a mining engineer, my father dealt with realities and yet was able to accept as facts arguments that were not even real when they came to him from outside his own experience and work.

I do not remember any of his sermons, nor how he graced the pulpit, for I was expelled from his home long before I was able to offer a judgement. He was not a perceptive politician. When he did accept Michael Heslop's advice to join the Tory Party he was far gone along the road to retirement.

As soon as Michael had eased himself up so as to lean forward and knock his pipe against the top bar of the fire my grandmother would rouse herself out of her dream and begin to set out a frugal meal 'for Bill and the lads' and 'get them on their way to the Grange', Michael would not linger against his departures. As he opened the back door he would throw back a word of farewell and be gone. The men of Hunwick were unacquainted with the niceties that pleased their hosts; they simply departed.

Michael gone, we would draw up to the table and eat the bread and cheese, and drink the tea, and then we, too, would get ready to go home. Beyond the yard door we would step into the lovely northern night. Above us the great dome of the sky, softly tinged with crimson from the flames of the dying coke ovens at the colliery, would show us its stars. The Milky Way would by then have gathered its myriads of constellations into a softly dusted stream of light and lain it across the heavens. It was a time for quiet breathings and soft treadings for we poached the beauty of our earth. About us the village would be making ready for the labours of another week, and it would be wrong to disturb those preparations for sleep and toil that would be going on in the kitchens in the houses along the street.

The cold meat would have been hacked from the sunday joint and the slices laid on the plates against the cold boiled potatoes, stiff pieces of cold Yorkshire pudding and soggy cabbage, and all would have been devoured in hungry peace. The father of the household would be having a last puff at his clay pipe before getting into bed in the kitchen. The mother of the household would be going about her tasks, filling the kettle at the outside tap and placing it beside the banked-up fire, seeking out the pit clothes and spreading them along the fender, putting the pit boots near the oven, setting out the water bottle and the 'midgies' – primitive little lamps used in the pit – and tying up the sandwiches of bread and cheese in the 'bait bags'. All this done she would undress and make herself ready to sleep without the benediction of a prayer. She would lower the wick of the paraffin lamp, blow across the top of the glass chimney, and extinguish the flame. The firelight, left now to play in the darkness, would illumine her path to the side of her husband.

As we walked up the road a pit buzzer screamed out its agonised wail, which was an intimation to the underworld to stir in its fastnesses.

Chapter Four

We were still living in Rough Lea when the Balfour adminis-tration handed over to Campbell-Bannerman without taking the trouble to seek the suffrages of the electorate. By that time I had passed out of the primary school along to the 'big' school by the church. All written work was done on slates, for our school life was not so very distant from the start of the elementary school system. The authorities had no idea, outside that of stark economy, of furnishing the schools. We sat on long forms, eight or ten children to the form. We each had an inkwell hole, but we had no inkwells. We cleaned our slates with spit and our jacket sleeves. We had no rulers. It was education on the cheap.

The day the voting took place in the Bishop Auckland division the little school had a holiday. As soon as we were set free from our school I made my way to the other school just to see what there was to see. I was soon deeply interested in the process. I stood in the porch to watch and wait for anybody I knew who might take me in. I was most impressed by the policeman who seemed to have nothing to do but stand about.

The Bishop Auckland constituency was a foregone Liberal seat. It remained so until 1918. The sitting member was James Paulton, who had represented the division since its enfranchise-ment away back in the eighties. Paulton was in the booth when my grandfather arrived to cast his vote. When Paulton emerged my father's father was deep in his interrogation of myself. He became highly amused. He came out just when I had told the old man I had not been home for my tea.

'Then thou'rt a bad lad,' said my grandfather. 'Your mother'll be worriting, won't she?'

'Who is the bairn, George?' the candidate asked.

'It's our Bill's lad,' he replied. 'Lives down at Roughey. He hasn't been home for his tea.'

'Perhaps he's interested, George,' Paulton suggested.

'Interested! What right has he to be interested? He wants his backside smacked for not going home.'

71

'It'll do the lad no harm, George,' said Paulton. 'Why don't you take him in and let him see how it's done?' He bent down and chucked me under the chin. 'Goodbye, my boy,' he said.

My grandfather did not take me into the booth with him. As soon as Paulton was gone he marched me to the gate and ordered me 'off home'. In the distance I could see my father. There was no need to tell me what to do.

Soon after that my father received his appointment at North Bitchburn colliery, and in time a farmer arrived at our door with his dray and a lad. With the help of the villagers they dismantled our home and packed it on the waggon. They found a place for the mangle, poss tub, garden spade, beds, everything but the clock and took it away to High Grange. My brother had to carry the clock, and a grievous burden he found it to be.

All this meant a change in our lives, but no change in our way of life. The colliery lay about a mile distant from the village, at the bottom of a steep hill. It was a replica of Rough Lea, a drift haulage, a large bank of coke ovens and an extensive brickyard. It polluted the atmosphere of Howden-le-Wear. High Grange was no better and no worse a village conception than any other village in the county. It lay exactly three miles from Bishop Auckland. The original frontage, which had been a bit of a speculative ribbon development, hid the three rows of houses which ran at right angles to it towards the foot of Grange Bank. Except that it was unpaved, it was fairly livable as a village.

Most of the miners were housed in North Bitchburn village, a collection of the most deplorable houses imaginable set on the brow of the hill that saw all that was to be seen of the fearful complex below and which accepted the smut and fumes and the roaring flames of the vast coking plant. North Bitchburn was the undelectable village.

There was a post office and general stores at the end of the frontage in High Grange. Next to it was a large house which was occupied by the clerk to the Bishop Auckland bench of magistrates, which was overlooked and over-ruled by Sir William Eden, Bart., the father of a son who eventually became Prime Minister and an earl, Anthony Eden.

At the top of the street was the school, which served the needs of the children of North Bitchburn, High Grange, Quarry Burn and the odd farms in between. The school was presided over by Charles Leonard Davies, B. Litt, the cruellest punisher of a delinquent child I have ever met. A sadist, if ever there was one. To see him stroke his cane before administering savage punishment of a male malefactor was to see the ultimate in disregard of childish suffering.

High Grange had its own advantages. It was a haven in a world devoted to coal production. It stood on a ledge of a steep hill where it could look out towards the distant Pennines. From the top of Grange Bank, upon which was built a reservoir for serving the habitations below with fresh water, one could on a clear day mark the march of the Pennine range from the glimmerings which broke over the Tees, then gently undulating and forever rising to parade on its lovely way into the mountains and then to dip into the lowliness of the distant Tyne country, beautiful beyond belief, wrapped eternally in a radiance that is ever ethereal to men.

The railway which had been laid from Darlington to Tow Law had branched off at a point half a mile distant from High Grange to enable a subsidiary line to climb the valley of the Wear as far as Wearhead. Wear Valley Junction served the villages and hamlets around. In the past the railway had had to be trestled from the old iron works at Witton Park in order to carry the line over the bed of the river. This had long been filled in with cinders and rubble. It stood like a rampart across the valley, but somehow it did not spoil the view. Over the road from High Grange to Witton-le-Wear had been constructed a tremendously high brick arched bridge. On the top of this bridge stood the station.

Our house was no better than any of the houses in the village, but, being the bottom house in Pipe Row, it had an incomparable view of the valley. The windows had been inserted in the gable, and so the view was our own. At any time of the day the mountains could be caught clinging to the shoulder of England. It was a vista to delight the lowliest heart, not because it was there, but simply because industry had not as yet laid its unclean paws on the field, fold or fell that stayed as they had always stayed long before Bede had lain down his pen. Before coal was spaded out of the earth of Durham the country must have been wonderful to gaze upon. In my early youth the country which had escaped molestation still lay in the gift of beauty. The wooded uplands rose gently out of a benediction breathed upon it from untroubled skies. Only the smoke of a solitary railway engine fluttered upwards as if afraid. From the bedroom window on a bright morning, and there were many bright mornings, I would look out upon it all, unaware that I would not find an excess of peace and stillness elsewhere in my wanderings. The valley cleaved gently to the remote fanes of the land and the mountains stood steadfast as they held up the white clouds above the deep purple of the heather cladding their slopes.

It was a glorious place to arrive at, for there was always the beckoning, if not the promise of fulfilment. It was somewhere in that valley where my mother had been born, in Wolsingham, a village that remains what it must have been when she was a child playing in its streets more than a century ago.

I recall that day she and I, and the newborn fourth son in the perambulator made a journey to Witton-le-Wear. The sun was warm as we walked along the road above the willow land that touches the river with a green gentleness. We got as far as the saw mill, but instead of walking on into the village she left the road by a path that edged the river along its pebbled reach. All was quiet and lonely. We walked until we came upon a fallen trunk, and there we sat down so that she could suckle the child. When he was sated she put him back into his sleep and then she began to weep. She wept silently in an uncontrolled sobbing as I sat beside her, wondering. If she had had tears to spare against her lot she must have shed them long ago. When she grew composed she rose, turned the pram round, and smiled at me.

'We'll go home now,' she said.

I expostulated, but she merely smiled my anger away. 'I cannot go on,' she said to me. 'It is too much like trying to go back home,' she told herself. 'I hope you will never have to go home and find that there isn't any home left, Harold,' she said, almost in a whisper, said it to her soul.

We retraced our way back to our village, back over the road that is wedded to the water that was destined to be muddied and polluted.

Never again did she pass that way.

I had not at that time gone to the grammar school at Bishop Auckland. Indeed it was not until after she had given birth to her fifth son that that happened. Life by then had become easier, although my father had not been given the undermanager's position at the colliery, and had had to settle for an overmanship. This meant that he went to work at six in the morning and finished at two in the afternoon one week, and commenced work the next week at one in the afternoon and continued until nine at night, carrying over his over-looking of the waste after coal production had ceased, to see that the return airway was functioning.

As children we always felt unhappy when he was on the afternoon shift, because he insisted on morning prayer before we went to school. We all had to kneel while he went through his performance. Mother hated all this 'rigamarole' as she called it. She did not sink to her knees at any of the sessions. My father did not appear to recognise the fatuity of his perform-ance. Nor was he consistent in his attitude to God. He only said grace before one meal, the Sunday dinner. Rarely did he explode into a swear word, but he always emphasised his dis-quiet caused by our misbehaviour by uttering a pompous and threatening enunciation of the punishment he would inflict if it occured again. Like all miners he went to the pit from January 2nd to December 31st without any break except such as were occasioned by recognised holidays, of which there were few. The pits did not 'hang on', as the term was, on New Year's Day, Good Friday, Easter Monday, Whit Monday, August Bank Holiday and Christmas Day. The week began on Monday morning and ended every other week at Saturday 1 p.m. On Pay Friday, which occurred fortnightly, the pit ceased to draw coal that night.

Once a year, on a workless Saturday, the Sunday School trip took place. The Church of England scholars went ann-ually to Redcar, while the eager scholars from the Primitive Methodist enclave went to South Shields. Both my parents preferred the trip to that port. There was a long pier to walk along and plenty of places upon which to rest on the pier. Father went in search of a healthy salmon roe. He knew the best shop where the roe was sold under the counter. Salmon roe made an excellent bait for trout, but it possessed the disadvantage that it was forbidden by the river authorities, whose bailiffs kept a strict watch on its being used. Neither my father nor my grandfather felt any compunction when they set about pre-paring the bait. The skinning of the eggs and the subsequent treatment which turned the roe into a thick paste which could be fixed to the hook already carrying a worm was a hush-hush job. Small jars of paste were passed among the fishers in a secrecy that would have done any set of spies proud. Where it was secreted on the person of the fisherman was a mystery to me. After a storm the catches of brown trout were sometimes remarkable.

The river flowed placidly once it had passed the Witton-le-Wear reaches. The flat country from Witton Park bridges to beyond Escombe, an old village which still treasured its most ancient church, was the happy ground for the delivery of the roe to the fish. Witton Park was the one bleak spot on the river's course, and one which a straying bailiff would avoid whenever possible. Once there had been a considerable ironworks close to the river. An iron bridge carried the road over the river under the span of the bridge which carried the railway line northwards.

It was this very iron works which cradled the movement which sent England scampering into the industrial age. The Pease family were the chief sponsors as well as the greatest beneficiaries of the movement. It was they who entertained George Stephenson when he came south from the Tyne to Darlington to discuss the project of a railway which would run from the iron works at Witton Park to the nearest port, Stockton-on-Tees. The railway was to be an open-ended affair, which was to take into its care the carrying of ironstone from the coast and the Cleveland deposits to the furnaces and the finished goods to the coast. The resulting birth of the railway system made it possible for the capitalist mode of production to break its fetters and expand over the face of the earth.

The furnaces had been dismantled and sold for scrap long before I was born. Even the industry that had been had faded from the memory of the people. The place upon which industry had stood was now clotted with the solidified contents of the great cauldrons which had been emptied right to the edge of the river. There they lay as they had lain when the puddling process had been ended. The place looked what it was, a hiding place for forgotten ghosts. Not a child played about that forsaken ground. Men did not fish from that side of the river. It was a dreadful place, fitting only for a hiding place for immovable masses taken from the smelters. As night fell, the fishermen sank upon their unkers to wait upon the fish. The old waste seemed to take on a strange, forgotten, dim aspect that was rather weird. Witton Park was outside our normal experiences, and had become a lingering slum left over from a near feudal era. The mechanisms had sunk into the dust and had left the large village half alive.

They were all bottom fishers, even my father. I never saw any of them cast a fly upon the water. I cannot say that any one of them was adept at the art. They were content to squat down on their heels and stay thus an interminable time without moving a muscle. It was a habit learned in the low seams. In the deep high seams the habit of squatting on the unkers was lost. James Heslop, who lived in Witton-le-Wear, was a master of the art of both kinds of fly fishing. He rarely fished otherwise, preferring to raise his trout rather than sneak it out of the muddied waters of the river. It was exciting to watch him stand in the middle of the river and bring out the fish that swarmed in and about him. The High Grange men rarely bothered to drop a line in clear water, but give them heavy rain up the valley and they went forth to harvest the fish. Sometimes a salmon was caught. Salmon rarely spawned in the Wear. On the Tyne it was different.

I was some eleven years of age when the days of the beehive coke-ovens came to an end. The first invasion to trouble us in High Grange was at Bank Foot, high above Crook. Here a German invention enabled men to extract all the by-products of coal, which escaped from the old fashioned ovens, and still produce saleable coke. The plant was technologically ingenious. Even the ovens were loaded automatically. All the salt, tar, benzine, saccharine and the like were harvested and purified in the chemical lodgements of the new process. The silver departed from the coke. Gone were the men who felled the beehive ovens. Coke was expelled from the ovens by a mechanical rammer and left to cool while the oven was loaded for the next turnover of production. All that was of little use, all the deadly poisonous waste, was sluiced into the nearest brook and left to find its way to the sea. The puss from the new method managed to pollute the lovely river Wear in a very short time, all the way from a mile below Witton Park Bridge. The poison swirled and killed all aquatic life in all the waters that roved by the ancient castles and the cathedral right to Wearmouth.

In little more than a year there was no fishing for anybody, yet no voice denounced, and no hand was raised against, a savage pollution which became total as new coking complexes were organised over the coalfield. The river died. Not a child paddled. No one bathed. No fish swam. Years later the higher reaches of the river were stocked with young trout, but all the simple pleasures had passed out of those waters.

It is admitted that the coal industry had contributed its portion to the pollution of the north country, but it ought to be remembered that even in the days of its worse excesses it did not lay hands upon the foundations of the churches and the noble buildings. Indeed, it left them unmolested.

Unbridled pollution of the atmosphere, the land and the rivers continued until the coalfield began to die. The shallow seams of the west were abandoned, and even the coking industry began to decay. The deep-mined coal in the east was found to be unsuitable for coking. So death laid its hand upon those areas where industry had been born. As the paralysis crept across the county it stamped the coking industry into decrepitude. Mining was driven under the sea. The river was left to the winds and the rains, and the snows of the fells. Of late the fish have begun to venture up the waterway to revisit their ancient places under the jutting stones, the shadows over the rippling water runs, and the roots of ancient willow. One day, perhaps, the river will recover most of its lost joys and there may be the whispering of the long forgotten songs. Perhaps, the birds will not fear to drink at the edges of the deep pools.

Sometimes I wonder if the peewits have come back and are at their old shrill sweepings of the pastures, and screaming over the fields along by the river, breeding after the manner of their kind, and holding court with the deepening dark. They still guide their young along the escape routes from the north's savage winters, for I go to watch them in a field near my home taking their pause before continuing on their inward and their outward journeys. I rest content to leave them all my envies and my memories of their freedoms and the departures which the north holds for me.

Apart from being fishermen, they were all politicians in those days in the Bishop Auckland area. Away in the seventies, the men of Morpeth elected Tom Burt to parliament, but it took the men of Durham a long time to change over from Liberalism to Labour. When they did make a break-through they found men of deep Liberal persuasion to represent them. Bishop Auckland remained Liberal until 1910.

High Grange was in the Bishop Auckland constituency. Howden-le-Wear, a mile away, was in the Barnard Castle constituency. That year there were two general elections, and in both of them Arthur Henderson kept the seat he had won in 1906. I remember both elections vividly. We were, as a family, part of the make-up of the village by that time. In both elections, a most respected leader of the miners, William House, contested the constituency as the Labour Candidate. He lost on both occasions to the Liberal.

My father was a keen asker of questions at the hustings. In the second election of that year, 1910, he asked me to accompany him to Howden in order to hear Henderson. There was only one large hall in the village, and on that night both Henderson and his Tory opponent had agreed to address the meeting in turn. The hall was crowded to the doors when we arrived, but somehow we got in. First show went to the Tory, and the first thing he did was to write on a conveniently placed blackboard the result of the Woolwich election in which Will Crooks had been defeated. Parliamentary elections at that time continued over a considerable period; indeed, some results were known before the nomination of candidates had taken place in other constituencies. It was once the privilege of Winston Churchill to state publicly that he regretted the law which had changed the old practice of elections on the grounds that unfought constituencies could repair the mistakes of those constituencies which had erred.

After the Tory meeting had ended and the candidate and his wife had departed, the meeting fell into some repose until Arthur Henderson and his wife appeared. He was a tall, angular man in those days. He had to fight down the enthusiastic hubbub before he could make himself heard. That he succeeded need not be insisted, but I have no recollection of his speech. The meeting over I walked homewards by the side of my father. It was a dark night. The ovens beyond the colliery were blazing like some superb hell. Everything was still. It was a hushed northern night that lifted itself up and beyond the stars.

A miner walking on ahead allowed us to get alongside of him before he spoke. 'Seed you at the meeting, Bill,' he said. 'I think the Tory'll get beat, but he'll take a lot of votes off Henderson.'

'I think you're right, Joe,' said my father. 'You know who you're voting for?'

'Nacherally,' said Joe. 'Folks the likes o' me dinna live in Witton Castle like the Tory. That leaves Henderson.'

'I suppose it does,' my father agreed.

Arthur Henderson kept the seat until 1918, when, for reasons known only to himself, he left Barnard Castle to fight a London constituency, which he lost. For years after he passed like Ishmael through the constituencies in England losing seats at general elections and winning by-elections. A miner, Jack Swan took over Barnard Castle. Bishop Auckland cast out the liberal in that year and returned Ben. C. Spoor, the son of James Spoor, a business man. Both father and son were preachers on the Primitive Methodist circuit, but old J.J. was regarded as the better preacher.

J.J. stuck 'to the book', but Ben was enamoured of the New Theology, much to the affrighted disgust of my grandparents. How the old couple fought against so outrageous a tampering with the 'old book'! Grandfather could find it in his heart to overlook the theological delinquency, and grandmother was able to bide her time.

And it came in the summer of the year 1919. She was marching down Newgate Street when she met the newly appointed Labour Agent. He held out his hand to her.

'I'm so glad to meet you Mrs Heslop,' he cried. 'Ben was only speaking about you the last time he was home. He particularly requested me to offer you his kindest regards if ever I should meet you. And this I do now, Mrs Heslop.'

'Did he the noo!' she cooed. 'An isn't it fine he should remember an auld body like me?'

'But he does,' he insisted. 'Why should he forget old friends now that he is in parliament? He is away a lot, you know, carrying out his duties to the people. I'll tell him that I met you.'

She crumped up her frail body and smiled at him. 'Aye' she assented. 'Ye do that, my canny man. Just ye do that. It's nice to be a mighty man o' valour, isn't it?'

'What do you mean, Mrs Heslop?' the poor man asked.

'Why, nice to be the captain o' the host,' she replied. 'Like Nahaamen, ye ken? Him in the Bible. Ye knaa…'

'But…Mrs Heslop…I don't get the inference…'

She smiled at his discomfiture. 'Ye forget the auld book,' she reminded him. 'Ye remember Nahaamen, surely…him that was a leper.'

It has been one of my pleasures to remember that little, old lady, her umbrella clutched across her breast by both arms, a little woman well in advance of the van of the Lord God of

Hosts. She denounced all those who sought to lay hands upon the Bible, of which she could not read a word.

Grandfather became grave when she reported her conversation to him.

'It wasn't so wise to say a thing like that to the poor man, Mar'get,' he pointed out. 'You didn't brawl?'

'I just said it an' walked away,' she assured him. Then she stamped her foot. She always stamped her foot when she was annoyed. 'Must one not defend the Word, George?' she cried out. 'Must one stay silent when men commit sin in wor pulpit?'

'A man can be forgiven,' he reminded her.

'Forgiven? Forgiven, George!' she cried out. 'For shame! He is beyond forgiveness.'

'But, Mar'get…'

'No, George! No!' she cried out. 'They that take the work o' the Lord into argyment, take His word in vain.' She raised her thin arm and shook her fist. 'God will not be mocked, George,' she assured him. 'Yon Ben Spoor! Hoots!'

Margaret Heslop was the daughter of a borderer, called Tom Glenwright. As his family had increased he had moved towards Newcastle, seeking work. He ended up in a small downstairs flat in George Potts Street, Westoe, South Shields, and there he eked out a livelihood as a donkeyman at the Mill Dam glass works. He was not a religious man. His family was born, and both sexes, six daughters and two sons moved over the north in their own right to work and eat. I was surprised when my father and I were walking in the Westoe area to learn that he knew the area. He was attending the synod of his church in the town of South Shields. I was taking him to my lodgings for tea. As we walked along George Potts Street he stopped at a door.

'Aye,' he said. 'This is the very house.'

I waited.

'I used to come here to stay with my grandfather Glenwright,' he explained. 'The last time I was here was to go to his funeral. He had his head cut off.'

'Cut off!' I cried. 'What do you mean?'

'Surprises you, eh?' he challenged. 'It's true, though. You see he was minding an engine at the glass works. It was a cauld night. His muffler got tangled up in the cogs as he was giving them a drop of oil. When they found him the engine was still running and he was without his head. What is a donkey engine?' he asked.

Life at High Grange was not unpleasant. There our family was increased to five boys. Grandmother Whitfield was not highly excited about the fecundity of her daughter, but, being a wise woman, she did not expostulate in the presence of my father. It was a bitterly cold night early in January when my third brother was born. Around that period there had been an unusually heavy fall of snow. All the country around was covered with a deep layer. Grange Bank was made impassable by the drifting so deep that it lingered against the hedges well into May.

In that January of 1907 a great comet blazed across the sky. A tremendously long tail of brilliance spread away from a single star. Nothing so spectacular had ever occured in our experience as that wonderful thing in the sky. It was as if that star had been disembowelled and was fleeing from its own catastrophe. In the day time it was visible, without its spectacular brilliance. When night came all its magnificent diamonds were set ablaze and the heavens held a delirium of light. To us it appeared stationary, even though it was moving away from earth at an incredible speed. When at last it faded away the sky seemed to be lonely, as if something had been snatched from its reach.

I was too young to pay more than passing heed to any of the discussions on the strange phenomenon. The old men and women were filled with apprehension. The argument died away as soon as the comet had gone away.

We were an average family, my parents and my three brothers. (Tom had not by then put in an appearance, but this he did in May of 1910.) Life went on without deep incident. My father went daily to the mine. Returning home, he washed his body in front of the kitchen fire, and, when it was possible, went along to Howden to gossip with Walter Hook, his brother-in-law, or to some chapel meeting or service at Hunwick. During the season he fished the Wear.

As boys we attended the council school at the top of the street, and we suffered the stinging slashes of the cane of the master. We rarely complained to our parents. We wept over our sore hands, and the class took as little notice of our grief as we took of the grief of other children. And there was plenty of grief to go round, for none escaped the righteous and dutiful anger of Charles Leonard Davies, B. Litt. And yet he thumped the permitted lessons into our heads. It is possible for me to look back and sympathise with him in the task he had undertaken. What became of him I do not know. In some ways he was a gifted man. Whatever knowledge I came to possess passed over the beginnings inculcated by him. He was the only headmaster but one I had.

In the year 1911 the miners came out on strike. My father being an official at North Bitchburn had to perform some of the important duties while the strike lasted. As the struggle was not expected to be protracted the management had decided to keep the ponies underground. This meant that the ventilatory tract had to be examined, and the air flow kept more or less constant. The rotary fan by which the working tract was ventilated had been shut down and recourse had had to be taken to bring the old fashioned furnace ventilation back into use. This was in actuality a huge fire near the foot of the ventilation shaft through which the fan drew air. Part of the duties of the officials was to stoke and refresh this furnace.

It was on a Saturday afternoon that I went along to the pit bank to meet my father. He was waiting for me near the drift mouth when I arrived, and without more ado he instructed me to follow him. I was not given a lamp, and I was told that there was only need for one, seeing that we were not going far. I kept close to him, sharing the dim light, as he led the way down a longish wet drift, which, as it lengthened, gradually discarded any semblance of tidyness. Soon the brick arch of the cavern was left behind us, and before long I found myself stumbling after my guide along a fairly low passage which seemed to be plentifully supported at either side with timber. What I could see of the roof appeared to be of a bluish white colour.

My father was a swift traveller underground; in fact, I do not recall any man or boy who could travel faster in a crouched position. He was a man of small stature, and yet he could stride, bent low almost to an obeisance, from sleeper to sleeper without trouble along any distance of track. When it is recalled that the distance between the sleepers was four feet it can be assumed that his walk was more of a lowly leap from sleeper to sleeper rather than a stepping forward. As for myself I was not able to step in such a manner all the time I worked below ground. We came at length to a wooden door that was set in a brick wall. This he pushed open and when I had passed through he closed it carefully. A little later we came into the furnace cavern.

The ancient bricklayers who had arched the cavern and created the fire hole and the fire arrangement had been meticulous craftsmen. There could have been no better walling to support so beautiful an arch in the upper world. Across the cavern were laid the great bars upon which the fire rested, a slow blaze of coal. Hanging his lamp on a nail he took up a long slicing bar and began to disturb the embers. Soon he had invigorated the fire, and when he was satisfied he laid on a large supply of coal. As the flame grew and the heat intensified the air began to stir about us perceptively. Before we left the wind was moving at a good speed.

'Isn't this all dangerous?' I asked.

He grinned at me, 'It might've been if I hadn't shut that door,' he said.

'But why a fire?' I asked.

'It's the only way we can ventilate the pit,' he explained. 'We'll have to carry on this way while the strike lasts. It wouldn't do to stop the ventilation. You need fresh air in a pit.'

Squatting on his unkers and lighting his pipe he gave me quite a little lecture that afternoon. He explained how before the invention of the rotary fan the mines were all ventilated by furnace draught. 'You see,' he began, 'beyond the furnace there is a shaft which runs up to the surface. You've seen that big wheel going round just beyond the pit pond?' He waited until I had nodded. 'Well, that wheel draws the air up that shaft. Now it isn't working, so we have got to keep this fire going. How does the fire shift the air? It heats the column of air in the shaft and this causes it to rise. When this is done air from this side of the furnace fills up the gap and passes on into the upper atmosphere. And so it goes on.'

'But how does the cold air get into the pit?' I asked.

'Through the other drift, the one we draw the coal out of,' he explained. 'But don't think that we allow it to come straight in here, my lad. We make it go all round the workings before we let it go free up the shaft here. We give it a circulatory movement. See?'

He took a piece of chalk out of one of his pockets, and then he invited me to come closer to the box, 'the kist', he called it, against which he stood. He commenced to draw lines on the lid of the kist. 'This is a plan of the pit,' he said. 'Here is the drift where the air comes in, and here is the place where you and I are now. They are not far apart, as you can guess. But before the air gets from that point to this point we make it travel.'

'But how?' I asked.

A flame shot up from the furnace and revealed to me the grin on his face. 'Thou'll nivver know what clever lads us miners is,' he said. He laughed at his own Durham witticism, and became serious. 'We don't allow the air to escape on its way in,' he said, 'and it has no way to escape on its way out except up the shaft. What we do is we stop up all escape routes on the way inbye. As a matter of fact we call them stoppings. Any place leading away from the intake is stopped up, built up with bricks and cemented. We control the air. Over the years we have mined coal this has been our main problem. We have to get the fresh air into the workings, give each man his share of it, and get it back up the shaft here. Getting the air in is the most difficult job. It means employing lots of bricks and mortar, lots of timber and doors, and a tremendous amount of brattice cloth.'

'Brattice cloth?'

'Aye. That's a lump lying there.'

I examined the stuff and found it to be thick, almost unworkable, tarred hempen weave. 'How do you hang it?' I asked him.

He laughed again. 'We nail it to props and planks,' he explained. 'It is a tetchy job. You can lose a lot of skin off your hands doing it. We have to split a going so that the air can go up one side, into the man, and then outside into the next place. You might call the job curtaining.' He paused. 'Curtaining' he reflected. 'I hadn't thought o' that.' He stood up. 'We must go now to the galloways. How-way!'

We left the furnace blazing merrily, closed the door after us, and made our way to the stables. As soon as the ponies, or galloways as they were called, became aware of our approaching light they began to stamp and scream.

This was the most impressive sight I had so far seen in all the years of my young life, impressive because of many things, chiefly its squalidity. As I entered the place my eyes began to smart on account of the strong admixture of foul air and ammonia. The place which housed the undersized ponies was simply an enlargement of one of the passages that had once been hewn, dirty, bible-black as the poet would have it, without light, an area of underground cruelty. Just the bare walls of the mine. The stalls in which the animals stood were simple and economic in their transgression of pity, a wooden manger, a halter, adequate roof support and a running prop to divide one stall from the other. The bare rock of the floor, dunged into a cake of discomfort was all the resting place granted to these creatures condemned as they were to so outrageous an exist-ence. On the wall behind each animal hung the leather trappings along with the exaggerated skull-cap which offered some pro-tection in the low places through which they dragged the tubs or waggons. The poor, defeated playthings of the winds and heathers had been taught to attune themselves to an awful existence.

The far end of the stables was the coal face. A hole at right angles permitted a vent through which the supersaturated air could pass. The heat of the bodies of the animals had raised the temperature considerably, uncomfortably for humans. The dung and urine recently excreted smelt horribly. There was the constant squeal of rats to be heard among the noises of the clamping hooves. I do not even think even now that there had been, or ever could be, larger and more sophisticated rats anywhere else in the world. They slunk out of our way, bellies to the ground, without hurry.

The first duty was to water each pony. In turn we took them to the trough, where they sank their heads deep into the water, almost to their eyes, in order to drink beneath the thick coat-ing of dust that lay upon it. It was a slow and tedious job water-ing all those thirsty animals. While I watered the ponies he set about filling the mangers with choppy from a tub.

'Gerrout! Gerrout! You brutes!' he shouted at some half dozen of the animals that had lingered too long in the choppy tub. They went at the behest of a shovel. Choppy was the standard mixture of hay, straw, oats and beans, used all over the coalfield. All the mass was passed through a chopper before being loaded into a choppy tub. A quantity of the stuff was put into each manger, which the pony shared with the rats. Since the miners had withdrawn their labour the rats which had con-trived to live on the food they could steal from the hewers and putters and the choppy in the mangers where the animals worked had migrated to the stables. The problem of feeding the ponies was intensified.

I watched my father fodder the ponies with eyes that brim-med with tears. I cried when he was kind to a rather small pony. 'This is Tip,' he said. 'We've got to be careful with Tip. We try to see that he never comes to harm.' He patted the little thing on its neck. 'He gets all the canny work, you see,' he went on. 'He's never seen the daylight. See how he shoves his head into the watter! He knows a thing or two, does Tip. Why, Harold, thou's crying!'

Later, when he had finished the task of replenishing the ponies, he went to Tip's stall, and there, to my surprise, he brushed out the stall. 'That's our favourite pony,' he told me. 'He was born in these very stables. We don't have mares below, but if you look carefully you'll see that some o' them are entire ponies. They stopped allowing mares below a long time ago, Tip's quite an old pony. We are all kind to Tip.'

I was glad when we reached the surface and he told me to go home.

Chapter Five

I was admitted to Bishop Auckland grammar school for the September term of 1911. I was then in my thirteenth year. The intake of students went straight from the elementary schools in the district into the lower fourth form. I do not think that I was unsuccessful in that first year, for I shared the form prize with a farmer's son, who came from Heighington, near Darlington. We were all day scholars. We passed into the upper fourth and there began our preparation for the Oxford local examinations.

The school was situated behind Newgate Street. It gloried in the name of 'James I Grammar School'. It could have been erected during that monarch's reign, for it was the most down-at-heel establishment in the British Isles. The elementary school at High Grange offered more in the way of ordinary amenities and considerably more in actual cleanliness. It most certainly possessed decent lavatory and ablutory amenities, which was more than the grammar school could offer. There were better facilities in a wayside pub. Actually there were three wash basins for the couple of hundred scholars, each with a cold water supply. The class windows were high, and were never cleaned. The bare deal floors were rarely swept. The one really decent offering was a five acre field.

Most of the scholars came from the far flung districts by train, and consequently assembly was a casual affair, carried out perfunctorily by the head master, Robert Bousefield, M.A., a tall, thin man with a balding head and a deep yellow complexion. He was assisted by a small staff which was grossly overworked.

During that year our family continued on its way, unaware of approaching dissolution. The Titanic disaster struck mankind with a devastating force. The world-wide sympathy evoked by the tragedy ebbed away as do all the great tides which assault the imagination of mankind. It was during my first term in the upper fourth that two important things happened to disturb our wonted domesticity. October was slowly abandoning its resistance to the forbidding embraces of November when my father received a request to meet a well-known mining engineer, William Walker of Hinderwell, in the first class waiting room at Middlesbrough railway station. There was tremendous excitement in the family. My father met Mr Walker and received the appointment to act as manager of Boulby Ironstone Mine, near Staithes. His actual employers were the Skinningrove Iron Company, Limited. The other, and, indeed, the most important happening was my mother's pregnancy.

I comfort my recollections of that time with the remembrance of the keen disappointment expressed by Mr Bousefield when I went to his study to tell him that I would not be returning to school after the Christmas recess.

During the years that have passed over me since that time many large forgettings have eased the many small wounds beyond regret. Things remembered not are of little consequence. My attendance at the Grammar School is one such. Our migration to Boulby ended a phase and begat another wherein our family life was shattered beyond repair. How my father reacted to it all I can only guess for he was not at any time a communicative father at the hearth. Before I presume to judge him I must take a close look at him as the man I came to know. I will not offer excuses for him, nor do I intend to reveal him in his nakedness, for scripture denies me that duty.

My father was a pharisee of small stature which is unusual, for to be a pharisee one must possess a commanding physical presence, else none will be attracted to glimpse him as he prostrates himself before the Lord. If any person or persons can be indicted for permitting him to develop as he did, they were his parents. Those two ancient posturers in a forbidding world were so attuned to, and so close to God, that they were convinced that out of all the universe He had chosen their backyard in a dirty Durham colliery village as the place in which He should dwell. Whenever they offered up their prayers it was to the top panes of the kitchen window. Theirs was a temple behind the doors of their home, and within it they committed all their goodnesses and all their sins. All through their joint lives an overwhelming religious conviction held them chained to an outwardly severe existence, which they stained with the lusts of the flesh and tired with the incontinences of temper. Together they sacrificed everything to their love of God, and, as a consequence, granted none of their offspring any pity.

My father was the first-born of this Methodist tribe, and upon him rested all the hopes of their begettings. He kept low in stature, like his mother. He was doomed to pass his days underground, like his father. His fate was as inescapable as that of a lump of hewn coal. As he moved into manhood he sought to conquer his increasing sense of frustration by exercising what he called his 'spiritual being' in the chapel. His environment was so circumscribed by a conglomeration of squalid, shoe-string enterprise that it was impossible for him to find anything more suitable than a chapel pulpit in which to express himself and liberate his yearning thoughts. He quite early set about the task of study in order to obtain the certificates of competency to manage coal mines. He offered himself to the mines and to God. It was beyond his imagination to realise that the omnipotent God might have no need of his confessions. Such trivial considertions are for the priest. He 'came on to the plan' at an early age. When the privilege of the pulpit was handed to him he accepted it with glee and never did he renounce it.

During all his life, my father did not entertain even the slightest doubt of the rightness or the permission to go forth and preach the gospel. What he did fail to realise was, that by doing so he alienated himself from those whom he sought to serve, the coal-owners. That is not to say that any of those remote and inestimable gentlemen rejected Methodism. Not at all, for they provided many of the chapels, and attended to the heating of them. There they stopped their charity. On the other hand they were not deaf to the rampaging that went on in the chapels. At a mean distance they could recognise the pulpit orator in the guise of a 'local official', or the active trade unionist. They were not in the least surprised when they saw that it generally was the same person under the cloth cap. They made no effort to strangle the movement. They recognised that the path to the high places in the working class movement passed through the vestries and the pulpits of the mean little chapels. What must have surprised them more than anything was the sight of a certificated man doing the same thing as the agitators...preaching in the chapels.

Had he subdued his passion to 'preach the word' my father might not have been overlooked by those who might have been willing to utilise his services as a mining engineer. During all the days of his existence he failed to realise that his propensity to orate, like any small Coleridge, was the reason why he was not allowed to scale the doleful heights of the underworld. He was a sound, practical miner, whose main specialisation was ventilation, and whose surname counted for something in the industry. I remember how, when we got to Boulby, how critical he became after he had had a good look at the ventilatory system. Life was made almost unbearable for man and horse during the shift when all the powder had been blasted. Each face man carried into the mine seven pounds of cordite, and with this in the course of his shift he blasted the stone from the seam. The reek thickened the slow-moving current of air into an appalling fog, and this irritated the olfactory passages of man and beast. Unfortunately, my father was not long enough at Boulby to alter the unbearable situation.

I once discussed it with him, and he showed me how expensive it would have been to ventilate the ironstone after the manner of a coal mine. The method of extraction was the same as that in the coal mines, that is on the 'board and pillar' system, by which the seam was split into huge blocks, some fifty yards square. Under such a method, the air could be circulated through the workings by hanging brattice lanes so that it could enter the place on one side of the hempen cloth barrier and be conducted out on the other side. It was always easy to set up these barriers by utilising the timber roof supports. But in the ironstone mine there was no such timber. One could walk for miles in such a mine under the superincumbent shale without seeing any timber at all. All that anybody could do under these circumstances was to let the mine reek.

He was a patient man in many respects. For years he wrote answers to advertisements in the mining journals, offering his services without even guessing that many of the recipients of his applications knew all about him. On Sundays he would climb into the pulpit at this or that chapel right on the heels of some agitator or politician who had paused to orate on the eternal theme of 'the men, the folk, aye! and the bairns, Lord! The slaves in the darknesses of Thy world!' Poor old dad! Not once did he stop to appreciate the dichotomy in the coalfields. He was unaware of his own 'guilt' by association. But the Lord did smile a half benediction upon him, and, small as he was, he set forth to claim his kingdom.

By the end of the first week in January 1913, our furniture had been packed into a pantechnicon and was on its way to

Boulby. My father had gone in the November, and my oldest brother had joined him before Xmas. Before we finally quitted High Grange, my grandfather Whitfield died. I attended his funeral as the lone representative of our household. I found it a most distressing experience, for the snow fell heavily all the time. A Methodist funeral is by no means an exhilarating service. There comes a time when the officiating minister must place his tongue firmly in his cheek and speak an obituary of the dead person. It is always an unhappy time for the mourners, whether they be bored with the business of grief or tired gazing upon a varnished coffin.

We stayed overnight with my mother's mother at Quarry Burn, and before noon of the next day we set out to walk to North Bitchburn and then down the hill to Howden-le-Wear, where we caught our train.

My father and my brother George were at the station to meet us when we arrived in Cleveland. It was a most beautiful day. There had been a soft fall of snow, and this had whitened the earth and lent it a happy radiance. We walked on to the Loftus road, turned right and climbed our way through the village of Grinkle on to the road that is proud to help the wayfarer to reach his first glimpse of the great cliffs that held the seas at bay. Halfway through the village the church peers through its rosary of trees and looks down at the passers-by. No church that I have ever known seems so reluctant in its offering of sanctuary. Even its gateway is forbidding. The sensitive traveller cannot evade the conviction that he is passing beneath the tombstones.

Looking back on that day I remain convinced that by the time we had arrived at the church my mother had become convinced that we had made a huge mistake in migrating to this area. Her tears were almost ready to fall. She was clinging to my father's arm when she paused in her stride to say to him:

'Promise me you won't bury me up there, Bill.'

I heard my father tell her not to talk daft.

It was a long walk to Boulby. We made it without further incident. Beyond the church and the farm, the road levels out as it drives along an escarpment overlooking the falling vision of land loaned to the plough and the rooks. The great sweep of country took the eye to the furthest point beyond Staithes and across in the track of the westering sun to the moors far away. Directly beyond us as we walked the land broke off and space was left to the sea. As we drew nearer we could see that the cliffs were holding back the intruding waters in wondrous peace. Not even the slightest swell was visible to us. We came to a turn in the road and beyond we found our new home.

'This is it,' said my father.

'That!' said my mother. 'Oh, Bill!'

He gave us the news in his gentlest manner. The pantechnicon was snowbound somewhere this side of Darlington. It was doubtful if they would get here in a couple of days. He had made arrangements for us all to stay in the farm where he was lodging. We would go there and have tea, and then my mother could have a rest.

By the time we had reached our temporary lodgings mother had reached a state of utter bewilderment. Her reactions to the almost desolate area into which she had been thrust established a disconsolation from which she never emerged. She sank into a state of silent weeping. Nothing, no one, could soothe her, not even father's unwonted gentleness. She was as a plant that had been plucked up by the roots and flung upon a compost heap in some neglected corner of life. She exasperated us all with her constant tears to such an extent that we failed to recognise her sorrowing heart. Nor could we see that all her joyous hopes of a new motherhood were being washed out of her by her tears. Our disappointment because of her strange, unaccustomed behaviour overlapped all our sympathy, and in the end we accepted it as being in the nature of things.

Monday came and with it the working round. The furniture eventually arrived and we were settled into the great house. I think that mother was afraid of the place, with all its windows staring out at the sea, unaware of the infinity of the offerings of its waters. It might have delighted a poet. For her, in all her forlorness, there was only her ache magnified by her incomprehension of the scene. The contrast with the life she had hitherto lived was too acute for her to rationalise. The passing vessels, however slowly they seemed to trudge across their own distances, were, to her ships that were passing by the barred windows of her prison. Their apparent stillness of progression were comments upon her solitude. When she lay down to rest her body they passed out of her vision, and she left them to their own relentless pursuit of great occasions. The fact that she was so high above the sea and forced to linger on a ledge that was the end of nowhere deadened her mind till she found compassion in the screaming of the gulls.

Boulby Head is a magnificent projection thrust against the sea for almost a thousand feet above it. The cliffs which cower at its feet and carry the tale of its immensity to the cove that shelters Staithes are a formidable rampart against the moving waters. They all rise from a basal rock formation with the same forbidding command as Boulby Head, and all have resisted all the tumults of a sea maddened by its monstrous engagements with the winds, and have held it at bay from beyond the memory of man.

This Boulby to which we came stood in a primeval desolation. Until the opening of the mine few had ventured to till the land close to the edges of the cliffs. It was an ill-farmed, wind-scored, almost uninhabited part of the coast, which seemed to hold but one purpose, that of paying quiet homage to the immense brow of England standing there, contemptuous of the savage waters. Here they had built a mine into its bowels. Nearer the top nineteenth-century excavators had robbed it of its alum shale. This new mine was discreetly placed, and little harm was done to the scene. To house the miners, the company had erected a row of mean, corrugated iron, semi-detached bungalow affairs, which rejoiced in the local appellation of the 'tin huts'. The rest of the manpower for the mine was drawn from the fishermen's sons in Staithes.

Boulby Grange was a vast house that stood some considerable distance from the edge of the cliff upon a sheltered escarpment. It stood as from its beginning, remote, almost stark, yet with impressive beauty, especially when viewed from the distance. Those who created it did a good job, as was meet that they should have done. When a man builds a house, no matter how mean might be the ultimate structure, he builds it into the belly of a century. When he does this deed he incorporates a vast amount of labour power into the finished home. And he must continue to lend it all his skill and aid. It behoves all men to build well. Christ, according to the scribes, had quite something to say on the subject that is still apposite. The men who built Boulby Grange did a sound job. They knew nothing about plumbing, for they attempted none. In an alcove on the first landing of the lovely staircase there was a water closet of later date than the house itself. It had a fixed mahogany seat. There was a handle at the side. Where the water might have come from or where the contents of the pan were carried, remained mysteries that we were unable to solve. There was a deep, lead-covered construction outside into which the rain-falls might have been directed, but this had long been abandoned. There was neither a cold water cistern for ordinary uses nor a sink to receive the water we might use. The water we needed we drew from the common tap in the outer yard. The tin huts had much better amenities than we had.

The great house had been divided into two dwellings. A family called Rowlands scratched some kind of existence from the soil which lay in measured acres over the area that had once been defined as the messuage of a ship building family called Richardson. Old Rowlands milked a small herd of non-descript kine, grazed a lowly flock of sheep, and fed a goodly number of hens. His two eldest sons worked in the Skinningrove iron works. The youngest boy worked in the mine as an electrician's mate. There were two daughters who helped the mother with the work of the steading.

Our part of the house was impressive. A deep garden ran round three sides of the house and was railed off with white palings. The front doorway, complete with pseudo-Grecian portico, was reached by a path from the garden gate. This path was curious in that it was made to follow the contortions of a fossilised snake-like monster that had been quarried unbroken from the alum shale quarry above the house. The actual thing must have been of monstrous proportions. My father was told by Mr Walker that some years ago it had been vandalised. When we were there most of the fossil lay intact, but broken into sections. The minor fossils which were found in the shale strata above and below the ironstone seam were impressive in their size and bulk. Some of the fossilised molluscs would have interested palaeontologists. I have seen some over fifteen inches across, and all were disregarded and thrown aside, the leavings of the acons.

Poor old Boulby Head! It has continued in its own majesty since pre-Cambrian times. Now it is threatened in this, our own, capitalist time. Uncounted centuries have not despoiled it. From it has been extracted its yield of alum shale, its jet and all its ironstone. And yet, so little damage can be seen to have been done. Now, as I write with some diffidence, for diffidence becomes an old man, the next breed of explorers and exploiters of the treasures of the earth, are getting ready to probe the deeps that have hitherto lain beyond and below the reach of the miners, and the fathers of the miners, a grim race now crumbling into social decrepitude. So far as I am aware, the purpose is to bore down, as they have borne down to the oil bearing strata, and extract the potash by wild-pumping with, I suppose, refining carried out in places erected unmindfully upon that ancient and unspoiled England. I tremble at the thought of men disembowelling the very foundtions of that formidable upper rock that is still Boulby Head. How great the deposits of potash may be is beyond my conjecture. If it reaches as far as Whitby, and if it stretches illimitably under land and sea, the prospect of unimaginable disaster becomes clear. All the land and sea floor above the deposits must in time become superincumbent, and in the end the hidden demesne must collapse under the formidable pressures. Thus it is possible that man will deliver over a little stretch of time all the destruction that the tumults of unimaginable aeons failed to achieve. Once the fissures are compelled to admit the sea the earth must retreat in despair.

The old alum shale deposits have long been gobbled up, but the elderly fishermen from Staithes often wandered over the few miles from the fishing village to search for the black dripp- ings of jet that had been overlooked. They came often to the old quarry to search for the weightless stuff, and whenever they did discover a sizeable blob they made their return journey a happy occasion. What they did with their findings of jet was not bruited abroad.

The view from any of our front windows was truly magni- ficent, for the eye was free to wander over delectable country lying away to the west where the moors sank into sweet com- posure under the wide skies. A land untroubled by industry. A primeval peace. From the moors went a lovely sweep back to the cliffs beyond Staithes. From headland to headland, with- out limning the eastern horizon very deeply, the vast arc held in still composure the great sea, shading the communications of the sunlit sky in all its hues. It was a shining pool that edged all the land of our European earth. Daily the sun gleamed over it, defying the clouds to do more than soften its radiance, its gentle radiance, over the waters as they rose out of the far beyond to gather power and purpose to hurl defiance at the foot of the immemorial cliffs, or gently stroke the shingle as the mood provoked it in its ageless war with the cliffs that held back all the weight of the earth and so encouraged the agri- cultural pursuits of the generations and the growth of the forests that lingered from eternity.

Those cliffs stood straight as the walls of shafts from the bare green earth to the sandless shore. Nothing brushed the manes of the waves but the soughing winds and the gusts of the storms as they held over their trackless wastes. Often the cobles danced as they held their brown sails square to all winds while the fishermen trailed their baited lines. There was a still magnificence about that vast stretch of water, a more impressive grandeur than any I have been privileged to see, and a grandeur that was masssive, imperturbable, eternal.

During the few short months that were left to her my mother wept all her tears in the presence of that lovely scene. She sobbed her soul into quietude over those cliffs and waters. How lonely she must have been. How apprehensive. How sad.

Chapter Six

There was no possibility of my being transferred to another grammar school. The nearest one was at Guisborough, too great a distance from my new home. The problem was quite easily solved by that accomplished pragmatist, my father. He would take me with him into the mine and, to use his favourite expression, I could get started to learn how to paddle my own canoe. One fine morning he touched me out of my dreams and told me to get up. I followed him downstairs to the kitchen. I dressed myself in my school clothes. I ate a tasteless breakfast which he had prepared. We left the house together and I followed him to the travelling drift mouth where I was handed a lamp which he had previously bought for me. After he had held a short conversation with the man in charge of the fan I followed him down the wet drift. And thus began my servitude in the underworld which was to last until the early months of 1928, when I and a thousand others were put on the dole.

I was not plunged into a coal mine, but rather I was offered a short apprenticeship to the mystery in an ironstone mine.

The men had all gone into the mine before us. I followed my father with some trepidation. When we reached the drift bottom we left the travelling way and emerged upon the track devoted to the haulage of the waggons. It was the same system as that at Rough Lea, the only difference being that the gauge of the tramway was wider. What did astonish me was the whiteness of everything, the roof, the timber, the ironstone behind the timber. The roof was quite high, for the seam was over six feet in thickness. The thick timbers stretched at intervals across the haulage way reduced the height considerably. This, as I noticed later, caused all the men who travelled it to hold their heads on one side. Everything about this new environment was white. There was a fungus very much like thick whitewash which spread over everything, which even invaded the floor before and behind the standing timber. It was all most astonishing.

Without uttering a word we walked in file along this underground tramway until we came to a space at right angles to the engine plane across which was a deal door. My father pushed this door open and walked into a sizeable room, an office it could be called, which had been excavated out of the rock. Inside, waiting, was a group of men, sitting on the rough forms along the walls of the cavity. They must have been there sometime prior to our arrival, for their lamps had raised the temperature quite considerably. Actually they were waiting for their orders for the day's work. Most of them were engaged on the tasks necessary to the continued flow of the stone to the surface.

My father offered a curt, 'Good morning', and immediately set about apportioning the work. As each received his orders he left the cabin, and my father ticked off his name in a notebook which he carried in his pocket. The last man gone, we left the cabin. I followed him. He set a brisk pace, stepping from sleeper to sleeper along the track. I tried to imitate him, but soon gave it up. I found it much easier to walk at the side of the track. I had not gone very far when he ordered me to get behind him. 'Your light is dazzling my eyes,' he said. I did as I was bidden.

This was my initiation into the most important rite of the men of the mine, the keeping in single file when travelling. Nowhere was it so rigorously forced as in the coal mines. A miner was not in ease when confronted by a stranger's light. I have known men stumble as if gone suddenly weak when confronted by a light coming towards them, a light so far along the tunnel as to shine like a dull star. I learned that this rigorous attention to light was conditioned by a nystagmus which begins to afflict him from the first moment of his entry into the mine. As the disease progresses the eyeballs appear to lapse from the control of their own muscles. I have often experienced the profound shock when I have unthinkingly held my light up so that it shone directly into the eyes of a nystagmatic miner. I have seen his irises literally revolve. While in the pit the miner was always constrained to behold his task by sideways glances through half-closed eyes. My father was not as bad as all that, but then he did not hew coal.

We came to a place where the railway divided at a set of points which permitted a haulage service to two districts, the one being further on along the plane and the other going at right angles after passing along a slow curve which was reinforced by a thick wrought iron rail against which the tubs leaned as they passed round the curve. All the time we had been travelling the engine plane the main rope had been moving, but the tail rope had lain slack. When we arrived at the junction the first wagon in the train was emerging into our view of the curve. We stepped aside and waited until the immensely heavy train of waggons was drawn on to the main track and brought to a halt. This achieved, the youth whose duty it was to attend to the junction coupled the tail rope to the last waggon and affixed the clumsy safety device that trailed behind from the waggon. He then gave the signal and the haulage was resumed. My father simply told me to 'bide here' with the youth and then walked away into the darkness.

It became clear to me that most of the ironstone was being drawn out of the area beyond this curve. That the landing was at the bottom of a rather steep incline was obvious to me on account of the free running of the empty trains down the dip, that is without the aid of the tail rope. I later discovered how steep that incline was, and how simple was the activation of the self-acting principle. Later I found that traction beyond the landing by the youths who skilfully manipulated iron 'dregs' which were thrust between the spokes of the waggons' wheels. The seam of ironstone at Boulby thus sloped away from near the surface to a depth where it must, and did, peter out. It was exciting to wander into places high up in the seam and find the miners there working in daylight as a result of their having 'holed out to day' as they had it.

I spent that first day with that youth, and I found it to be the longest eight hours I had so far counted. I could not imagine anything more boring than sitting for hours in that cold wind and waiting on ten or eleven trains of waggons. The next day there was a diversion. Joe Willerby and his mate came upon the scene. Joe was the powderman at the mine, and in the odd hours when he was not attending to his stores of explosive in a cabin near the cliff top he did odd and important jobs in the mine. He handed me a whitewash brush and a pail of whitewash, and, with a smile, enjoined me to carry it, not paint the floor. Before moving on he made anemometer readings of the current passing to the junction and those passing down the dip and along to the level landing. I watched him with some interest. While his mate measured the areas he took the readings. When his calculations were ended he entered the results in a book and then he led the way down into the dip. I followed him. I was in a state of rebellion, that first condition through which all miners must pass and from which all must emerge.

Arrived at the landing we reported our presence to the deputy in charge and Joe took his instructions for the marking of some half dozen headings that were getting beyond the lines. It was quite a simple job. A heading proved to be simply the place where two miners were extracting stone. When we arrived at the first one they were busy boring holes. After a cursory joke the work proceeded. I noticed that running the length of the gallery to some distance from the face were three white lines seven feet apart painted starkly on the still blue roof. The job was to carry these lines as near to the face as was possible. By a simple sighting along two suspended boblines to a light held near the roof the required distance to the face, the centre line could be marked and whitewashed. I held my candle near the roof and shifted it as I was directed until I received instructions to 'mark her there!' This done, a chalked string was passed from the bobline to my mark, each end held while the chalked string was drawn like a bowstring and let go against the roof. The resulting mark was covered with white-wash. The two side lines were simply marked off from a seven foot stick and after the same string procedure were duly coated.

What did interest me was the fact that I had not noticed even one stick of timber in support of the roof all along the roads we had travelled since we left the engine plane. This set me wondering and it brought me to cogitating the use of the lines on the roof. Why so much care in directing this cleavage of the stone? And why no timber? That there was great importance to the lines became apparent when Joe pointed out to any couple of miners that they had strayed to right or to left, and what did puzzle me was their consternation when this was made clear to them. My father gave me the correct explanation, which was that the conservation of expensive timber could only receive sanction within the permitted limits of super-incumbency. To stray outside those limits would be to imperil the men working beneath an unsafe roof.

I marvelled at such empirically obtained exactitude of the stone, the straightness of direction and the sanctity of width, things I was not to encounter in the coal mines. Coal mining, I found, was more slap-happy than I thought. Perhaps it was because timber was cheap. Perhaps it was because there was no need to drive haulage roads to an exact survey line. I was relieved of these presuppositions when I held a conversation with an old man of the pits far below the county borough of South Shields. How astonished I was after I had finished boasting about the straight engine planes I had seen in Cleveland, when he said to me: 'You only have explosions in coal pits.'

'Explosions!' I was almost too surprised to grin. 'What have explosions got to do with straight engine planes?'

'There, see! You don't know, so I'll tell you.' He spat copiously into the pack. 'In a coal pit it is dangerous to keep an engine plane in a dead straight line. 'Cos why? 'Cos it is the intake for the fresh air. And, 'Cos an explosion allus runs along a straight line. If an explosion has a straight run along a straight engine plane it'll not stop till it gets to the shaft bottom. But if you bend your plane here and there the explosion will flatten itself against the far wall. I've known explosions flatten themselves against a set of full tubs. You see, lad, you've got to prevent an explosion doing all the damage it would like to do. Now, do you see?'

The pragmatism of those whom nature schools!

Being the son of the manager, I was not asked to undergo the exacting and laborious conditions that were imposed upon other men's sons. Compared with the experiences I was to undergo in the coal measures it was never as exacting as might be thought. While I was at Boulby I had yet to become a miner. At that initial confrontation I was not brought into any painful contact with labour. My inauguration had yet to come, and it was to precede my maturisation. I could only watch.

What struck me most forcibly was the soft nature of ironstone. It was extracted by blasting. The shot holes were bored by an ingenious, yet simple, drilling machine which could be operated by one man using one hand. The skill of the miner lay in his ability to appreciate the contour of the face and the depth of the hole to be drilled. The soft nature of the stone and the lack of any grain such as is found in coal established conditions of production which had to be overcome by art and guile. Once the hole was drilled it had to be cleaned out with a copper scraper. A calculated amount of black powder was then inserted and pressed up to the far end of the hole. The borings from the hole were then pressed into a sausage shaped core and then rammed into the hole right up against the powder, and gently tapped into a solid mass. When the hole was thus tamped to almost its length a copper pricker was driven carefully through the tamping until the point found the hole in the powder. The rest of the hole was tamped and then the pricker was withdrawn. A slow fuse was next inserted into the hole, and after a shouted warning, it was lit and the two miners made their ways back to safety.

Immediately the shot was fired the working place became fogged to suffocation with acrid fumes. The shortest possible time was allocated for the ascertaining of the result of the shot, and then the roof was tapped, and the work of loading begun. Respiration was taken for granted. Long before the end of the shift the atmosphere became so vitiated that water – tears they might be – escaped from the eyes of the noble shire horses which had been compelled to lend their existence along with their immense beauty to the act of this torturing employment.

Even after this so immense lapse of time I still find myself pitying those great, silent horses toiling out their lives at that abysmal initial point of the transfer of the ironstone to the blast furnaces at Skinningrove even though I am able to remember and to smile at the recollections of their own impositions of their own limitations which they set upon those brutal conditions. Unlike the pit ponies I was to come into contact with they had to be shown an adequate light as they were being led about their business by the younger members of the mining tribe, which was to apply their unimaginable strength to the pulling of the high-piled waggons of stone, encouraged by the older youths whose tasks it was to keep the waggons on the right rails. They also had to be given the privilege of eating and drinking, a privilege rarely granted to a pit pony. Upon so sombre an industrial scene those magnificent beasts imposed their own slow haulage tempos regardless of the exasperated hurryings and anxieties of the underworld. In return they had but one offering, that of immense strength but always did they grant it as they had granted it to the plough and the harrow.

They did not develop any observable attitude to their surroundings as did the pit ponies I was yet to encounter.

In the coal seams the smaller breeds of ponies not only exercised but revealed an indubitable intelligence. I once saw a pit pony actually *kneel down* on his forelegs and *crawl under* a low portion of a gallery, and shuffle his legs behind him until he was free from an obstruction. I have seen sheep, far gone in foot-rot, crawling to the slaughterhouse in a like manner on their knees, but that was under the open sky. When I 'lost my light' in the pit – and there were many times when I lost my light – I have merely held on to some part of my pony's harness and gone with him through the blank walls of darkness without once his barging into an obstruction.

Not only was this strange sense highly developed in a pit

pony. There was also his sense of hearing. In some ponies it was highly exaggerated. Miners were always aware of any disturbance made by a pony during a 'waiting-on' period when there was silence. I have listened to many tales of men about the ability of pit ponies to hear the distant cracks of disturbances in the high strata, and of the miraculous, in some cases, and the disastrous occurrences in others, that followed a pony's 'misbehaviour' in certain circumstances. At Harton Colliery we had a splendid pony called Devon, one of the most beautiful as well as the most intelligent creatures that was ever crucified in the living darkness. He could, and did, inform his driver by pawing with his foot on the rail, of the approach of another pony dragging a tub of coal long before one could see the approaching light. He would only go forward with his own tub under compulsion. One could sense his scorn when the confrontation was not avoided.

But to return to this Boulby mine. There was a considerable band of shale running through the middle of the seam. In actual fact the shale separated two distinct layers of the ironstone. The condition of employment repudiated the right of any miner to include any of this shale in any delivered waggon and consequently a scale of fines was operated against those who contravened the rule. At the pit head the contents of each waggon were spilled into a chute and passed down to a long moving belt where the offending shale was extracted from the output by a gang of youths working on the belt or at the side. The shale so recovered was loaded into waiting waggons at the fall of the chute and when a train of such waggons was made up it was taken back into the mine, run down the 'shale drift' which outcropped about halfway down the cliff. Here a tipping arrangement had been contrived and a cabin which housed it had been marvellously constructed so that it jutted out from the sheer face of the cliff. The contents of each waggon were hurled down on to the unoffending beach below.

At times when I felt the urge to escape I would wander into the shale drift just to look through that window of the earth and out upon the gleaming sea. To walk under the earth and then to emerge above the waters was thrilling to the very edge of the soul.

It was an experience I was not to know again after we left Boulby.

Chapter Seven

Easter having passed without trouble, my mother appeared to be passing into the final stages of her pregnancy without deep incident. The repeated visits of the doctor from Hinderwell betokened a careful consideration of her health. So far mother had not insisted on sending for her own mother to come from Quarry Burn, and, residing in her belief that 'it would be just one of those things that she had to go through' Grandmother showed no anxiety to make her way to Boulby. One thing did trouble me, and that was the visit of a Mrs Pearson, who was to act as the doctor's help at the confinement. I did not care a great deal for Mrs Pearson, especially after that night when my father escorted her to her home at Dale House, a hamlet set beautifully in the woods a mile or so deep from Staithes.

'Do you like Mrs Pearson, Harold?' my mother said to me.

She was sitting on the sofa by the great window. The darkness was beginning to blot out the lovely scene she had by now grown to evaluate as something unusual in her life. I was sitting on the piano stool toying with the keys. 'Not very much,' I replied, 'Why do you ask, Mother?'

She was a little while in answering. 'That woman will be your next mother,' she said. 'I will soon be gone now,' she added.

I was too surprised to offer her a rebuke. Since then I have often thought about it all.

My father did at last write to Uncle Ralph, my mother's youngest brother, suggesting that it might be as well if Grandmother Whitfield came to Boulby. He was asking a great deal of the old woman to be sure, for she had now gone past her eightieth birthday. A few days later my uncle appraised my father that his mother would make the journey on the following Saturday and that he would feel easier if some member of the family would meet her at Saltburn station and escort her to Boulby. As I had always been the messenger of the family I was sent to Saltburn to convoy the old lady to the Grange.

I met Big Grandma at Saltburn. We called her 'big' to identify her from Grandma Heslop, whom we called Little Grandma. She had not changed much since I had last seen her. She was still the same tall, taut, straight-backed woman I had always known. Her black clothes and her black bonnet, without a spray, betokened her widowhood. She wore no veil.

We greeted each other with a kiss, and then we crossed down to the platform and climbed into the train for Whitby. It pulled out a few minutes later. When we were comfortably seated she said to me:

'Thou hasna grown much.'

She could see that I felt reproved for avoiding the fact of physical growth, and so she offered me a smile that was as charming as the winter's sun. 'You take after the Heslops,' she went on. 'They don't make big bones.' And then to ease the situation she said:

'How's your Ma?'

'All right, I think,' I replied, and I added: 'She still cries a lot.'

'Aye! I warrant she does,' she reflected. 'She's had bairns enough, without this one. How's your Da?'

'All right.' I said.

She sniffed. 'I reckoned he would be,' she said, almost to herself.

We left the train at Easington. I took her straw travelling case, and we set off to walk the two miles to our home. 'What's this place called?' she asked.

'Grinkle,' I said. 'They changed the name of the station to Easington, but I don't know why.'

We toiled up the rise upon which the village is built.

'Yon looks a dowly place, yon church,' she observed. 'Is it far to your house?'

'A tidy step,' I conceded.

'That bag's none too heavy for you, is it?' she asked. 'I'll lend you a hand. I didn't think it would be so far.'

'I can manage a thing like this,' I said. 'No fear o' that.'

'It's only got my own bits o' things in it,' she said. 'I allus travel light. Allus have…me an' your grandfather.'

'It's light enough,' I assured her.

'You like living here?' she enquired a furlong later.

'Yes,' I said.

'What school are you going to now?'

I gave her a short laugh, almost like a scoff. 'I haven't been to school since we left High Grange,' I told her. 'I work down the pit'.

'Down the pit!' she stopped in her stride. 'He put you in the pit...your Da?' She waited on my nod, and strode on. 'Now, isn't that like Billie Heslop to put you in the pit! Do you like it?'

'I'd much rather have stayed at school,' I confessed. 'I wanted to be a solicitor.'

She walked on sturdily and around the bend of the road. The great sweep of view must have startled her, for she stopped to look at it. But it was not within her appreciation, for she spoke more to herself than to me or the lovely countryside.

'Just like the Heslops,' she muttered. 'They all talk big about eddication. They allus did. And when they have their chance they send the scholar into the pit like any driver-laddie wi' a pony! Shame! Shame, I call it. A great shame.'

We trudged on and in time we came into the view of the cliffs. I led her to the white gate and opened it. She passed through it and I closed it after her. I was glad to set her 'travelling case' down on the ground. As I picked it up she asked:

'Which is your house?'

I pointed to the great house. 'That one,' I said.

'The big one?' There was incredulity in her voice. 'You mean the one wi' the big winders an' the fancy door steps?' She did not hear my answer. 'My canny, canny bairn!' she breathed. 'To come to all them winders an' all this loneliness.'

She becalmed herself. She became herself. Until that moment she had been but a very old lady walking and talking with her grandson. Now she became herself in the role of the matriarch. Her step became firm. I found myself having to quicken my own step in order to keep up with her. Suddenly, as she walked, she spoke to me. 'Did they have to have *all* that sea?' she demanded.

I left her question unanswered. We mounted the steps and walked into the house. Deftly she undid the ribbons of her bonnet and took it from her head. I noticed that her skull was balding a little. Without her hat and cloak she looked very old. I stood and watched her, still holding her case. She walked into the room where my mother was by right of her own possession of her own daughter. Mother had not left the window, but she was standing, huge and formidable, in her condition. There was a wintry smile upon her eyes. She began to cry. Grandmother went to her and took her into her embrace – the first time I had ever seen her do such a thing.

'Nu! Nu!' she said softly. 'Thou maunna cry, my bairn. Thou't be all right after we get thou to bed. Nowt to cry about... another bairn, surely!' She made her sit down, and then she sat beside her, soothing her, whispering all the lore of her being as a midwife into her cheerless face. 'I couldn't come till I was sent for,' she said. She turned to my father. 'Thou knows, lad, that I never went where I wasna bid. Thou could've sent for me sooner.'

Things became too intimate, so I slipped out of the room and went across the yard to the byre where the maid was milking one of the cows.

The next fortnight passed.

The weather was most benign, and the days passed in splendour across the water within the soft smile of the sun. The sea glistened with light as it rolled with unwonted gentleness to the feet of the cliffs, where the gulls screamed and floated and began the round of breeding.

Friday night came, the third of the month of May 1913, and settled upon the quiet earth. I was digging in the garden when I saw my mother come to the door. I watched her. She looked past me and across the filthy farmyard, tired, irresolute, filled with pain. She stood huge and pendulous, her hands resting on the huge bulge of the new life, as if she were bidding her alien world a long farewell, a last goodbye. She turned heavily and walked slowly into the house. When I came in from the garden I found that she had gone upstairs. Some time later my Grandmother came down and began to brew a pot of tea. She offered me no word, no tea. She walked out of the kitchen and went upstairs.

The night, with its peace, fell upon the household, and lasted until the early hours of the morning. And then the crucifixion began.

It was a long way for my father to have to walk to fetch the doctor. The telephone in those days was a novelty, not a public amenity. For my father it was an oft repeated task 'going for the doctor'. There were many miles lying between our door and that of the doctor. When he did at last arrive at Boulby Grange everything was almost over. Alone, at her great age, my grandmother had brought into the world, as she put it, twin girls. Alone. Unaided. Magnificent old grandmother.

Later, when I was growing into manhood, she said to me: 'Nobody will ever know how I got her back into bed after the second one came.'

A tortuous delivery. After the passage of almost six decades

I can still lie in my bed and listen, as I did on that night, to the screams of a woman in childbirth. Even today I try to imagine that agony when remembering those scalding screams.

Not until the doctor did arrive did my grandmother attend to anything but her soothing of the woman in crucifixion.

I got out of bed and went downstairs to prepare for the Saturday shift in the mine. I found my grandmother sitting over the fire, her feet resting on the steel fender. The kettle was boiling on the hob. Beside her was a bowl of warm water, and in her lap lay a female child as yet unwashed after the journey from the womb. There was a life time of experience enfolded in that washing of a babe. Her hands, scored with the labours and toils of a lifetime in the back streets of the coal industry, aged beyond belief, still held a careful cunning and a copious deftness. The little thing lay in her lap and there it fitted as if it had been measured for the fitment.

'It'll dee,' she informed me through her lips that held a large safety-pin. 'It's sure to dee. It were born gone three, and now its after five. They should 'a' been washed hours ago. They'll both dee.'

'Both!' I exclaimed.

'Aye. Two lassies. They'll both dee.'

She dried the babe in a softly dabbing movement. Still nestling the little thing in her lap, she cut a piece of linen from a clean piece she had obtained from somewhere, put it on the points of her scissors and scorched it near the grate. After cooling this scorched cloth by waving it, and after testing it against her withered old cheek she placed it upon the umbilical cord that depended strangely blue from the body of the child. Then she firmly wrapped the little thing in a binding sheet and pinned it carefully. Swiftly she dressed the babe and laid it in a clothes basket and placed it near the fire. Not a sound issued from the baby.

Without pausing, she took up the other bundle from somewhere on the far side of her and repeated her careful, skilful performance. This done, she tied a piece of blue wool on the arm of the second baby, and then she laid it beside her sister.

Not a whimper came from either child.

'That bit o' thread marks the one that come last,' she informed me. 'But I needn't've bothered. She'll dee first. Sure to. I needn't've bothered at all for they'll both dee.'

'Why?' I asked.

'How can they live?' she demanded.

We sat together in our misery. I had nothing to offer the old woman but my company. I could only sit and listen.

'That doctor,' she said. 'He wanted to know all about the confinement. 'Look,' I said to him. 'You save my bairn, never mind how the little things came. I've 'livered hundreds o' bairns in my life. Hundreds an' hundreds'.

She spoke again. 'I want to know all,' he said. So I said to him, 'You save my lass. The bairns'll dee, but what does that matter? A bairn's nobbut a bairn.'

We sat until my father came into the kitchen. He was torn with anxiety that was crushed under his grief. 'You'd better come up, grandma,' he said.

Grandmother got up and went out of the kitchen, followed by my father. At the door he said to me: 'You'd better come up as well, Harold.'

I followed them upstairs, and into the bedroom. My brother George was there on the other side of the bed, a picture of awful woe. On the bed my mother lay still. My father went and stood by my brother George. I remained with my grandmother. She had seen many women die. She had administered to countless mothers as they dwindled into death in like circumstances.

As she went up to the bed a great gush of pain escaped from her old lips. 'Goodbye, my bairn,' she sobbed softly, 'goodbye my own lass.' She bent forward and put her hands upon the dead face, fondling it, granting it if she could a new lease of life. She put her lips to the unfeeling mouth and kissed it. As her sorrow broke, my father took her away, gently, kindly.

'Come away, grandma,' he said. 'Let her sleep.'

The doctor helped to lead her to a chair, and then he went and drew the sheet over the dead face.

The sensation which the death of my mother caused in the district was immense, in the village of Staithes, where sentiment was always as copious as the waters from which they rarely drew more than a sparse sustenance. The death had taken place in the early hours of the morning, and by the afternoon strangers were knocking at our door and begging permission to view the corpse and to see the babies. As a family we had not met with such morbid curiosity. In the end my father refused to grant any further privilege.

That Saturday afternoon it was once again imposed upon me to travel to Saltburn and meet the train which was to bring my paternal grandparents to the scene of our domestic disaster. I went with some reluctance, but as the day turned fine I was glad to explore the quaint town. I met my grand-parents and convoyed them from Easington station to Boulby Grange.

The weather became exceedingly warm, and my father had to accept the force of the argument in favour of an early interment. This had to take place on the Monday, and, consequently, meant another journey for me to the Post Office in Staithes in order to despatch the telegram to Hunwick.

At that time Staithes was celebrating its annual fair, one of the features of which was an extraordinary visitation of men who possessed horse-drawn, open landaus. With these they touted for passengers 'for rides into the country', which, in fact, were no more than rides from Staithes railway station to Hinderwell churchyard and back. Naturally the good folks of Staithes hired practically all the landaus at the fair for the purpose of attending the funeral. Clad in their best blue jerseys, the wives in their best funeral outfits, they succeeded in enlarging the cortège to an immense length. It most certainly made an impressive procession.

A scattering of my father's family, and a goodly number of my mother's, came along to the funeral from various parts of the north country. Michael Heslop, clad in important clothes and high hat, held close to my father, as did my uncle Stephen Whitfield, but he held close to his mother. Both men's immaculate dress caused much interest, for such rare attire was not seen in the locality.

The practice of singing a hymn over the coffin before enhearsing it was one which was observed in Cleveland. The hired local preacher, a rank below that of full minister, took charge of this ceremony at the door of our home. Standing by the coffin, which now rested on two chairs, he gave out the first verse of the hymn. A blue-clad fisherman gave the note, and the large crowd sang the hymn with much fervour. When it was ended the coffin was lifted into the hearse, and we all climbed into our separate mourning coaches, and the long cortege moved off slowly along the highroad to Grinkle.

The obsequies ended, our relations walked down to the railway station where they caught the train northwards. The rest of us, weary and forlorn went back to Boulby Grange, there to make the best of our lives.

Death had removed the gentle personality of our mother from the family circle. Her going left us in a hopeless domestic situation. Had Mrs Pearson not agreed to stay 'for at least a fortnight' I do not know what might have happened. A few days after the funeral Grandmother Whitfield departed for her own home in Quarry Burn. My other grandparents stayed a little longer, and then they went back to Hunwick. On the day following the funeral, my father's sister Margaret carried the eldest of the twins to Saltburn. Some days later another of his sisters, Rhoda, came and took the other child to Durham City. Thus they passed conclusively from the broken family circle. They did not die to fulfill the prognostication of Grandmother Whitfield. As a matter of fact they both lived to bear their own children.

My father was by no means transfigured by his passage through his woeful experience. He remained unchanged. If ever he mourned, he mourned in other people's houses, never in ours. Old Isaac Theaker, a fine, well-bearded fisherman in Staithes, did tell me that he often sat in his house and cried 'beyond comforting'. He rarely spoke of my mother to any of us five boys during the time he was conducting us into humanity's term, which in any case was not of long duration for most of us. That he may have felt determined to fulfil in that intention can be assumed; that he failed in his mission cannot be left fully to his charge. He was a helpless man in any contingency in the world above the coal-measures. He was a man of peace when he chose; he was a great squabbler over religion always. Being an official in the deplorable world of coal he had no reason to show just how many Achilles heels he really did possess. He was always courageous enough to hide them somewhere before he entered the pulpit. All through his life he went on his way preaching what he called the living gospel.

The Boulby ironstone mine belonged to the Skinningrove Iron and Steel Company Limited. The works were installed on the other side of Boulby Head along the edge of a vast combe. The houses of the workers, as fateful as any in industrial Britain, cluttered close to the inferno of noise, clamour and heat during winter, and sweltered throughout the long-drawn summer. All the ore that was blasted out of the mine was sent direct to the works there. How advanced the techniques were at that time it is impossible to say. That the organisation is still in existence testifies that it was of some importance. Where the ore comes from now is of no importance.

My father did not realise the danger he was in. He had always taken it for granted that he was a pulpit man by the grace of the Lord God and the leaders of the Primitive Methodist Church. The reason why he had been tolerated as a preacher in Hunwick could only have been because he was a Heslop. The name did count for something in coal. It did not occur to him that his new employers might not appreciate his position in the clan, and that they might disapprove of his exercises in biblical exegeses. Unmindful of his own mortal danger, he soldiered on in the van of the army of the Lord.

The Cleveland iron deposits were being exhausted rapidly when we arrived in the district. The iron content of the stone was by no means high. The area under exploitation lacked all the ingrained social purposes of the coal fields. There was no formidable proletarian activity. What trade union organisation there was was woefully weak. The Labour Party was not even in a formative state. In such circumstances it was quite clear to everybody but my father that the directorate of the company would have much preferred that the people should remain undisturbed by agitation of any kind, even that of religion.

I have often wondered if those unseen people ever did place observers in the places where my father went to preach. They need not have troubled themselves, for my father accepted the capitalist mode of production as being ordained by God. Nevertheless, in a short while, they did get rid of him. They showed him no pity. He was cast aside with his motherless children. By the middle of October, 1913, we were scattered about Hunwick and made to wait upon a turn in family fortunes.

During this rather prolonged hiatus I went to live with my aunt and uncle in Saltburn, and was made nurse to my sister. I was unhappy there. I did not like staying away from my brothers. In due time things did begin to happen. My father received a new appointment, this time in Northumberland, in the district that once nurtured men like Thomas Bewick and George Stephenson.

Before setting out on his new adventure, my father married Mrs Pearson. When I was apprised of this in a letter from my father I set off to walk from Saltburn to Staithes. I do not know why. I presume that I wanted to express my disapproval of the marriage. When I did arrive at Dale House I soon realised that I had better keep my mouth closed. The next morning, being a Sunday, I watched the unhappy couple depart for Grinkle Church, where they were married by the rector who had officiated at the burial of my mother some five months previously.

The good lady had had three daughters by her earlier marriage, but only one of them was brought into our family.

Within a fortnight we had passed out of Cleveland for ever.

Chapter Eight

The family reassembled at No. 9 Stephenson Terrace, Wylam-on-Tyne one dark, gloomy November day in the year 1913.

Although Wylam had lost all memory of Thomas Bewick, it still felt some pride in George Stephenson. Outside the village, some distance along the river bank towards Heddon-on-the-Wall railway station, stood the cottage in which the great man had been born. If that cottage has any tourist value today, it certainly possessed none when I lived in the village. As it then existed, Wylam possessed two faces. On the Durham side of the Tyne, clad the low heights beyond the railway station, in complete bourgeois isolation, were the tree-enfolded residences of those who either commuted to Newcastle in the better class jobs, and those without reason to commute to any place and do any work at all. A toll bridge spanned the river and brought one part of Wylam into association with the other part should the need arise, which was not often. Although the bridge joined the two parts, the railway from Newcastle to Carlisle severed them without compunction or pity. Curiously enough the Northumberland site had little use for the railway on the Durham side, for another railway from Newcastle to Wylam did all that was needful for the transportation of the folk to the 'canny toon'.

The less residential part of Wylam was the real village. It had always been there, and it had developed somewhat when men began to exploit the coal measures lying under the land on the north bank of the river. During the nineteenth century shafts had been sunk to the considerable seams lying in a forty fathom shallow. These were the 'Six Quarter', the 'Five Quarter', the 'Yard Seam' and the 'Brockwell Seam', each resting within the earth in that order of descent, and at workable levels. Below the Brockwell seam lay a thinner streak of coal, called the Victoria Seam. It was twenty-two inches thick. It had been left untroubled through time until about a year before we made our entrance into the village. The top three seams had all been exhausted by the end of the century. Trouble had not been encountered underground until the hewers began to remove the Brockwell Seam from Mother Earth to the fireside. Pragmatic mining engineering had laid this wonderful seam in hazard, for all the water at higher levels in the area, to say nothing of that flowing in the Tyne, found its way to the deepest levels, and mining had had to be abandoned.

A year before we happened on the Northumbrian scene, a Newcastle company had been registered for the mining of the remaining coal. That it was a shoe-string affair can be judged from the fact that before making an attempt to clean out one of the abandoned shafts, they had caused a drift to be driven into the Victoria Seam from a point in a valley through which dimpled a stream that was tributary to the Tyne. A ramshackle pit head had been set up for the purpose of easing the strain upon finances by mining and selling at 'land-sale' the coal, with the consequence that the loveliness of the valley, clothed in beauty by tall conifers, was debauched.

When we arrived at the pit the shaft near the land-sale pit had been cleaned out almost to the Yard Seam. The drift was producing some thirty tons of coal per day. My introduction to the pit was horrifying. No place anywhere in the pit was a yard high. Economy was the first consideration. A small producing force and hopelessly primitive transportation. There was a pony, a pitiful little thing that did not possess the strength of a collie dog, and was fit for nothing better than a knacker's yard. Two young fellows – putters, they were called – shoved and pushed the tubs from landing to coal-face, and from coal-face to landing, and did all the chores of the landing, making up the small trains of tubs and receiving them from bank.

Our job was to produce as much coal as possible and get the shaft cleaned out with a minimum of delay. When all was said and done, it was a most miserable job, but that was not the worst of our troubles. Our stepmother had not bargained for life in the distant North when she had married my father, and now that she realised what it all meant she became more and more soured as the days passed. Looking back over those years I can see now how valiantly my father tried to climb a broken ladder. Had he been a more courageous man he would have refused to accept the appointment, and would have gone to the deep measures on the Durham coast and there 'chanced his arm', as the Geordies have it. Surely, a man possessed of his qualifications would not have been buried in the deep seams.

As soon as it was possible I was assigned to the sinkers.

In those days, all work began at six in the morning. It was a bleak one when I arrived at the cabin near the mouth of the shaft. A squat headgear had been erected to engage the purpose of a hand-worked winch. The rope ran from the winch over the pulley wheel and down into the shaft. At the end of the rope was a box-like arrangement, called a 'kibble'. Two men rode in this thing at a time, one foot in the box and the other out. The kibble was loaded, or unloaded, of its human freight at the top on to a wheeled platform, which enclosed the mouth of the shaft. In accordance with the provisions of the Mine Act of 1911 men and boys travelling in such a contrivance had to be securely fastened to the rope by a leathern belt. All-in-all, it was a most doleful method of transport.

There were two sinkers, a datal-hand (or 'shifter') and myself. My father's new brother-in-law had accompanied us from Cleveland, and was now a member of our family. He had charge of the sinking. The other two were local men who had forsaken the hewers' picks to work in the shaft. Dick, my new uncle, said he would take me down after the other two men had gone down. I stood aside to watch the proceedings, and I was more than a little discomfited. When the kibble had received its human freight in accordance with the law, it was raised a few inches to allow the bogey to be withdrawn. As soon as this was done the kibble began to spin. I noticed that one of the men, Jack Cheesman had a long stick in his free hand, and with this he was able to bring the gyrations under something approaching control. And down they went.

After some time the kibble was drawn up, the bogey wheeled over the apperture, and things made ready for a fresh load. Dick told me to get in with both feet, and this I did. He strapped me to the rope and made sure that I was safe before he did the same service to himself. He then gave the signal. I felt myself being gently raised. I heard the bogey being gently withdrawn. I felt myself spinning round. I held on grimly to the rope. We began to drop down the monstrous throat of the earth. Our ludicrous spinning was brought to a halt. I opened my eyes and for the first time in my life I became acquainted with a mine shaft. Dick kept holding the kibble away from the sides of the shaft. As he did so he examined the shaft. Water bled from it at many points of our descent. As we got further down I could hear the plopping noises of water. It was weird, uncanny and frightening.

'There's nothing to fear,' I heard Dick say to me. 'We'll soon be at the bottom.'

At the five quarter seam he gave a loud shout and the kibble came to rest. Jack Cheesman thrust out his arm and caught the rope, and brought it to the side. 'Lower,' he roared up the shaft. We came to the side and finally we settled on the jutting platform. Garvie Reynolds undid my belt and helped me on to the landing. 'Nowt to fear, was there, hinney?' he said.

I did not give him an answering smile. I had yet to recover myself. Dick did not get out of the kibble, but went on down the shaft to the point of that morning's work. After examining the sides he declared everything to be all right, and very soon after, Cheesman joined him in the sump of the shaft and the day's work began. Both men wore thick rubber 'back skins'.

It was my job to shout the signals up the shaft and help to land the full kibble on to the platform and help Garvie to get it shoved to the place where he could stow the contents at the far end of the tunnel. Dick and Jack tore at the rubble and muck beneath their feet and loaded it into the kibble. When it was full it was hoisted up to where I was and they went on digging at the cloying mess in the shaft.

The shaft was some fourteen feet in diameter. It was a well shaped hole and much craft had been expended upon fashioning it. When work had ceased in it many years ago, it had been filled to the throat with all kinds of rubbish, logs, tree trunks, great stones, blocks of masonry, clay, ashes, lavatory contents, and ordinary soil. When the sinkers had a large obstruction to move, Garvie and I could only stand on the platform and watch those two immensely strong men extract it from the cloying muck. It was dangerous work, for neither of them could go anywhere to get out of danger when anything was being pulled up the shaft. All they could do was cower against the dripping sides of the shaft and watch the ascent of the loaded kibble, the slung timber, or the slung stone, and be ready to spring out of harm's way should anything untoward happen. And all the time this tedious work went on great blobs of water fell like stones.

As the stuff was excavated it was taken along the old working road between the shaft pillars of the seam, which, curiously enough, had not collapsed during the decades which had lapsed since they were mined. Our illumination came from two candles – mine and Garvie's.

A shaft is a construction inserted *into* the earth, a construction in reverse, so to speak. And like all structures it must have a sure foundation. Those seams of coal through which it will be made to pass, as well as the final seam of coal it will reach, must be broken only from two opposite sides of the shaft, and they must proceed at right angles to the shaft along one line, and one line only. No deviation from these initial excisions must be allowed. Any branching off from these two incursions into the seam can take place after a carefully calculated distance in ratio to the depth of the shaft. No circumvention of this rule can be allowed that might weaken the coal seam foundation upon which the shaft rests, for any such probing would weaken the shaft as a structure.

In that Five Quarter seam the coal stood in all its primordial and pristine loveliness, blinking back at our simple lighted candles like a shy maiden. Coal is always beautiful when it reflects such light. I can still recall the stillness of that coal as it stood before us in the presence of its own enormous centuries. It was beautiful. And yet we walled it up with the filthy debris that had been inserted by unclean hands into as straight a shaft as ever was shot through the northern earth, walled it up and left it standing in unclean shrouds, safe forever from the consuming fires. In all probability no one has touched it since we covered it up without pity.

All through those days we worked on that shaft. Early in the New Year we reached the Yard Seam. The shaft was bleeding copiously at this point, but this did not impede our progress. We became intensely interested when the sinkers uncovered an iron collar inserted in the throat of the shaft. My father identified it as 'a ring of tubbing' which, apart from its power to reinforce a crumbling section of the stratum through which the shaft had passed was also a defence against water. Later examination showed that the tubbing had been inserted as a defence against inundation.

The tubbing was in actuality a huge collar made of thick segments of cast iron, and had been inserted into the shaft some distance above the Yard Seam down to some distance below it. When bolted together it formed a continuous tube over its length. It was one of the most interesting adjuncts to mining

I had so far come across. In all my experience I have not encountered such another in any shaft I have travelled. The only other ring of tubbing I have noticed was in a deep lift shaft in a London underground station. I did once work on the sinking of a shallow shaft, or staple, which we gave a thick collar of cement as we descended. This staple, however, was passing through a fault or a 'hitch' which had flung the seam of coal some fathoms below its own level. The stone through which we dug the shaft was soft and crumbly, and so we had to build the wall as we went down. It was rather an interesting piece of mining engineering. This tubbing at Wylam must have been calculated to the finest fractions. The bolting was meticulous. We examined it in awe and wonder. When we had uncovered it and cleaned the dirt off it and sunk below it we could see it hanging, and gripping the throat of the shaft like time grips existence.

Ingress to the Yard Seam was to be gained through that iron barrier in the shaft, but we had to find out where it was exactly before we attempted to break through the tubbing. All that we knew was that the roads into the seam would be the same as those in the two upper seams, for no other conformation could be conceived in relation to the cage or cages which once ran up and down the shaft itself. Dick assessed that the best place to break through the iron collar would be in the centre, and after much careful jowling, or tapping, with a heavy hammer he marked a precise spot and forthwith began his assault upon the middle of the chosen segment. It was a laborious job breaking through that formidable barrier, but in this he succeeded. By the time this had been achieved an old-fashioned winding engine had been installed, and it became possible for us to raise all the excavated rubbish and filth to the surface and tip it over the unprotesting face of the nearby field that was already down to corn.

Down and down we sank that shaft. Garvie and I enjoyed our new task up in the daylight. We went on tipping the age-old refuse over the field until the day of the catastrophe. The sinkers had by then almost reached the Brockwell Seam. Dick and Jack were loading a kibble when the water broke through from below. It was Jack's huge shout which brought us all running to the mouth of the shaft. After the commotion had been softened out, one of us was able to speak to the two men working in the shaft, and we soon understood the disastrous situation into which our mates had been plunged. Unfortunately, just at that time the winding engine took upon itself to break down, and from that moment we were all in great trepidation. Luckily the hand winch had not been moved from its original place, and we were able to carry the rope over the old wheel and drop the old wooden kibble to the two men now gradually becoming more and more anxious. Luckily the water rose slowly, and in the end we were able to extricate the two men from their predicament.

The water rose slowly in the shaft. The next day it was still rising. By that time the machinery had been put to rights, and Dick and I went down to assess the situation. It was most strange looking down on that baleful eye of water. There was no sound, no bubbling, just a slow, gentle rising in the shaft, as if the water were *climbing* up the shaft. There was no sound. And yet, we were in the presence of an enormous force, a force that was raising a huge column of water upwards and away from the darkness. It was eerie watching the level of the water rising in the shaft, not filling it, but rising. That water, which had been imprisoned for decades, was simply rising as silently and as purposefully as a column of mercury in a barometer. We both sat there on our unkers fascinated, horrified. It was stretching the imagination to the limit to accept what was happening there, below us, in the light cast by our candles. There, down there, it went on, soundlessly pursuing its own purpose. If it came up to the point where it could flow over and into the Yard Seam what would we be able to do?

The water stopped rising when it reached a point a few feet below the gantry upon which we squatted. There was an old wooden joist which Dick and his marrow had left undisturbed as they had sunk below it, and which in the past had carried one side of the cage slide. We accepted it as a mark to be submerged. It did not disappear. We waited, watching, and at last we became assured that the force behind that water had become exhausted.

My father came down the shaft some time later.

'She's stopped rising,' Dick told him.

'We'd better make sure,' said my father.

We made sure.

That night, at home, we discussed the phenomenon.

'What does it mean?' I asked.

'Mean!' cried my father. 'How can water mean anything of itself?'

I blushed. 'But why has it stopped rising?' I demanded.

My father winged me an apologetic smile. 'It becomes quite simple to understand,' he said. 'The water has risen in the shaft because it has been liberated from one of the things that constricted its purpose to flow downhill. That is obvious. Filling the shaft in kept the water in the seam.'

'But what has stopped it flowing away?' I asked.

He shook his head. 'Harold,' he said, and I knew that he was unable to provide all the answers to his own question. 'Harold! Ever since I've know thou, tha's always wanted to know the far end of a fart and where the stink goes.'

'I'm sorry,' I said as I rose to leave the room. He laid his hand upon me, and I resumed my seat. 'The water has obviously been forced up the shaft by immense pressure. There's only two answers to the problem we have before us. Either the Brockwell seam is filled to the brim with water, or it isn't and the water is damned back somewhere, somehow.'

Dick came between us. 'Then there's a hell of a lot o' water behind that dam,' he said. He rose and put on his jacket. 'I'm off for a drink at the Fox and Hounds,' he said.

When he had gone, my father said to me: 'I can't think the seam is drowned out. In my opinion there is a dam holding the water, and what is more the dam cannot be very far away from the bottom of the shaft.' He gave me one of his rare grins. 'Whoever built that dam knew what he was about,' he said to me, and then he added, 'There's nowt beats good workmanship in a pit. I'd like to meet the man who thought it out.' He paused for a considerable moment. 'We've been lucky,' he said.

'And what do we do now?' I asked.

'Find that dam, and find it quick,' he replied. 'I don't know what they'll think at Newcastle when I tell them.'

'And in the meantime?' I asked.

'We'll go down to the Yard seam and see what we can see,' he said. 'It is the only way to get to the Brockwell. The old plan shows a drift.' He smiled again. 'If we don't find it Harold,' he said, 'We'll both be out of a job.'

Later that night Dick returned from his foray among the beer barrels at The Fox and Hounds Inn, eager to consider further the problems which now faced my father. 'We'll have to find some way of tapping that water,' he said in his slurring Cleveland drawl. 'But when we do that, what are we going to do with all that water? It'll have to go somewhere, and one thing we can be sure of, Bill, and that is it won't flow up the shaft.'

'That's just what bothers me, Dick,' my father confided. 'If we do find the dam and we can tap it we might find ourselves doing more damage than the royalty is worth.' He reflected a moment. 'I wouldn't like to drown out any of Harry Richardson's districts at Clara Vale. He's a decent chap. Goes to the chapel at Crawcrook. Doesn't preach, though.'

'He might,' I suggested.

My father shook his head. 'It isn't every man who is fitted to preach the gospel,' he said. 'And it's about time you knew that, my lad.'

I waited and then I asked, 'What is a royalty, Dad?'

'The area of the coal we are permitted by the landlord above ground to mine the coal underneath,' he said. 'He owns the royalty, and what we pay him for the privilege of mining the coal is called a royalty payment. Sometimes it's as high as sixpence a ton.'

'But…' I began.

He wagged his finger. 'Now! Now! It is the way of men wiser than you, my canny lad! So hadn't we best leave it like that?'

Chapter Nine

The Yard Seam was a revelation to any of us who ventured into it. About a furlong away from the shaft we came upon the entrance to a drift, and after clearing our way into it we discovered that it went fairly steeply through the intervening strata of various interesting kinds of stone into the Brockwell. I have seen much better constructed drifts. We descended it carefully and emerged upon the seam, which subsequent exploration proved to be standing, as it had been left, in unbroken pillars of some thirty yards square. My father had brought his safety lamp, which had been presented to him when he left North Bitchburn colliery, but after making a few examinations, he handed it to me to carry, for there was no methane present in the atmosphere.

To our great surprise we found a free flow of air coursing along the main waggonway running at right angles to the drift. However, we were still unconfirmed in our assumptions about the place which had been left unvisited a great long time. We spoke to each other in undertones, as if we were afraid that noise might disturb the roof. All the timber that once had supported this roof had long disappeared. The entire travelling way, and the entire seam, as we later discovered, had been denuded of every stick of timber that might have been left by those forgotten miners. Nothing had escaped dissolution but the coal and stone. Careful examination of the standing coal showed that it was undisturbed by overhead pressure. It did not look like coal, for everything was coated with a reddish slime, which when disturbed revealed a blue, shale-like clay nature under-neath, and thick. The floors of all the passages through which we trudged lay inches deep under that ancient coating of slime. The little hillocks, into which the standing props and neglected pieces of timber had disintegrated, were of the same detestable filth.

We had ventured into a forgotten world, a damp, silent world which had been abandoned far back into the century. The imperturbability of eternity rested coldly within those tomb-like places through which we walked. It was uncanny.

We sat down on our unkers to rest awhile, and, fearlessly enough, to smoke. Jack Cheesman soon had his clay pipe going, and was the first to break silence.

'Know what I think?' he demanded of nobody in particular. 'I think this beats hen-racing. It does, be buggered! Look! Whoever was in a pit where there was no timber?'

My father gave a short laugh. 'Dick and me are used to it,' he assured the huge Geordie. 'At the last pit we worked in we could take you for miles and you would not see a stick of timber, not even lying near the deputy's kist.'

'Well! I'll be buggered!' he snorted.

'It's a good sandstone top,' my father observed. 'There's been nothing to disturb it. If we started taking out those pillars of coal you'd find we would want quite a lot of timber,' He got up and measured the height of the seam. 'Just under four foot,' he said. He lunged at a piece of coal jutting out with his foot and broke it off. 'Grand coal, this,' he said.

'You could tell that in the other seams,' said Jack 'She was ower good to abandon, this coal.'

Dick held out his candle into the stream of air and watched the flame blow over on to its side. 'What bothers me,' he said, 'is where the air is coming from. As I reckon it,' he went on, 'we're away from the shaft, so how does the air get past all that water?'

'Aye! That's the problem,' said my father.

We walked along the 'main going', as we now termed the passage, for a long time, stopping at intervals to judge the air flow. No one spoke, for no one was inclined to disturb the graveyard silence. We might be walking into danger, like ill-equipped pot-holers. And, yet, there was nothing for us to fear. The roof had little need for any support at that particular time, for it had edged itself solidly upon its coal supports as the timbers had decayed. The chief danger lay in the appalling silence, the lack of any sound, the deep soundlessness, the absolute lack of vibration that is such a part of a mine. Nothing, it seemed, was interfering with the sleep of this entire seam.

We came upon a well excavated place about twelve feet high, gouged out of the upper rock. The act of disembowelling had been done by meticulous surgeons. It had been almost sculpted into space, and there it continued to exist, as if it had been fashioned in love.

'Now we'll see,' exclaimed my father. The exploding of the word 'now' was peculiar to the speech of the man, and betokened finality. Perhaps he had learned to use it when he was drawing a large trout out of the Wear. He stood up and carried a lighted candle as high as he could up to the roof. We all offered him the lights of our own candles. For some time he examined the roof. 'That's what I call a sandstone top,' he said when he had finished his examination.

The men discussed the place, and I listened. They all arrived at the conclusion that this place had been the housing of the wheel of a self-acting incline. The gallery running at right angles to the incline was much wider, and looked as if it had fed the landing with the furnished waggons for the incline. It must run to a good dip, a steep gradient. It was obvious that the train of full tubs of coal would be lowered against an ascending train of empty tubs, and that the hewers would be supplied with the tubs when excavating the coal. It was an old method of haulage underground.

We explored the incline carefully. Here the width of the passage allowed the roof to collapse at various points. We went on and on until we reached a fall of roof that prevented our further progress. And so we called it a day, and we retraced our steps to the shaft.

That night I asked my father why we had explored the area so meticulously. He gave his reply rather reluctantly. 'You see,' he said, 'when we tap that watter' – he always used the Durham pronunciation of the word – 'it will have to go somewhere. I was anxious to see if that area was big enough to hold it when we break down the dam…'

'Which we haven't found yet,' I said.

Without speaking, he reached for his pipe, lit it, and picked up the latest copy of the *Hibbert Journal*, and began to read.

Our search for that elusive dam occupied us many days. The 'shoe-string' directors daily became more and more exasperated. We toiled on, and the day did come when we discovered it.

What did surprise us was that the same lavish care had been applied to the construction of the dam as had been on the 'engine house' further in-bye. We might never have discovered the dam had my father not surveyed the immediate area around the shaft top and the area near to the bottom of the shaft. I helped him in all this work, dragging the chain, holding the candle, marking the place and all the insignificant chores that belong to accurate surveying. I learned an immense respect for him during those most anxious days.

The day came when he had to make his decisions. Drawing his own plan to the scale of the old plan of the mine, he posited the exact position of the dam. The next day we went and worked under his direction. I watched him carefully, vaguely aware of, and wonderfully appreciative of his mining knowledge. We came to the wall of the mine. Beyond this wall lay our quarry, a monstrous reservoir of stinking water. We could go no further.

'Gan back an' find a stopping,' he said to Cheesman.

Cheesman found the single brick stopping and kicked his way through it.

'Thou shouldn't've done that, Jack!' my father cried.

But Jack had gone through the hole he had made.

It was safe.

We followed him, slowly, carefully. At the end of the pillar of coal we turned right, and came into an enlarged area. Beyond it was a fall of stone, but under that fall flowed a stream of water.

My father sat down on his unkers and lit his pipe. For some minutes he smoked, without speaking. Then, scrambling to his feet and taking his stick, he spoke to the men.

'You'll find her through t'other side o' the fall,' he said. 'I'll away to bank now.'

And with that he departed.

The fall was not extensive and after two or three days' work we were able to go up to the face of the dam. This confirmed our supposition that the mine beyond the dam had been deliberately drowned by the owners of the mine on our side of the dam, drowned by those ancient private enterprisers.

We attacked the face of the dam. It had been massively constructed out of squared logs of oak. The workmanship was superb, and often engaged our glances of admiration. Each block was a foot square and four feet long. There were two sets of blocks embedded in the aperture, all wedged exquisitely into the space. The water had swelled them into an almost immovable mass of oak. An augur was brought and with difficulty was driven through the middle block of the almost impermeable wood. Dick was the arbiter of the process. When the augur had been thrust as far into the wood as it would go it was withdrawn and the hole scraped out for blasting. Then he inserted it and tamped the hole with softened blue shale. He sent us all out of the tunnel before he lit the fuse. The explosion provided the underground with a vast noise. Examination showed that little damage had been done to the dam.

Undeterred, Dick began a fresh borehole as soon as the reek had gone out of the cavern.

We literally burned out that first block of oak with dynamite and gelignite. When we had cleared the first four feet of oaken wood from the hole, we set about removing the second four feet. This, however, proved to be not so difficult as the first one. Once the oak was removed we came face to face with the actual dam, which proved to be twenty three feet thick, and was built of massive stone concreted into position.

Here we toiled to undo the evil that had been so cheerfully done by those forgotten men. Once we had removed the oak barrage we had to take action against the new barrier of concreted stone. This was more in the privilege of the miner. True, there was very little room in which to work, but that was overcome. Dick Atkinson knew all there was to know about using a hand drill, and so he bored his holes into the concreted mass quite cheerfully. And he succeeded, despite all the difficulties attendant upon a man in a constricted space, holding a primitive drill with one hand hammering it home with a heavy hammer in the other hand. To my surprise, he had the ability to repeat the action when changing hands. Dick had worked with the more powerful of the explosives since leaving school. He was a consummate miner, one of the best I ever encountered. He was never averse to lending a hand to clean away the debris after the explosion.

Excitement mounted when the barricade was fractured. We sat in safety gloating over the increased flow of water. We knew that all the water had to be liberated, and that our time was short. At first the water flowed more sluggishly than we had anticipated, and we came to the conclusion that the breach would have to be made much wider. But how? The problem was solved by the engineer. He had some cast iron pipes of a small diameter, and he suggested that we ought to screw them together to make a ramrod and batter the fracture from a fairly safe distance. We laboured mightily and at last the dam became fully breached. We scrambled to safety and left the water to sweep to its own unknown destination.

'We'd better get back to bank,' said Dick. 'There's nothing to be gained watching that little lot.'

'Bloody big lot, I call it,' said Cheesman.

Nothing loath, we went to the shaft and rode away from the water.

The next morning we went down the shaft anticipating a dramatic lowering of the column of water in the shaft. We were bitterly disappointed. It had not lowered a great deal.

'We'll go and see what's happening at the dam,' he said to me.

This we did.

We found the water still flowing with the fury of yesterday.

'Think we've done the trick, Dick?' I asked him.

'If we haven't I don't know what else we will have to do,' he replied.

The next morning we discovered that the water had almost cleared the shaft, and we were all very happy. I was not so elated when I was told that there was little else I could do, and that I had better get over to the land-sale drift where I would find plenty to do. I soon disliked the pit, its forlorn shabbiness and its eternally bleeding roof.

It was all so different from the ironstone mine at Boulby. It was mining in severely constricted conditions. In Boulby all action was proposed and disposed in terms of physical strength. There, a man of mean stature could lay hold of a piece of rock up to three hundredweight and hoist it, first on to his knees, and then upwards, the dead weight laying upon bended arms and forward chest, and heave it into the waggon, all in one flowing movement. It was a trick I learned and never forgot. In the coal measures strength was of lesser consideration than skill. The picks used by hewers were light affairs, never under two and a half pounds and never over four, with points sharpened to the finest degree. It is forbidden to tackle an uncut seam of coal with explosives, for the coal, so finely grained and lain in the earth is impervious to such revolting action. Skill, measured skill, is all that is needed, even today. The great hewers of the past were not mighty men physically; they were skilful and enduring craftsmen.

To watch a hewer was always a revelation for me, especially when in the low seams. In a place only twenty-two inches from floor to roof, a man had to be agile and sure as he assumed the posture suitable for such a constriction of space. Before presenting himself to his task 'on the caunch' the hewer had first to divest himself of most of his garments, and so to free his arms and legs from all encumbrance. He then inserted his body wholly into the space and shuffled his back, taking his pick and shovel with him as he so shuffled, until he reached the point of his production. Within hewing distance of the face he turned himself on his side, drew up one knee to make a cushion for his shoulder, and thus be in a position to manipulate his pick. Then, without more ado, after a careful assessment of the coal that had to be hewed, the hewing commenced. The coal glinted in the light of the candle. The hacked pieces of coal began to encumber the little space, and when the heap over his legs began to impede his work, the hewer would pause to push it aside, using his legs only. It was all a matter of hacking, just hacking, gently, forcibly *feeling* the mineral out of its fastness. The incision was made close to the caunch, or the floor, a promotion of superincumbency. At the right moment there would be dealt the measured blow, the sinking of the pick point into the upper band of coal. No levering. No angry smashing. Just a gentle trembling of the pick shaft, a given temptation to it to fall. And thus he proceeded until the coal so hewn became an encumbrance, and then he would manipulate his shovel and get the coal to that point where it could be thrown into the waggon.

As he hewed the coal so he progressed into the seam. At times he would suspend his operations and tap the roof over with his pick. It was for him to judge whether a support should be set or not. If it was necessary to do so he took a sawn prop and a headtree and hammered it into an upright position between floor and roof with his pick. When it became uneconomical for him to continue hewing and having to throw the coal long distances to the waggon, he would set up a drilling contrivance and set about boring the necessary holes in the now intruding caunch. When this was done, the deputy would come with his box of powder and slow matches, tamp the holes and fire them. The dislodged stone – it could be taken down from the roof, or up from the floor – was then thrown into the space which had resulted from the act of hewing. It thus was made to serve as a 'pack', a support for the roof. Such an act was recompensed by a yardage payment.

All this strange contortion of the labouring body fascinated me. I often spoke of it to my father. It was rare for him to be in an expansive mood when I questioned him, for, I think, it had been his intention to make me other than a miner. He told me on that occasion that in the beginnings of commercial mining men hewed coal without the aid or sanction of timber.

Why? Because timber was needed for charcoaling, and was not only expensive but a particular commodity in the reserve of the landowners. Consequently men had to arch the coal, no matter how long it was as a seam. To reinforce his argument – against my disbelief – he took me one day to the other side of the little valley and showed me such a place. The seam was actually arched for a considerable distance into the outcropped coal. It stunk of foxes, to be sure. How any man could have managed to arch so low a seam and take it to such a distance still entrances me.

The Victoria was a wretched little seam of a very good quality. It dipped away at a fairly steep angle, and as a result a very simple one rope haulage system operated the output. The hauling engine was a ramshackle affair that might have started its career drawing a threshing machine about the countryside. It stood, or rocked, on its four wheels, and was fired in a box that might have been originated by George Stephenson. It had a large flywheel, which the engineman often had to help round whenever the steam pressure was low. The screens were as pitifully inadequate as the hauling engine. Everything was worse than secondhand. Even the pump at the drift mouth was scarcely adequate to keep the main heading dry. The water it managed to pour into the tumbling beck was black, sour and stinking.

I learned to hew coal, and to my surprise I experienced no discomfort when I had coiled myself into the correct postures against the glittering coal face. I absorbed all the simple tricks. They were there for any male to learn. All he needed was strength.

Over at the shaft things went on quite well. The work went on. Dick and Jack dug down through the shaft towards the brow of the seam. The weight of the dropping water was countered by their wearing 'back sheets', great rubber capes. They were anxious to get the job finished. They worked like slaves.

It was Cheesman who made the discovery. His candle had burnt itself out, or so he thought, and he decided to relight it and place it nearer to the floor of the shaft. As he lowered it, the light was snuffed out.

'Yer bugger o' hell!' he exclaimed. 'See that, Dick. Look!'

He relit his candle and lowered it gently until it became extinguished.

'That's queer,' said Dick.

They worked on for some time and then they discovered that at knee height the candle died out. Both men went down to smell.

That's stythe,' said Jack. 'I ken that bloody stuff.'

Dick nodded. 'I think we'd better get out of here,' he said.

And so it was stythe. Mining engineers dignified it with the name of 'choke damp'. Scientists called it carbonic acid gas.

'We'll get up on the Yard Seam gantry and watch it before we do anything about it,' said Dick. 'Bill Heslop won't like this,'

'You bet your bottom dollar on that!' exclaimed Jack. 'Poor little bugger! He gets all the knocks!'

They were raised to the surface, where Dick got a flare lamp and a considerable length of twine. After a brief conversation with the engineer, they were lowered to the Yard Seam. A man was set to wait-on at the shaft top for any orders.

Down on the gantry the two intrepid men carried out their survey of the rising gas. The flare was lit and dropped down into the suffocating atmosphere until it was extinguished. The point in the shaft was registered, the lamp withdrawn, and a period of waiting set. Repetition proved the slow ascent of the stythe.

My father was sent for and after he had confirmed the new visitation he went home, a sadly disappointed man. He was angry, and remained angry long after Dick and I got back home. There was no point to be gained by discussing something that was present, which could not be wished away, and which had to be overcome.

The office at Newcastle went into panic. Reason did emerge and in due time a small suction fan was delivered at the pit head and erected. A large number of long, tarred, sheetmetal tubes, each a foot in diameter, were brought to the place. The first one was securely attached to a side rope and lowered to a point where the next one was similarly slung and joined to its predecessor. In this way a tube was constructed which reached from the fan to almost near the floor of the shaft. The fan was set in motion and left to do its own work.

Each morning Dick lowered his flare lamp to the point where it was extinguished summarily. Each morning Dick cursed the fate that had sent him into the land of George Stephenson. But the morning did come when the flare lamp did not go out.

The shaft was ultimately cleaned out.

The summer blazed over the land.

The Great War seized the world by the throat. Coal was being drawn up the shaft we had sunk.

The year was 1914.

The month was August.

Chapter Ten

By the New Year our family had reached crisis point and was in danger of imminent collapse. It had long been apparent that the lady my father had taken to wife had arrived at the conclusion that she had made a profound mistake. The life she had visualised when she stood by his side before the altar had not turned out at all well. Her ukase was published at a family gathering. I was her chosen victim. If I did not depart from under the parental roof, she would forthwith 'take her 'ook'.

I had no alternative, and so I packed my belongings into a couple of brown paper parcels and departed, leaving my elder brother to join the army. The eldest of the three youngest sons was soon to go, leaving my father to enjoy the luxury of keeping up appearances with a woman who luxuriated an ungovernable temper.

I found a job at Harton Colliery, Tyne Dock, South Shields.

At the age of sixteen I was on my own in a strange town. Luckily I found lodgings with a good proletarian family. I still consider that I was fortunate to be granted a lifelong place at the fireside of Billie and Emily Gibson, at 23 Marsden Street, Westoe, South Shields. Billie was a small-boned, ginger-headed man who hewed coal at Marsden Colliery. Emily was a fine, intelligent and courageous woman. I think that they took me in as a replacement for one of their two eldest sons who had died some time just before the war commenced. Under their roof I crouched among the turmoils of mine and adolescence, alone, stupendously bereaved of my family, without friends, relatives and confidants.

I still recall vividly my introduction to Harton Colliery.

The Harton Coal Company Limited was a vast mining operation carried out in the rich seams of excellent coal lying under the county borough and the rural district of Shields. The tremendous seams were mined at four separate pits, St Hilda, Harton, Marsden and Boldon. Each pit was geared to a daily production of three thousand tons of coal. It was at that time the most majestic complex in the county of Durham. Each pit was powered by electricity throughout. The economic basis of the structure was a secure and satisfactory coalfield. All the produced coal was screened before being loaded into the company's own waggons, carried on its own electrified railway to its own staithes near the mouth of the Tyne, where it was loaded by its own coal trimmers into colliers, big and small. The company's own railway serviced three of the collieries, and the fourth, Boldon, had to obtain the services of the then North Eastern Railway. The entire county borough was conscribed, transport-wise, by the colliery railway.

Not one chimney honoured the company with a belch of smoke. Each colliery was drawn by an impressive winding engine and an enormous headgear that imposed its ever revolving wheels over a scene of incessant labour activity. Even the subsiduary appurtenances complemental to the task of creating the coal commodity were impressive. The pit buzzer was an electrified screech. Coal drawing at each pit commenced at precisely six o'clock in the morning and continued without pause until nine o'clock in the evening, five days one week and an extra few hours on the Saturday of next. During the year the pit made holiday on Xmas Day, New Year's Day, Good Friday, Easter Monday, Whit Monday and August Bank Holiday Monday, and on no other day of the year, except, of course the alternative Saturday morning. No miner ever took a holiday; none had the money for such an easement.

Three seams were being worked during the time I was there, the Yard Seam, the Bensham Seam and the Hutton Seam. The shaft, which was sunk to the middle seam, the Bensham, was two hundred and forty fathoms deep. The coal won in the Yard Seam was dropped to the Bensham, and that won in the Hutton Seam was drawn up through a long drift. All the coal was a shining, beautiful mineral.

It was on a Sunday night round about half past ten when I set off from my new home to work my first shift in the colliery. I made my way rather tentatively to the lamp cabin where I handed over my permission to take a safety lamp. It was a huge, tiled place holding well over two thousand safety lamps, all of one pattern, all made to burn oil. I received my lamp at the counter that ran the length of the room, and followed the men and boys into what proved to be a huge waiting room. At the doorway stood two men whose duties it was to test the lamps.

This was done by thrusting the lamp into a chamber filled with gas from the local gas supply. The lamp was merely extinguished. At the other side of the room a youth manipulated an electrical gadget which relighted the lamp by creating an inner flame at the end of a piece of wire near the wick of the lamp.

After I had received my lamp from the youth another young fellow approached me and told me to stick by him. This I was most content to do, for I was feeling strangely perturbed by the immense crowd of men and youths. I was conducted through a set of revolving doors, up a flight of steps, through another door and on to the pit head. The steel headgear ran up from some place hidden below and out to the wheels, which were still enclosed within the huge building. A buzzer tore a great leaf out of the closing day and the ropes began to move. Over all there was the continuous roaring of the suction fan which was located some distance below the pit head. All this noise overpowered any which the cages and ropes might make. They seemed to slip silently upwards to receive their human freight.

Each cage carried two decks, and each deck accommodated twenty people. I accompanied my mentor into the bottom deck of the cage. The descent was quite slow. We passed into the great wind created by the suction fan, and at last we were stayed in our progress by a slight bump on to the timbers over the sump. The gates were opened and we all filed out into an arched cavern that was flooded with electric light. Here was space in which one could move. I was totally impressed, for this was something I had not expected. This was mining on an immense scale, novel and to me incomprehensible.

The air moving against me was quite warm. It flowed over the clad body like tepid liquid.

I kept close behind my new companion as we passed under the arched cavern. We passed through a series of wooden doors whose purpose was to isolate the intake from the return. To have had all six doors open at the same time would have caused a ventilatory catastrophe. We emerged upon a section of the shaft landing. Here there were more coal tubs standing on the one side fully laden and on the other side empty than I had ever seen in my life. I calculated that in a mine of the size of this one there must have been some thousands of such springless boxes. Each carried exactly ten hundredweight of coal. There was no noise. A gale of cold, fresh wind caught my breath as I slipped into the passage between the rows of tubs.

We were not a great distance from the bottom of the downcast shaft where the coal was drawn. Here again I noticed that the bricklayer and the mason had been busy years before I intruded upon the scene. The tunnel was magnificently arched and safe. Its entire length was illuminated by electricity.

We walked against the wind. Everything about me was built on the large scale, and was set for rapid, unimpeded transportation. There was a neatness of organisation, a simple efficiency, about the place that fascinated me, almost shocked me. There was a total absence of squalor. There was quality as well as quantity embodied in this underground scene, tending towards the intensification of a process that could be felt although everything was still. Later I became used to this shaft bottom and able to appreciate the orderliness of the work. There were two levels of approach to the shaft, the upper one into which the loaded streams of tubs discharged themselves, and the lower into which the empty tubs were received from the cages. There were four decks to each cage, which carried two tubs to each deck. The act at the bottom was an almost automatic one of inserting the two tubs from each deck and expelling the two empty ones in one movement. The act at the top was the same in reverse. The actual run through of the cages occupied fifty eight seconds. Such organised activity for me was beyond the phenomenal.

I wondered, and I still wonder, just why my father had not tried his own fortune in a pit such as this one. Why had he chosen to scramble about such primitive organisations as Rough Lea and North Bitchburn? Just how reluctant to adventure could he have been?

It was the stabling of the ponies that astonished me.

For the first time in my life I found some endeavour to behave with humanity below ground. Those stables could not have been improved upon. The entrance was arched with the same careful craft as the tunnels through which I had passed. At the end of the arch which continued up the gentle gradient the stabling was organised along a passage running at right angles to it. A clean flow of air was borrowed from the main stream and passed through the accommodation for some forty ponies, all of which were munching the same old choppy mixture of the mines. The flooring throughout was cemented, and the stalls were separated by stoutly built brick walls. Light flooded all the stabling. The saddlery was hung across the passage behind the pony. All the walls and ceiling were lime-washed. The feeding boxes were copious and clean within the conditions of the place. There was no infestation of vermin. As a matter of fact rats were unknown in that colliery during the time I worked there. Mice existed in large numbers. The water trough was deep and clean, that is, so far as cleanliness can be observed in a mine. There were brooms and shovels to deal with the droppings. The runnels were kept brushed. Everything that could be done within reason was done for those imprisoned creatures. The horsekeepers kept a stern eye on youths and beasts. They examined each pony as it was returned to their keeping after the shift was ended.

I had not seen anything to compare with these underground stables. Obviously somebody did have some care for the little things. At Boulby the transport of the produced commodity was carried out by magnificent Shires and Clydesdales, which were returned after each shift to the stables near the edge of the cliff, like farm horses. But Boulby had been something special, and was a long way from Harton.

We geared our pony, a superannuated old fellow who had been withdrawn from actual coal-putting, and was kept to do the odd jobs with the repairers on the night shift. We let him drink his fill at the trough before we set out to our destination, the landing in the Dandy Bank. The area supplied by this landing was 'coming back broken', that is, the pillars of coal which had been hewn many years ago were now being removed. This operation set free the pressures which had been contained over the years by the coal pillars. The space resulting from this extraction was called 'the goaf', and as this became enlarged by further extractions so the strata bore down against the obstructing coal and reached along the areas reserved for transport. Such illimitable pressure disrupted the ordinary life of the mine. The roof supports, even the great timber baulks set closely along the main transport avenues were crunched and snapped, and where this was held the floor of the mine was forced towards the roof. Consequently, the broken baulks had to be renewed and new ones inserted, and where the pressure could only 'find vent' by disturbing the floor and the tramway had to be taken up and relaid, and the debris carted away to some nearby pack.

Carting away was our task.

We arrived at the place of work and limbered the pony. This done we attached the limber lock to a small waggon, curiously enough called a 'kibble'. When this was filled with stone and rubble we made the pony drag it to the pack, the place, where it could be stowed out of the way. A great baulk, which had been summarily broken, was taken down and carried away, and when this was done the jutting stone was hacked down and a place cleared for the insertion of a fresh baulk.

The night passed slowly. I felt like a stranger who had strayed into a very strange land. The shift ended. We put the kibble out of the way near the deputy's kist, and led the pony back to the stables, where we unharnessed him, tied him up, and left him. Then we went to the shaft and joined the queue of men and boys waiting to be hoisted to the day.

As I left the cage an official drew me aside and told me that I would not be required to come to work until Tuesday morning at ten o'clock, and that when I did return I would ask for a Mr Simons and he would tell me what I had to do. I nodded acquiescence and walked on to the lamp cabin where I handed in my lamp, and out into the morning air. The air tasted sweet. The morning had yet to break. I walked away without haste. The air was blowing fresh from the seas.

Thus I began my new life in an underground from which I would not break free for thirteen long years.

I awaited the coming of Tuesday morning with some trepidation, for I had a feeling that I might be setting out on some strange adventure. I need not have worried, for in any coal mine there is no place for adventure. There is time and space only for hard and difficult labour. When I arrived at the lamp cabin I met three grown men and a youth a year or so older than myself. The charge hand of the lamp cabin identified me, almost triumphantly, as 'the lad'. He gave me my lamp and I followed the four into the waiting room. Jack Simons did the examination of the safety lamps.

All my new fellow-workers were of Irish extraction, descendants from those immigrants who had fled the poverty of Ireland and who had caused great dissatisfaction among the proletariat living and working north of a line drawn from Liverpool to Hull. I belonged to that generation which had forgotten to be angry with the invasion. In my time Roman Catholic churches had lost themselves in the clutter of housing where men and women lived and bred. They were the first Irishmen I had met. Later I was to recognise many of them as consummate miners and far-seeing trade union leaders, even though I was more than aware of their being disgruntled, land-less peasants.

We went on to 'the heap' and got into the cage. It sank silently into the ooze of the shaft. We left it and set off for our new place of work. Once again I passed through those six wooden doors. When I emerged I found transportation going full blast. I followed Tommy Simons to the stables and helped him to 'yoke the galloway', which proved to be an old animal which ought to have been offered the freedom of some field before he eventually died.

Transport to the shaft cages was in full swing. In all my life I had seen nothing to compare with this orderly manipulation of tubs, hooked in batches to an endless rope going one way to the shaft and hooked to another and coming towards me. The mine is not a place for sightseeing.

We walked behind our pony for more than half a mile to the point where the two shifts changed over. There was some hearty chaff among the men. I was placed on view, examined under the concentrated light of their safety lamps, accepted and dismissed to labour. We limbered the pony and set about dragging a loaded kibble into some disused passage where we helped to upend it so that its contents could be 'tossed on to the pack', by the smaller and more diffident member of our group who was a shifter, or datal hand.

After a few days I had sorted out my new impressions and I had accustomed myself to the nature of my task. The young Simons disappeared from the work party. I had merely been his displacement.

Before very long I had grown aware of the fact that our task, which was the sinking of a staple, a short shaft, was nothing other than a calculated waste of money. It was a prestige project. In a mine! The seam of coal had struck a deep hitch, or a fault, which had snapped it off abruptly from its own level, and thrust it down some sixty feet or so to a deeper level from which point it continued. Such aberrations are often disclosed in mining operations and when they are they must be over-come. The excavations upon which we were employed was the sinking of this staple, but the one which would have occurred to most engineers would have been to slant a drift from the one level to the other and so continued the established mode of main and tail, or endless rope, haulage.

It was most curious that we were doing this in a world at

war. We had not by then succeeded in getting on level terms with the Kaiser's army, and here we were building a complicated thing like a minehead in a faulted region which could have been so easily overcome by straight drifting. The excavation these three shifts of men were engaged upon was almost fantastic in its conception. A great deal of work had been accomplished before I came on the scene.

The approach to the proposed site of the staple was already accomplished. The height of the tunnel was almost ten feet. The side had been walled by the bricklayers and the roof laced with enormous iron girders. It was the most careful bricklaying I had seen so far. At the end of the tunnel the wall had been continued through a much wider excavation and then narrowed down to a further excavation, suitably girdered, to admit of a splendid winding engine. Two immense steel girders, two and a half feet in depth already stretched against the lip of the ascending excavation, which, when finished, would enclose the pit head gearing. A wall of considerable thickness was to be raised upon these two closely set girders. When fully constructed the gearing would stand in a space forty feet high at the wheel heads and sloping down to the winding engine.

It was a stupendous waste of money and labour, in a time of war.

Everything was almost fashioned fully in anticipation of the day when the roof supports would be withdrawn and the great cavern could be shaped and made ready for coal transportations. Until that day arrived it was the duty of us all to keep the road of escape clear of all things that might impede flight.

I waited the actual felling with deep interest.

To my astonishment and delight it was performed during one of the shifts when I was on, the late, night shift. Bill Corner, the master shifter, came to superintend on the work. He was a small, loquacious, experienced old miner. I watched him examine the forest of timber that held up the dangerous roof, and I noted how nimbly he shielded his lamp from being extinguished as he made his assessment of the task. How carefully he examined that place, how minutely, I still recall with admiration. He singled out five thick props and marked them with a piece of chalk, exactly like a forester when selecting the trees and fating them to the axe.

'If we draw these five buggers we'll get the lot down,' he announced.

None of us present reflected upon his observation. Bill was the boss and his word was sufficient.

'We ought to get these three down with a mell,' he said.

He picked up the heavy hammer, set it down, and then took off his coat. He did not ask any man to undertake the work. He walked back and hung up his discarded garments, spat upon his hands, and walked back to the point of action.

He took the mell, and struck each of the props separately. Then he called for the axe. I have said that he was an experienced miner, but now I will say that he was a most courageous miner. With the axe he disabled both the forward props and left them. Despite the fact that above him there came an ominous remonstration, he stepped back to deal with the third one. This one he overpowered and when it was free, he threw it back for one of us to take away.

'She's gannen nicelies,' he said. 'Set the anchor here, Jack,' he told Simons.

Jack hacked a hold fairly deeply into the floor, and then inserted a stout prop into it and fastened the top securely against one of the encaged girders. When this was done an instrument was produced which was new to me. The miners called it 'the joss'. The main part was attached to the base of the prop by a chain, which locked on the appropriate hook. A lever was then set within the slots on the basic frame and a long chain attached to this lever, was carried to the next prop due for demolition and fastened to it. When all was ready the handle of the lever was brought into play and this tightened the chain and asserted great pressure upon the prop. When the full extent of the leverage was exhausted a fresh hold was taken on the shortened chain. As soon as the prop holding the roof began 'to give' the mass resting upon it went into loud protest, offering to the bystander the sensation of being concerned with an earth tremor. The noise was not awesome, but was minatory and menacing. As the links were drawn against the prop the protest developed, and catastrophe became imminent.

'Give way, Jack,' said Corner to Simons who was working the machine.

Jack released the lever and let the chain go slack.

'Let her settle,' said Corner.

We all sat down to eat the food we had brought with us. As we ate, we talked and joked. The water in my bottle was deliciously cold, steel cold. I suppose we all enjoyed the recess.

When the half hour was sped, Corner stood up and said it was time to see the other, the last, prop.

'But what about the prop we're on?' demanded Bill Vaughan.

Corner smiled. 'About as much use now as an old man's cock,' he told him.

'You oughter know,' muttered Bill Vaughan.

Corner walked towards the confusion, boldly, to where the felled prop was staggering under unbearable weight, tossing in the throes of the impending fall and calmly detached the chain. Without fear he went to the final prop and passed the chain about it and made it secure. Then he walked back. 'Let her have it,' he said.

As the prop began to give way the mass of rock above began to roar out its exasperation at its slow disembowelling. With each engagement of another link in the chain by the lever the roar increased. Thunder bellowed over us and tore out of the cavern beyond. And then quite suddenly the deed was done. The chain went slack. There was one gigantic crack, as if the skull of the mine had been broken, and then the silence of prehistory settled again into its wonted sleep

We all stood, entranced and horrified by the deed we had done.

'That's finished that bugger,' said Bill Corner, and with that he put on his garments, picked up his stick and lamp, and took a step forward. 'Now,' he said, 'I'll go and see about getting some real work done.'

The girdered space at each side of the gearing cavern held, and the newly fitted roof supports took up the new weight. Now work was to begin in earnest. The rock left above had to be made safe, and this could only be done by confining within a stoutly built wall and a tracery of ascending girders. We had to uncover the tops of the finished walls so that the bricklayers could carry the walls to the required heights. Much of the fallen rubble had to be carted away in order to affect the entrance above the huge mound of rock and rubble. Timber had to be set on the mound against the threatening roof. Danger began to lurk.

As soon as it was possible for them to do so, the bricklayers moved in and vast quantities of building material, bricks, cement and a special dispensation called pug was incorporated into the structure. Obdurate masses of stone which had not fallen had to be removed by hand and pick. Explosives were not used for as much of the mass in the roof had to be kept where it was, which called for more care and attention than is generally offered by skilled miners.

The war went on and we continued to labour.

We triumphed without much injury.

When the space for the headgear was completed we proceeded to sink the staple. This took us some three or four months. No one could have imagined so time wasting an occupation as this one, the one we delivered to the lore of mining engineering, the Boldon Way Staple.

There were two mentors in this sinking – an exactly centered plumb line and a sawn measuring rod the full extent of the permitted radius of the shaft. After sinking the first five feet, the floor of the shaft was levelled and a tube of cement tubbing laid on the levelled floor. The space between the outer edge of the tubbing was filled with cement of the best quality and mixture. When this was finished and the cement had solidified, the tubbing was removed and another six feet of rock extracted, and the tubbing reset to continue the walling of the shaft. The space between the top of one ring and the bottom of the other was filled in with bricks and then faced off with the plaster's trowel.

We reached the seam and from that point we laid out a suitable shaft bottom. Rope guides were slung in the shaft, the cages inserted, and the magnificent winding-engine installed. Before very long the staple was vomitting coal out of the Boldon Way.

By the end of the year, progress into this part of the royalty was further impeded by an enormous hitch which flung the seam further down some fifty or sixty fathoms, and work had to stop until the management had driven a drift to the lower level.

Boldon Way was abandoned before I left the Colliery.

The years flowed on and I became a single unimportant unit in the productive organisation of the colliery. There is nothing to be gained by setting down the story of those bleak and barren years made painful by conditions which frustrated the adolescent and made observable the unreality of a distorted labour activity. Life was an unremitting exercise of the muscles and a recuperation in sleep, a search for some kind of enjoyment and the stark reality of labour. I was not a huge physical specimen that could shrug off the effects of heavy labour. The joys that attend the exploitation of physical strength is only partially known to the man of small stature. In the pit there were men and youths of greater attributes. Work in a mine of the vast dimensions and excellent technological equipment like Harton was of a far different nature to those which I had known in Cleveland and Northumberland. In the ironstone field skill lay in the computing of the effects of so many grammes of powder. Strength was ancilliary to the act. In the simple connotations of the ridiculously low seams an adaptation of physical exercise within the limitations conditioned by the awful constriction of space, as at Wylam, were not imagined at Harton, where men simply clobbered the immaculate seams of coal and turned them into low-priced commodity producing agencies. And yet, within the coal measures, there was a sacred operation of the principle of fair shares which I had not hitherto experienced.

This sharing of opportunity was made on each 'cavilling day', which occured every quarter. All the jobs done on piecework in the act of coal production were 'put into the cap' and drawn for as lots. The man who worked in a difficult place was then able to escape from it and pass it on to some other unfortunate man by drawing a favourable cavil. The first Monday after cavilling day, which was always on a Friday, was shifting gear day. On that day the men affected carried their picks and shovels from one part of the mine to the other. Such a practice could only be carried out where the old fashioned modes and manners of coal production existed. When machinery came to be introduced, the board and pillar process ceased to be viable, and the longwall system was introduced, a system which destroyed the old individual methods and imposed a collective arrangement underground. Under this system loading at the face became organised, and the need for ponies and pony-putters was no longer felt. Mechanism of the production stamped ruthlessly upon the old ways of men.

I was gone from the mines before the new method was adopted at Harton.

I must confess that my upbringing within the mining industry had not produced me as a person an overman would be eager to help along. I had little to offer in the matter of great strength and skill, but much to proffer in that of observation and, later, politics. I remained with the repairing gangs and stayed on the night shift until I was caught up in the war machine at the end of 1917 and found myself at Tidworth Camp as a private in the Fifth Reserve Cavalry Regiment, and wearing the badges of the 10th Royal Hussars.

We were examined *en masse* at Sunderland, and trans-shipped to Newcastle where we rested on the bare concrete floors, without blanket or covering during the most miserable night I had so far spent. The next morning we were appointed to our places in the forces, and by nightfall we were on our way to Tidworth.

At Tidworth we were not expected in such numbers. The RSM, a dapper little Irishman, passed us all off as the best joke he had come across. We stood on the square in front of the Alliwal Barracks until he had laughed his head off, and then we were found places to sleep. The next morning we were fed. It took the military authorities the better part of a fortnight before we were assimilated into the various squads, and much longer before they had us satisfactorily inoculated and vaccinated.

For all the good we did ourselves or our country while we were at Tidworth we may as well have never left the mines. I was put in 'A' Squadron, Troop 3. I was trained as a cavalry man. I was taught how to fight with a sword. I was introduced to a rifle and a bayonet because a cavalry man carried all three weapons. We went through a course of physical training. We drilled for hours on the square, drilling with swords while attaining and sustaining the posture of mounted men. We cleaned stables and we groomed horses. We added not a scrap to the fighting of the war.

The summer simply drooled on.

Men died in Flanders while we played at being soldiers in and around Tidworth. None of us was ever granted any leave. The north country was far away. We abode in Tidworth. We contributed nothing.

Grandfather Heslop wrote to me of the far distant happenings in the old village. John, his youngest son died when the Fifth Army fought the flood of Germans early in 1918. During that year Aunt Rhoda's husband was killed, and so my little sister was bereaved of another father. The tale of disaster went on and on, killing ruthlessly the young men, while we stayed in Tidworth.

They made us sit our horses like Cavalry men. They taught us how to drive a sword through the body of a sack of straw dangling from a contraption like a gallows, while we were at full gallop. They taught us how to fight as men had fought at Balaclava while the holocaust exhausted itself.

There was a morning when an officer came round us while we were clipping horses to ask for volunteers for the Tank Corps. I hesitated and he passed me by. I have always regretted losing that chance to see just what was happening in France. Many of the lads went, and found out.

We cloistered in Tidworth away from the war all through that blazing summer and autumn of 1918.

We were the lost men of the Great War.

The Armistice came and long before Christmas we of the mines were summarily despatched to the demobilisation centre at Winchester. That same night we were on the train at King's Cross bound for Newcastle Central, free from the irk of the military authorities.

By the turn of the New Year I was back again in South Shields. The town had escaped most of the ravages of the war. I was able to pick up the threads of my life, and within a fortnight I was back once more to the old grind at the colliery.

It was strange, but unexciting, travelling the shaft again, taking in new gulps of the foetid atmosphere of the upcast sky. My absence had not been long enough to enable me to become revolted by the warm, clammy breath of the mine. It soon became clear that our repatriation to civilian life had come as a surprise to the management, and for a while they could find very little for us all to do. We got the chance to harden our hands slowly, and so 'get used to it all'.

I enjoyed those few early and easy days, and I was sorry when I did find myself undertaking a task that called for resolution as well as skill in its performance.

Nothing had changed during my absence in the Forces. It was the same old Harton Colliery, the same bleak, desolate habitation of the imprisoned people.

The cage slid upwards out of the damp, foetid atmosphere in the shaft and settled on the keps to receive its load of humanity. The doors were opened and once again I passed with nineteen other comrades on to the deck of the cage. I hung my head against my arm as we went on and on to the bottom of the shaft. Once again I felt that utter forlorness that follows after the shearing of individual freedom, as I became a piece, a part of a pawn, in the majestic purpose of the capitalist mode of production.

Was I near to rebelling? It did not occur to me to make the assessment. And yet there was a grim feeling of doom upon me. Was it doom, or was it a fracture of purpose? Before I enlisted I had responded to an urge to write what I thought might turn out to be a novel. I do not recall that early effort of mine now except the denouement which was a spectacular suicide of the heroine by throwing herself from the topmost tower of Durham Cathedral. I forget it all but that savage ending. And yet the urge was there. I had always wanted to write. All the time I had been at Tidworth the flicker had not died out. I still felt the urge to write, even in the furthest reaches of the mine, close against the goaf. Now that I was back where I belonged I might feel the urge again.

They did not treat us roughly on that first shift. Indeed, the management was as non-plussed as the military authorities at Tidworth had been, as to how to fit us into the machine. As the days wore on we were sorted out and in the end we were fully established within the dimly illuminated anonymity of the pit.

The year 1919 was a year of intense proletarian dreaming. The general election had taken place just before we were demobilised. I voted for the first time in my life at that election. The voting paper came to me by post. To my surprise I found that I had been put on the electoral role of the Blaydon constituency. William Whiteley, who later became Mr. Attlee's chief whip, was the Labour candidate. He did not win, but he did win at the next election, in 1922, and he held the seat until he died.

Despite the overwhelming victory of Lloyd George and his coalition, the proletarian world of men did not cease to dream. The most outrageous fantasy was the Sankey Commission. How patiently and particularly did we drool over the reports of that famous clash of personalities. Bob Smillie rose up before us all as the greatest phantom of endeavour so far produced. We gloried in his battles with the Marquis of Londonderry. How we gloated over the possibility of the mines becoming nationalised. How we dreamed. How we stretched out our hands towards the towering pit head gearing to take it, and all it signified, into our own dear keeping. Poor, soft, deluded people that we were.

When Bob Smillie and Chiozza Money came to address the first Durham Gala after the war, we carried our banners and escorted our brass bands with the deepest of reverence. In those days the Gala was a sight for all men to witness. The enormity of the proceedings outstripped the imagination. Perhaps it was the setting that lent privilege to the proletarian display. Maybe the vast mustering of the colliery tribes under the arches of the massive, brick-built viaduct, that spans the yonder part of the city and carries the great railway, grants a piquancy to the subsequent proceedings. The booming of the drums provoking the attention of the tribes and then the double tap which unleashes the brazen sound into an almost dreamlike unreality and sets men and women marching. Repeated almost two hundred times, the resultant noise and slashings of colour provoke an almost spiritual aura that hangs like a proud destiny over the immense beauty and the rich colour of the city.

The narrow streets – that were then – forced an intermingling of marchers and amused watchers. The crossing of the bridge over the Wear, that cowers like a coward within the ample shade of the great cliff that holds both castle and cathedral up to the arms of God, was always a strain lain upon the carriers of the banners. The passing over the bridge beneath the lovely scene evoked by tree-clad heights and glory-crowned buildings always evoked for me some strangely murmured benediction wailing softly into unreality. There is nothing so magnificent within Christendom that compares with the loveliness of Durham's cathedral. Ordinary men must have built it, but they must have been men filled with an extraordinary vision, for they left it where it stands encompassing, and encompassed by, its own earth, rising upwards to immortality like a prayer passing the lips of a woman suckling her babe.

It is this cathedral which has softened the harsh lines of the men of coal every time they have ventured into the city to listen to the orators. It is never forbidding, never minatory. It watches them marching to their venue, and when it is all over it beckons them back to their possession of their own lives. It is this half-church, half-refuge that softens the spirit after the pains of unremitting toil, and tempers the thunderings of exhortation into croonings and beliefs.

Leo Chiozza Money removed his hat and stood up to speak to us on that day. The gala had been a revelation to him to such a degree that he was still astonished and bewildered. Bob Smillie sat smiling. Both had been fighters at the hearings of the Sankey Commission. Bob could understand the little man's bewilderment. And when Money had breathed his prayer over the vast crowd, 'God bless you all,' Bob reached over and patted him on the shoulder. Bob was a showman in his own right. He stood

147

up and accepted the acclamations of the concourse. While it boomed over the city, and stilled the rowers in the boats on the lovely breast of the Wear that flowed nearby, he mounted a chair, and when the noise had died away he began to speak.

Monday came, and with it came disillusion. The Sankey Report was rejected by that prince of Prime Ministers, and the war was begun. Frank Hodges was the secretary of the Miners' Federation of Great Britain at that time. He too, had played a valiant part in the Sankey charade. He had yet to guide the Datum Line struggle of the year 1920.

The troubles of 1920 were succeeded by the hunger of 1921. We struck and we failed. The ten millions subvention were swallowed up, the strike came and the sun blazed down over the earth so that we could laze in idleness. The corn withered on the stalk in the fields around the collieries. We lazed upon the shores of the sea, loitered with the girls, spent all our savings – those of us who had any – and in the end we went back to work.

After that we turned to politics.

My grandfather Heslop died just before the 1922 election took place. We gathered as a clan, and we carried him to the chapel on the hill overlooking New Hunwick, and then we bore him to the churchyard and there we left him under a huge cross which he had raised to the memory of his sibling, John, of John, his grandson, and of William, his son-in-law, all of whom had not returned from the war.

'They wouldn't build a memorial to the fallen of the village,' he told me when I went, at his call, to Hunwick to see it. 'So I built one for them.'

I did not argue with him about the stone, nor did I tell him that I thought it was an awful piece of statuary. I was pained deeply when he said to me as we walked back to his home:

'I paid a hundred and twenty pounds for that stone. Aye! A hundred and twenty pounds, in gold, in a bag…all golden sovereigns.'

Poor grandfather!

He and Margaret, his wife, lie beneath it in Hunwick church-yard, resting in the Lord.

Chapter Eleven

Work in the colliery brought friendship as well as comradeship. Strangely enough this never came to me until I became a coal-putter. To this day I have never been able to understand why I undertook to become a piece worker at the coal face, for I was neither physically, mentally or emotionally equipped for the sterling dialectics of sweat-laden production. In the first instance, pony-putting required a sanguine temperament, consummate skill and commendable strength. A man can possess all these attributes and yet be unable to co-ordinate them adequately enough to be pronounced efficient. In the second instance, a pony putter required but a modicum of imagination, an attribute which I possessed to such a degree as to exist within the borderland of actual fear. But I will not excuse myself, for I must admit that I was not a very good putter.

The act is monotonous. The pony is yoked to an empty tub. After the putter has hung his token inside the tub he must squeeze himself between the pony's rump and the tub and utilise his posterior to go one way and his knee to go the other way. At the same time he must urge a not always unreluctant animal to make haste to the coal face and greater haste on the way back to the landing. Near the coal face the pony is detached from the tub, and the tub rolled on its side clear of the tram line. The putter then follows the pony to the point where he can attach it to the full tub and get the pony to exert his strength in order to start locomotion. After he has got past the over-turned tub, the putter puts it back on the line and runs it to the face. He then joins the pony and proceeds to the landing. There were young men who enjoyed so unimaginative a task.

It was when I suffered an accident which laid me off work for some time that I made friends with Jos Mackey.

Jos was my first real friend, and as he was deeply embroiled in friendship with Bill Blyton, we made a fast friendship for the rest of our time. We were deeply interested in trade unionism, and so our initial friendship found fundamental cement in the lodge activities. A miner's trade union branch is called 'a lodge'. Jos Mackey became the general managing factotum of the four collieries in the Harton group under nationalisation, and retained that position until he died. Bill Blyton ended up in the House of Lords.

The members of the lodge chose me to be their Council Delegate for the year 1923/24. This was quite an onerous duty, performed every five or six weeks by attending at the head-quarters of the Durham Miners' Association in Durham.

At that time there were some two hundred lodges in the Association. The council meetings were days out of the usual rut for the delegates. Each man was given an honorarium and expenses for attending, which added to the joy of comradeship in the pub that still stands under the arch at Durham station.

The meetings were formal. Council met in a rather splendid oak panelled, comfortably furnished hall large enough to accommodate a good sized public meeting. On the platform were seated the elected leaders of the association, six or seven shrewd men who had worked themselves up from the coal face to the checkweigh cabin at their local collieries, on through the chapel vestries and pulpits, or the bar room of the working-men's clubs, to the high regality of Red Hill, Durham.

The meetings ambled at leisure through the printed agenda. The treasurer offered a financial statement if ever one was requested, and the rest of the officials – agents, they were called – conducted such debates which called in question their actions or the actions of the departments for which they were respon-sible. Jim Robson, the President at that time, a huge, powerfully built man, with a voice to match on all occasions, better dressed at all times than any trade union leader I ever met, except Frank Hodges, could always iron out any decent sized rumpus on the floor. He was a great addresser of mourners at a grave side. He possessed a fine flow of words, and a manner of delivery that suited every aspirate. Had he been trained he might have come up somewhere near to Chaliapin. He had that kind of figure, stupendous. He never forgot to call the council to its feet when he spoke an obituary. He was a presence. He was formidable. I was present at the grave side of Jack Thomp-son, the doyen of the Marsden miners, and saw and heard his mastery of the spoken obituary. There was a great crowd present on that occasion. We bore three banners before the coffin. We followed two brass bands. He held us transfixed as he spoke of a man he had never liked in all his life. He left all of us in tears, for Jack was one of those really impressive men who from the days of their youth are not privileged to spend their own days in the shadows.

Generally the agenda was soon disposed of and we all were at liberty to go about our own businesses. There was Jimmy Glanville, who later became the member of parliament for Consett. It was a privilege to watch him consume beer. The last occasion on which I indulged that privilege was the night when Will Owen, once member of parliament for Morpeth, paid 'his footing to the lads' after his introduction to the house. There have been many enormous drinkers in Durham, but I never saw Jimmy's equal. He was also the possessor of the most extensive vocabulary of cuss-words in the North Country, and what is more, he could express them like any poet. There was also Will Lawther, who was always a canny drinker of pints, but preferred the more elegant mouthfuls.

I took part in the debate on a resolution proposed by Lawther that sought to instruct the association to finance four two-year scholarships at the Labour College, London. The resolution was agreed and in due course the examinations were held over the county, a preliminary one to choose fifty to sit a final examination under strict invigilation.

Bill Blyton and myself took part in the first examination in the Miners' Hall, Tyne Dock. A local school mistress undertook the invigilation. Some weeks later we went to Red Hill, Durham to sit the final examination.

Bill was not successful. I received the highest mark. Three other young men were successful. Jack Lonsdale, John McCutcheon and Philip Williams. All are now dead. Phil reached a high position in the Co-op movement and held it until he died. Jack MacCutcheon became a protégé of the then Mr and Mrs Sidney Webb. When he married he received a wedding present from the old couple of a splendid copy of each book published by them up to that moment. Upon the fly leaf of each book was expressed the congratulation of both of them.

We were all asked to attend the meeting of the Executive Committee of the Durham Miners' Association on the day prior to our departure for London in order to receive the congratulations of the officials and members. I had not met any of my new colleagues and I looked forward to make their acquaintance. In due time we were called into the committee chamber to be presented to the members by the President, Mr James Robson. After the Treasurer had reimbursed us for expenses incurred in coming to Durham, Jim stood up with all the massive dignity of the office to charge us to be careful when we got to London. Communism, we gathered was a greater evil than prostitution. After that we were ushered out.

The four of us joined forces at Durham station and journeyed to Earls Court.

The Labour College, as it was then styled – had been known previously as the Central Labour College, when it was founded by Denis Hurd on the breakaway from Ruskin College, Oxford. It was styled so in order to distinguish it from the National Council of Labour Colleges, an effete, end of the world organisation devoted to the inculcation of independent working class education over the trade union world. The College occupied two houses, numbers eleven and thirteen, in Penywern Road, a street off Earls Court Road, close to the underground station, all quite given over to flats and habitations of the higher income groups of the lower capitalist organisations within London, widely built, spacious and down-at-heel. At that time Earls Court had become somewhat de-classed as a result of the establishment of high class emporia in Kensington High Street. It was interesting to watch the after-dinner exodus of the Penywernians. Clothed appropriately they set off ingloriously on foot to their theatre or place of entertainment. They walked with the airs and graces of those who had touched affluence. The men with something approaching dignity, the women with that grace and charm that comes after the possession of a male with indubitable right to take a consort.

The College, despite its rather shabby frontage, stuck like any sore thumb from any grubby hand amongst such gracious people. The Lord knows that it housed a rapscallion crew drawn from the grim valleys of South Wales, and the far flung depots of the railway system. After a year of residence all were ready to storm heaven, except some of the railway men. J.T. Walton Newbold, who often came to lecture, and oftener called in for a free meal, cast an amused glance from his great height upon 'the young bucks from the Rhondda.'

The Welsh students interested me. For the first time in my life I had met up with that peculiar lilt that hungers in their speech. Most of them spoke Welsh, especially at the dinner table. It was a hopeless task trying to come to terms with their

Celtic speech, for it was almost impossible to glean a word, let alone a phrase, which one might incorporate into one's conversation with them. And yet, one could identify English words that had been incorporated into their own dialect. It occurred to me that a nation so devoted to the Rugby Union code would have found a Welsh term for 'goal posts'!

As a race, the Welsh are impressively materialistic. Naturally, a chap like myself could judge them only from a mining point of view, for that was the main basis upon which we met. Politically, industrially, it had to be objected that the Welsh revolutionary attitudes by no means squared with their social attributes whenever a struggle had to be waged.

I do not write this in anger. Nor in sorrow. In all probability, most of my colleagues at the college are long since dead, but that apart I feel that I must set down these observations.

As we young North countrymen wandered about London we were astonished to find so many files of 'Welsh Miners' plodding along the gutters of the main streets singing and beseeching for coppers. Heaven knows that at that time London had more than its share of gutter beggars. Such behaviour was beneath the consideration of the men of the north east, and far beneath their dignity, deeply sunk beneath all that they held to be sacred in their class natures. I once got into conversation with a file of such Welsh mendicants when they had paused to rest and refresh their throats. I asked them why they went about cajoling and begging.

'We got to bach,' said one. 'We got to send money back home. How do you expect Mam to manage if we didn't?'

London was at peace in those pre-National Strike times.

As the struggle deepened the invasion got worse, and London had to accommodate itself to an ever increasing mass of importunate singers of 'Sospan Fach'. It was affrighting. This was a social happening unknown in the north, outside the social behaviour of the proletariat. To borrow, yes; to beg, no. It became pitiful. Whatever happened, and much did happen in those now distant years, had happened within and as the result of the heavy bombardment of invective and discontent of the South Wales miners. To us organised mendicancy was not industrial struggle. It was not even fighting and suffering – it was 'greeding' as the northerner has it. In all probability the act was the result of the close proximity of the Welsh to the large towns, Bristol, Birmingham, London. The world beyond their borders was there to be sucked, and suck they did, so that the revolutionaries might survive. It did not matter if one survived on the crusts of charity, so long as one could lean on the wisdom of Moscow.

When the general strike fizzled out on its tenth day of existence, and the attitude of the miners solidified into a prolonged struggle, the swarms came down from the hills and up from the valleys of Glamorgan. A group, complete with an astonishing bass and a tenor who could hold a loud and prolonged high note arrived at 13 Penywern Road to rehearse for the gutters and for such concerts as might be arranged. After a while they moved into the attack upon the susceptibilities of the general public so that Mam and those back home could survive.

As northerners we stood aghast at the temerity of these singers from Wales. It was an aspect of the class struggle that was completely new to us, and we just had to accept it. Later, I was to discover that not only the big towns were exploited, but the whole of the south west. They went wherever they could in order to tap the charity of the people. They sought and captured alms from the west country from the people who had never experienced the normal wages and affluence of the miners.

Chapter Twelve

William White Craik was the Principal of the college. He had succeeded Denis Hurd. When I entered the institution there were two other paid lecturers, Alex Robertson, M.A., and Thomas Ashcroft, an ex-student who had been appointed as lecturer on economics following the translation of the previous lecturer to membership of the House of Commons. Craik dealt with marxism and philosophy, while Robertson undertook history. Outside lecturers came in on invitation. Belfort Bax, a contemporary of Marx and Engels, and a long-forgotten writer on ethics, had been a constant visitor up to 1923. Eden and Cedar Paul often came to lecture on psychology. Their contributions to the translations of the Marx classics is now somewhat overlooked, but those who would sample the work of Marx in translation had better be advised to have a look at the work of Eden and Cedar Paul. Whenever Eden lectured, Cedar was in attendance. He was not an accomplished lecturer, but his lectures were always carefully prepared. Cedar was a good-looking, full-busted woman, affable and helpful. She could sing, and she often sang to the students. One could see that Eden always deferred to Cedar much the same way as Sidney always deferred to Beatrice Webb. In all probability they copied the older couple, but they never achieved their intellectual isolation within the Labour Movement.

Henry Noel Brailsford, a rotund, serious, little man, happened along a time or two, and so did Raymond Postgate, who at that time was trying to become an authority on revolution, if not on Marx. J.T. Walton Newbold was quite a fixture after he lost his seat in parliament until he drifted away. He was a strange personality with a large propensity to make humorous observations. He was exceedingly tall, almost as tall as Henri Barbusse, but not so much burnt out. His most remarkable feature was his exceedingly small head, which was small enough to appear grossly out of proportion to his broad frame.

The mouth was rather weakened by his protruding upper teeth. His small eyes squinted merrily.

Other important members of the working class movement came along and spoke and departed. A.J. Cook, an old student, liked to come, for there he found deep rapport with the Welsh students. George Hicks, of the bricklayers often came, and was most helpful when the question sought to discuss the General Council of the Trade Union Congress. J.H. Thomas, though head of the National Union of Railwaymen, which sponsored the college along with the South Wales Miners' Federation, spurned the place. The Board of Governors of the college had as its secretary a nominee of Thomas called Foote.

For most of its sponsors, the College was much more than an exceedingly sore thumb, more of the nature of a diseased hand. The Associated Society of Locomotive Engineers and Firemen had nothing to do with it. The National Union of Railwaymen waited patiently for the opportunity to shuffle out of its responsibilities. The Miners had as their representative a small man who throughout his life flamed across the coal-field and who often contrived to ignite fires when the fuel was wet, Noah Ablett. He was a more luminous figure than ever Aneurin Bevan was. By the time I arrived at the College, Mark Starr, a sadly disappointed man because he was never given the lecturer's job, had gone off to America, without his wife, who was a sister of that charming man, Frank Horrabin, the Dot and Carrie cartoonist of *The Star*, and the illustrator of H.G. Wells' *Outline of History*.

The main entry of students was the alternative year. All the railwaymen and all but three of the South Wales Miners, entered for the same semester. The other three came the next year along with the other students who found their ways thither. All this meant double work for the lecturers, but luckily for them lecturing ceased with the morning. The rest of the day was given over to study, conducted tours, individual visits to galleries and museums, and searchings in the London book-shops. There was no rapport between the College and other educational establishments, not even the London School of Economics. It can be said that the Labour College was content to hide itself behind its own sore thumb, but better let it be asserted that it was *independent* education.

In the first volume of his life of Aneurin Bevan, Michael Foot describes the College as being situated in one of the back streets in Earls Court, which proves that Mr Foot had not yet taken the trouble to find out exactly where it was situated. Perhaps he is right not to search for the place, for the denizens of that 'back street' might become infuriated should they identify him as he passed by, for, in all probability, he has done a great deal in the matter of infuriating them. He was right when he talked about the 'bed-sitters' of the students. What can be said for them is that they were far superior to many of the bed sitters that accomomodate a lot of students and to contain their immense arguments. There were eight single rooms, too.

London blazed during that first September. We all felt that we had been liberated from some awful, dark doom. Had we not won our scholarships we would have been working underground, or in railway sheds, scratching for a living. We soon discovered our new environment, and we gazed upon it in a transport of amazement. This affluence and this total disregard for actual value staggered us. To watch a woman doing her shopping in Kensington High Street *by proxy* while she reclined on the back seat of a limousine and instructed her chaffeur, was to undergo an experience hitherto alien to our imagination. To wander in Hyde Park, or Kensington Gardens, and to become increasingly aware of the squalor that encompasses the deliberate wastage of social wealth, the odious contempt for time and application, the riot of splendid horses carrying their indifferent riders, the unenchanted display of clothes and opportunity, added up to an exploration that almost choked us. Nothing that we read in *Capital* shocked and benumbed our poor proletarian souls as did the ferocity and violence of the West End of London.

Existence, even life itself, had taken on a fresh meaning for us exiles from the mines. We were now able to measure the distance that stretched away from the pits we had abandoned, the ponies and youths we had left to the kindnesses of other men, to this world of wealth. What hurt us most was the cool assumption of privilege, the ghastly unawareness of these panoplied people, the translation of actual values. Not only was all the work of the world done for them, but that infatuation with the belief that their wealth was *our* privilege, that without their ministrations and their administrations there would be no work for any of us to perform. It astonished us to learn in our simplicity that work was not the buying and selling of a commodity which we possessed, our labour-power, but that the privilege to exercise it was the condition of our survival, and for our survival. These people, so strange, so suave, so unfamiliar, so removed from our simple manners and ways of life, these glittering females, these men with their tall silk hats, their low bowlers, their umbrellas, their brief-cases and their portfolios, were the people, or the creatures of those people who sat on the tap-root of society, guarding the flow of sap into the domestic offices and the shrines of their own lives. It was incredible, so we thought, that these people should be so privileged of wealth and so ignorant of the act of labour as are the toiling ants of sociology. It brought to my own mind that occasion when I paused at the coal face with poor Jimmy Strachan a few weeks before he was killed by a fall of stone.

The coal was desperately hard in the cavil he had drawn at the recent ballot of places. Not only was it hard, but the roof was treacherous. All the ancient wit he had inherited from his Irish ancestors, and all the skill he had garnered into his being, and earned and stolen from other men, helped him to cajole a few tubs of coal from a face that was as forbidding as a steel wall. Every advantage won from the glinting, unprotesting, beautifully polished mass before him had to be seized and enlarged upon if he were to live. He stopped tapping at the almost impregnable barrier before him, and he stood smiling at me, as he gave the points of his pick a careful caress with his forefinger and thumb.

'Know what, Harold?' he said to me, 'In my 'umble opinion all the wealth that's gotten in this bloody world comes from that pick point, an' millions like it. I may be wrong, lad, but that's my opinion, an' I sticks to ut.'

Perhaps he was not so far wrong. I have wondered at times when I have recalled that little conversation, and remembered that almost nude body, vexed with much wastage by labour, streaming with a mixture of fine coal dust and gently exuding sweat, who was the social man – little Jimmy Strachan or the man with the tightly rolled umbrella, and the shining black brief-case?

We had not been there very long when Joe Batey, the member for Spennymoor, an old friend of mine when he was check-weighman at St Hilda colliery and I was a delegate to the Labour Party and Trades Council, invited us to meet him at the House of Commons. The Labour Government was then teeter-ing on the edge of disaster and MacDonald was apprehensively awaiting the kick which Lloyd George would deliver that would send them all back to the hustings. Joe was a short, stout unsmiling miner. He once observed to me in his sweet Tyneside dialect:

'The reason why I don't smile often, Harold, is I have so little to smile about.'

When we got into the outer lobby and had sent in a green card he came out almost immediately. He must have been standing near Annie's Bar waiting for the messenger who carried a brass harness about his neck.

'Have ye had your tea?' he asked.

We told him we didn't want any, and he conducted us around the bits and pieces of the great building.

'Why all the pictures, Joe?' enquired Jack Lonsdale, who was a constituent of his.

Joe was always serious. He stopped and held our gazes. 'Would ye like to live all your working life among a lot o' statues?' he demanded. 'Don't ye think a bad picshure is better to look at than a good statcher of a man who should've been drowned when the midwife got him oot?'

He saw us to the clerk at the entrance to the gallery and left us.

An unimportant debate was going on at the time, and, as usual, a small spatter of members dozed about in the chamber, some with their feet up, none taking the slightest notice of what the member on his feet was talking about. The Speaker, bewigged and solemn as an owl after venting all his hoots, sat behind the clerks, clad like barristers proud of their briefs, immovable on their chairs. The mace lay on its rest at the foot of the table. A member who had grown tired of the charade of debate crept down the gangway, paused to bow to the Speaker, and strolled out of the chamber. It was the most solemn farce we had ever seen. Surely, somebody did the governing of the country somewhere other than in that place. A lone figure sat on the government front bench, and he appeared to be fast asleep. I was reminded of that quip by George Bernard Shaw that a socialist majority in the House of Commons would be as in-capable of producing socialism as a sewing machine of producing fried eggs.

Suddenly interest became stirred. Lloyd George had come into the chamber. The Speaker acknowledged his bow. We all recognised him, and we all strained to overcome the inhibition imposed by the uncomfortable seats in the gallery and see just what he was doing. A small, white-haired physically insignificant man, and not all that good-looking either, was now amongst us. He had strolled, aged-worthied, and gone to his place, a man who had defied the tempests and forced the winds to quit their ragings. Soon his name was called, but we all had to wait until the chamber had filled up before we could hear what he was saying. Ramsay MacDonald and John Wheatley came in, as did Stanley Baldwin. It was quite an important speech, quite short, quite clearly enunciated as is all Welsh speech. When he sat down another member was called, but we could not hear his voice or what he was saying until the chamber had emptied again.

We fled the place.

The college was altogether a strangely casual affair. There was no published syllabus of lectures. Everything that happened came about without any apparent design. Our basic instruction, as we soon found out, was to take place *after* we had listened to the initiatory lectures of the Principal, and that until we got over that hurdle we would have to make do with what we could glean from the lectures on the Theory of Value by Ashcroft and on History by Robertson.

There was no introductory lecture on Economics. We entered the college precincts as innocent as new-born babes. We were unaware of the writings of Adam Smith, David Ricardo, or even John Stuart Mill. We were a small group of eight, and we sat down to read the first pages of the first volume of *Capital* in pure innocence. We were simply introduced to a world of thought that existed outside the very world of men. What is more, we were given to understand that what we were about to study was the epitome of all the thought of men, the thought of Karl Marx, wherein was embalmed his theory of value, of historical materialism and of the materialist conception of history. Conjointly there was the philosophy of Joseph Dietzgen, a German tanner, a contemporary of Karl Marx and Friedrich Engels, and who died in America.

We did not wait upon Marx, we were made to wait for the Principal who would, in the fullness of time, show us how to wait upon Marx. He was a very busy man, who had to make constant forays into the outside proletarian sphere to gain credence for the college. In other words he was a propagandist. Whether he was or was not a brilliant lecturer is of no importance. He was incapable of overcoming a deep hesitancy when he was searching for the right word. At times his guttural hesitations were painful to listen to. One felt impatient with him, just as one did with Winston Churchill and his three word and one halt in all his passages of oratory. The day came when we sat down to Craik's first lecture, which was on working class education, a lecture so perfectly rounded as to make sure that he had delivered it hundreds of times before. The lecture did not raise the question: what is the working class? nor did it define the Marxist view of the class nature of society of which we formed a part.

The working class was taken for granted, which, in the future, was to stand in receipt of all power, and which, consequently, stood in dire need of a fully independent working class education. The next lecture was a historical excursion which brought to our notice that ever since civilisation began men had striven to think philosophically, and that such an action had begot a love of wisdom. The third lecture hit us where it most certainly hurt. We were left rolling about the lecture room in a state of utter bewilderment. All the second year students had made it their business to attend this particular lecture, mainly, as I suspected, to savour our bewilderment. Hitherto none of us had ever heard of Joseph Dietzgen, and none of us had ever asked ourselves what exactly we were doing when we were thinking. To make matters more confusing how were we to understand understanding, even if we were to agree that he who understands understanding cannot misunderstand. I think that Craik thoroughly enjoyed delivering that lecture. He could, I am certain, assess the degree of consternation he managed to cause. He did not know at the time that it would be the last time he would ever deliver that lecture in the College.

It is still strange to me after the passing of almost half a century why Craik thrust us simple young men into so savage an association with philosophy, we who had not gained possession of an inkling of the arguments of philosophers. We might have heard of Plato, Socrates or Aristotle, but even if we had done so there was no reason why any of us should have considered them to be all that important. For us, Aristotle was some ancient Greek who had written a book about babies. We were thrust even deeper into the morass, but never were we offered a potted biography of Kant, Locke, Butler, Hume,

Hegel and all the tribe of German philosophers. All we were instructed to do was to locate them and reject them on the grounds that they were not relevant to the needs of the working class. We could have told Craik that ourselves, because we could assume that even if they were entirely relevant to our intellectual needs they would not help us at all in the coal face.

What were we all doing when we were thinking? What is thought? Does the brain secrete thought in the same way that the liver secretes bile? How Craik toyed with us and our relations with the objective world. It is still very hard to forget our tortures. Craik idealised Dietzgen. He was on correspondence terms with Eugen, the son of the great old man. We toiled over the pages of *The Positive Outcome of Philosophy* and *The Nature of Human Brainwork* as well as *The Philosophical Essays*. During our discussion periods he met all our questions with all the adamantine arguments that lay embalmed in the Dietzgen corpus, and in the end we memorised all the formidable clichés and wrapped them in our own mental parcels.

We toiled at our Dietzgen more than we did at *Capital* that first term. We did our best to accept the old tanner's castigations of the spiritual world. We argued and angered. Michael Foot will never be able to understand our disastrous predicaments. Aneurin Bevan had to go through all of our experience, and because he did so with his bright mind he reframed his intellectual approach to politics because of his individual mastery of the Dietzgen approach to the general and the particular, the relevance of the real and the unreality of the relevant, the relevance of every thought, every thing. Such glib reasoning fitted the volatile mind and illuminated for the Welshman his own semantic power.

What it all was going to lead up to we never found out, for Craik was gone from the College before the year 1925 was fairly begun. We had returned to the coalfields for the Christmas holiday, and if we hoped at all it was that our studies would take us on a long and searching study of sociology that would link up with Marx's teachings as these had been embalmed in the English language through the kind offices of Charles Kerr and Co., publishers, Chicago, Ill.

But we did not make it. Craik was gone to Germany to escape retribution for his own folly. We were left without a Principal. Alex Robertson was persuaded to assume the mantle of Craik.

He kept to his own branch of study. A miner from the Rhondda, Jack Jones, stepped in to carry on where Craik had left off.

The departure of Craik did not deeply affect the College, and we got through the first year with the help of some of the second year students. During the first term two important things happened – the Labour Party Conference took place in London, and the Labour Government was defeated on the Campbell Case. MacDonald was chairman that year. He opened the Conference, and he closed the Conference. Between his two speeches C.T. Cramp, a railwayman, conducted the conference proceedings. Will Lawther was a member of the NEC of the Party at that time, and the ticket he gave me at the beginning of the affair enabled me to occupy a seat on the platform. One of the visitors to that strange conference was Karl Kautsky, an exceedingly old man who now and then sat close to me. It was the last open fight by the Communist Party for affiliation. Harry Pollitt and Saklatvala led the debate, and appealed over the head of Herbert Morrison. But all in vain. On the last day the conference listened with respect and attention to what Sir Patrick Hastings had to say about the Campbell affair. When MacDonald closed the conference there was still hope that the Liberals would relent. They did not. The first MacDonald Labour Government was blown away.

We came back to the College and settled in for the new term. A couple of weeks later Craik was gone. I did not meet up with him again until one day in 1935 when I went down to attend the demarkation of a Soviet ship at Hays Wharf, which he, his wife and daughter had joined at Hamburg. He recognised me, greatly cheerful. I gave him Bob Ellis's address and left him to his fate, which proved to be most kind. He was not long in getting a niche somewhere in the fast growing BBC.

Today, as I look back upon those years of study in the College, and on the half century which has followed during which I have continued a close reading of the Marx corpus, I am convinced that few, so very few, have made any sustained attempt to come to terms with the author of *Capital*. No one, so far as I have discovered, who has made an effort to study the man, has felt impelled to pronounce upon the magnetism of the man, and yet, it is something one cannot escape once one has broken the seven seals of *Capital*. Once this is done, the fascination becomes enslavement. In the field of economy, despite all the mumblings of the micro-economists as well as the macro-economists, Marx stands as a giant. The brilliance of conjecture as well as analysis and the subsequent phrasing dazzle even the loiterer upon his pages. I was a mere youth come to some penitent form obsessed by a deeper hunger than ever I had hitherto known for salvation, and yet doubtful of attaining a deep enough understanding. Marx is persuasive, even when what he writes is clothed in terms which must be taken apart and subjected to meticulous examination. There is always a crashing force in the simplest of his observations.

Marx never argued about God: he simply arraigned Him. Often, very often, the priest, and the arbitraments of the priest, come forth to be assessed by Marx. Today, I agree with him; yesterday I had to learn to understand. What I did squirm against was the irony of the man, his own particular Jewish irony, as inescapable as all Israel. It was always an immense relief to find him touched to a deeply concealed pity. That came when he accepted the simplicity of the simple men as they moved out of the magnificently cruel oppressions of the capitalist and pre-capitalist social arrangements and into the newer and more startlingly pitiless cruelties of an established pre-democratic period of capitalism. In the pages of *Capital* there is more concentrated human anger, more pity, and infinitely more understanding than there is in all the pages of political economy since the publication of *The Wealth of Nations*. What Marx appreciated as being innate, formidable and simply relevant in the capitalist process of production, Adam Smith and David Ricardo never discovered in all their work.

I did not realise at the time that my discovery of economics was as profound as was that moment when I actually became a member of the underworld of mining men. Both discoveries were shattering. In the College I passed out of a phase of ordinary, almost unintellectual life into one which held the imperative demands for understanding. It was almost as catastrophic as that day when I passed out of the still lingering habitudes of childhood into the actual existence of a man.

It occured one morning after we had discovered the dam at the bottom of the drowned shaft at Wylam, when my father came to see how we were faring and what progress we were making. After a careful examination of the place he expressed himself as satisfied.

'I'll go now,' he said. 'You chaps get on with the dam. The sooner it's busted the better.' He turned to me. 'You, Harold,' he said, 'can come with me and set me up the shaft.'

I followed him into the air and then we retraced our steps back to the Yard Seam. Arrived there, I saw him into the kibble and gave the signal of 'men to ride', which was three distinct raps on the pit head hammer. My father strapped himself to the rope. I handed him the shaft stick. The shaft was silent. The enormous eye of the water glared up at us, unblinking, malevolent. Occasionally a stone loosened itself from the side of the shaft and dropped with a plop into the water. My father ready, I gave the hoist signal.

'You needn't go back empty handed,' he said. 'Take a couple of those planks back with you.'

The kibble began to rise.

I stood on the wet gantry watching the kibble ascend. I stood there until the bogey was drawn over the aperture at the top, excluding most of the light of day, leaving me alone.

It was then that fear seized me. I was alone, a few feet above that most dreadful monster in the shaft. I had to turn and face the more malevolent monsters that lay between me, that prowled about the distance I was to travel, and the dam. I had to leave it there and go back to the dam. I think I moaned before I picked up the two planks of wood. Placing one under each arm I paused long enough to settle the clay bob holding my lighted candle between my fingers in such a fashion that the palm of my hand shielded the light of the candle against the wind. I marched fearfully into that maw of darkness. Each step I took burgeoned my fear. I was alone, terribly alone, in a mine that contained all my fears. Once or twice I stumbled over a piece of stone or a lump of coal. I went on and on and on into fear.

I came to the top of the drift. The road lost its black gloss and took on a white sheen, and made a fitting habitation for any ghost. I felt a scream rising in my throat, but I choked it back. Down the gradient I stumbled. The planks eased themselves of some of their weight as I plunged on. The gaunt fingers of my fear squeezed into my flesh, my very being. I began to sob as I went on.

At the bottom of the drift I had to turn left and pass over a small barrier of stone. As I did so I lost hold of the plank in my right arm. It fell and knocked the candle out of my hand. The darkness fell over me. I sat down, alive with fear, at the mercy of all the phantoms that hid themselves in the everlasting darkness. I groped about for my piece of candle among the wet muck, and at last I found it. I had no matches upon me. They were in my coat pocket at the dam.

I tried to compose myself. I did not weep. I was too far gone in spiritual abjectness to do anything but clutch my aloneness against my palpitating heart. I was stupendously alone in that darkness which held all the ferocious fears of my existence as they had built up since I was born. I could only hope that nothing, nothing would assault me. It did not occur to me to try to feel my way through the darkness to where I could call for aid from my comrades. Had I done so I would have been compelled to carry my two planks with me. I sat still. There was nothing else that I could do but sit in that darkness which weighed down upon me.

My head drooped and I fell asleep.

I awoke.

A voice was calling my name along the passage. I opened my eyes and felt the dreadful shock of candle light, a long way off. And my fear fell from me like a cloak.

'Harold! Harold!'

I picked up my burden and started to walk forward. 'Coming,' I yelled.

'Where the hell have you been?' Dick demanded.

'I lost my light, and I had no matches,' I explained.

I knew then that I had become a member of the fraternity of men who sought their livings beneath the fields.

I had become a miner.

Somehow I felt the same sensation of fulfilment when I came into the territory of Karl Marx. I offer no apology for this, for I am convinced that all mankind must come to terms with him. I offer no suggestion as to the manner of that coming.

It is when one discovers Marx in a contemplative mood that one begins to assess his immense stature as a thinker. Watch him observing the social arrangements which men have produced over the illimitable aeons of industrial creation, especially 'the social production of ancient days…which are far simpler, enormously more easy to understand than bourgeois society'. Follow him closely and attend to his explanations of such productive purposes 'based upon the immaturity of the individual being (who has not yet severed the umbilical cord, which, under primitive conditions, unites the members of the human species one with another) or upon the direct relations of dominion and satisfaction.'

This revelation brought its own shocks which were as impressive as my own individual experience with and within myself in that solitary pit in Wylam. It held me just as spellbound in delight as the other had held me so forlorn in loneliness.

I was free from all economic worries for at least two years. I was at liberty to make the most and best of my studies. I could do that, or I could make a countenance of studying and idle my time among the social catacombs of the West End of London. It was impossible to escape the impact of this London. Not only was it shattering, it was new. So far as I was objectively aware, Earls Court had not yet learned how the other half contrived to gain a livelihood, and how it connived at the sustenance of Earls Court. It was a place wherein was exposed the insensitive privateness of existence. In the daytime Earls Court was deserted, smitten by a plague of achievement in other places. In the evening, its denizens clad themselves in raiment more appropriate to the charade than to the purposes of living. Pleasures were systematically sampled, pleasures unknown to me or my contemporaries of the coal measures, be they wanton or intellectual, be they moral or merely wrong. The contrast was at first almost paralysing, but it soon appeared ordinary and tawdry. We who had forsaken industrial turmoil for the time being had to turn to Marx if we were to discover some rationale for this contrast that was made so manifest. Even so, he did not provide us with all the answers.

As the years have passed and as I explored the literature that has concentrated on the working class ways and manners of life, Gissing and the lesser breed, I have found it difficult to understand how and why London made such an impact upon me. And yet it did. If one were to judge the London of the '20s and compare it with that which lies exposed on the pages of that splendid author, one must accept the fact that in the main it is merely a hell-hole under revision. Why must the contrast between riches and poverty be so stark?

The student of Marx can present his own reasons for the deplorable conditions with which he had to contend in order to sustain his importance as a writer on economics. It is, today, useless bemoaning the conditions which in the end prevented his bringing his work to its conclusion, and so giving mankind all the refinement of his thought. If only...But was his entire work basic to the complete understanding of the capitalist mode of production, or does the capitalistic mode of production remain basic to the understanding of Karl Marx?

There was that moment when I came upon a reflection by Marx. Allow me to set it down:

> Whatever view we take of the masks in which the different personalities strut about the feudal stage, at any rate the social relations between individuals at work appear in their natural guise as personal relations, and are not dressed up as social relations between things, between the products of labour.

When I had successfully grappled with that flaming thought, I found myself compelled to refrain from further contemplation of my own lot. It explained the family that had bred me. I had been conditioned within the terms of their own lives' begettings. Their lives, their religion, their beliefs and their tortuous assumptions were all securely anchored, and had always been so anchored, to a productive process that went into the makeup of the capitalist mode of production. The pity was for them that it was all embedded in an indubitably personal relation with God and His priests.

The Labour College had little to teach any of us. That is the conclusion at which I arrived along with many of my fellow students. Did we react to Marx, or did Marxism simply sweep over us like a shower of rain? I believe that we had no other option but to allow it to do so. The fact was that the purveyors of the Labour College brand of Marxism-Dietzgenism were not particularly well-schooled for their tasks. They broke off all our hitherto intellectual development the moment we crossed the threshold in Penywern Road. They insisted that there was no viable reasoning on economics before Marx, and none whatever since. They insisted that history could only be understood from the point of the materialist conception. They insisted that philosophy ended when Dietzgen published his works. They made us start afresh.

Chapter Thirteen

When I left South Shields at the end of the Christmas vacation, 1924, I took back with me my typewriter and the typescript of a novel I had toiled over for many months. When I got back I left the manuscript in the outer office of Herbert Jenkins Ltd. This firm had published a couple of novels by James C. Welsh, MP and it occurred to me that they might show some interest in what I had written. In due time it was returned to me with a longish letter in which they offered a reasoned excuse for not proceeding with publication.

A little dejected, I put the thing away among my clothes and tried to forget about it. I might have done so, but one morning I received a letter which bore the embossed address of the Embassy of the USSR on the flap of the envelope. In my room I read the enclosed letter with mounting interest. It read:

> Dear Sir,
>
> From a friend I have learned that you have written a novel dealing with mining life in the North. This novel might be of interest to readers in my country, so would you care to call at the Embassy at 3 p.m. on Thursday afternoon, and, if possible, bring the m.s. with you? I do hope that this will be convenient for you.
>
> Yours sincerely,
>
> IVAN MAISKY.
> *Secretary to the Soviet Legation.*

I was rooming with Horace Morgan, a miner from Cwmtwrch, a village in the Swansea Valley. Horace finished up with an M.A. degree at some Welsh university and became a schoolmaster. At that time he aimed at becoming a dramatist. If he ever did become one the fact has escaped me. The last time I saw him was on the occasion of the Old Boy's of the Labour College annual dinner. This took place in the House of Commons dining room somewhere near the members' bar room. The meal was so bad that I refrained thereafter from any of the college jamborees. Nye Bevan was the star of the affair, and this, somehow, did not suit Will Lawther, who possessed a positive dislike for the member for Ebbw Vale. Lawther told me that night of his impending knighthood.

Horace came with me to Sloane Square. We paused awhile at the entrance to admire a huge photograph of a meeting which was being addressed by Lenin in Petrograd. Standing beneath Lenin was Leon Trotsky. I thought it was a magnificent photograph. I have often seen that same photograph since, but so doctored that Trotsky was completely removed from his stance.

We were ushered into Maisky's room. He asked us to be seated after we had introduced ourselves. This was the first time I had met the man. Indeed, prior to the receipt of that letter I was unaware of his existence. Small of stature, rotund, moustached, smiling, he was a most charming man. He spoke English well, although there were occasions when he had to to search for the appropriate word. I now think it would have been better had I gone alone, for he was most reluctant to engage me in conversation. He asked me if I had brought the typescript with me, and I forthwith handed over the parcel I had under my arm. He told me that he would read it and find out if he could recommend it to a Russian publisher. Did I agree to that course of action? he asked, and when I nodded he rose from his chair, came round the table, shook our hands and ushered us from the room.

I did ask him how he came to know of my book, but he merely smiled, and told me that a friend had suggested he should read it. Some time later I did learn that my good friend was Rochelle Townsend. She was then reading for Jenkins. Mrs Townsend had a comprehensive knowledge of the Russian language. She was friendly with Maisky. Later she became employed by the Russian Trade Delegation and held a comparatively important position until our friendship drifted away.

A publishing house in Leningrad, Priboj, agreed to publish the book on Maisky's recommendation, and he accordingly handed the novel to a Madame Zina Vengerova-Minsky. She was a small, energetic, bronchitic person who had one passion, and one passion only, literature. She knew most of the European languages and had spent all her mature years doing translations for Russian publishing houses.

During the time she was busy on my novel I was often called to her home in Bloomsbury to elucidate some mining term or some north country cliché. It was in her house that I made the acquaintance of Mrs Townsend. A warm friendship sprang up between us, and this solidified after Phyllis Varndell and I were married.

The latter event occurred at Brixton Registry Office on 26th

March 1926, a few weeks before the General Strike and while I was still resident at the Labour College.

After a short weekend at a Thamesside hotel near Maidenhead, I took my wife north to meet my family. She was not deeply impressed by the north country, but she did impress all the people she was introduced to. We made our way back to London for me to take the last term of my stay at the college.

The strike came and went, and a bleak future stretched away into the infinity for us both. We made the best of it, and in some way we enjoyed ourselves.

There was that occasion when the Minskys suggested that we should undertake an excursion to Stoke Poges, and pay our respects to the shade of Thomas Gray. We all met at Earls Court station and from there we went to Hounslow. We caught a bus outside Hounslow station which took us to Slough. At the junction of the road going west and the one diverging to Eton there stood a hotel which offered us lunch. While we were seated Zina made a long study of the menu, of which Nicolai took no notice until she mentioned the word 'salmon'.

'Is it fresh salmon?' he asked the waitress.

She nodded. 'And you have lettuce, much lettuce, nice lettuce?' he demanded of her, and when she had indicated that there was, he said to her: 'Bring it in some abundance, please. Lettuce, tomato, salmon, onion, oil, vinegar, and much mustard.'

When the girl had gone he smiled beatifically upon us. 'When she bring it all I will make you a salad just like Peter Kropotkin showed me how to make. No man could make salad like Peter …no man in all Russia. Peter was my friend.'

Zina leaned towards me. 'Peter and Nicky were inseparable friends,' she told me. 'Now Kola will surprise you.'

We watched the old man prepare his salad, the basis of which was a copious dollop of mustard. His salad, prepared with such meticulous care on that small table, became a blissful luncheon.

We walked to Stoke Poges, and made our obeisances to the ghost that still haunts the churchyard. Kola signed the book that lay on a table in the church. As I watched him I felt envious of his small, beautiful handwriting. He must have produced a lovely manuscript.

The day remained beautiful all the way back to London.

But to the book. It was published in Leningrad and carried a warm preface by Ivan Maisky. The publishers honoured their agreement and I received sufficient valuta to enable me to get married and furnish our home at Cleadon, South Shields. Some years later the book was published in a mass edition, of a half a million copies, not in book form, but in the format of a magazine. By then Maisky was the Russian ambassador to Finland, and when I drew his attention to the fact of the new edition, he demanded of the publishers that the agreement be honoured. It was, in part, and I made no further attempt to obtain the rest of the 'honorarium'.

I did not learn how much Zina received for the translation of the novel. She once told me that if she went back to the Soviet Union she would be a millionaire in roubles. In all probability she had to live on the salary she obtained from the Trade Delegation and the Embassy, and that all her earnings from her literary activities were kept for her in Russia. When I suggested that they should go back to Russia they both shuddered. Never, she said. Nicky merely smiled.

Nicky's real name was Nicolai Maximovitch Vilenkin. His pseudonym was 'Minsky'. He was a considerable pre-revolutionary poet. When I first met him he was writing a vast 'philosophy'. I believe that he completed it before he died. Rochelle Townsend did begin to translate it, but in all probability she discontinued her task after the old man's ashes came to rest in Père Lachaise. He was a very old man when I first met him. The Russian colony in London held a great affection for the old man, mainly because he had had to flee from Tsarist Russia long before the revolution. Zina did tell me how she and her sister Bella managed to get him across the border just in time to avoid arrest. He remained in exile until the end of his life. He and Zina were married, but I do not know if it was ever a successful affair, for Nicolai had an eye for beauty, and nobody could have called Zina even good-looking.

When I met them they were great friends with Madame Stepniak, the widow of the writer and anti-Tsarist. When I met her she was a vastly ancient creature, and dreadfully poor. She had retained possession of all Stepniak's papers, and was holding out for a better offer from the Embassy for them. Discussions on the papers went on without much pause. I believe that in the end the Russian authorities did gain possession of the papers. The poor old lady had been a widow from long before I was born. Her husband was knocked down by a train and killed as he was returning from the cremation ceremony of Friedrich Engels, in 1895.

Chapter Fourteen

The scholarship terminated at the end of July, 1926, and I left Penywern Road to those students who had still another year in which to study and to serve. Morgan Phillips was one of the incoming students, but I never met him personally, nor did I ever hold a conversation with him during the years that remained to him.

The miners strike continued under the effervescent leadership of Arthur J. Cook, but by the end of the year it began to founder into disaster. The first crack in the facade appeared in Nottinghamshire, and from that moment the militancy of the men began to fade away. A strike becomes useless when it is seen to lose its basis of power. One by one the local leadership sought accommodation with the local coal owners, and the coal industry began to stir to life. But, as an industry, it was never to be the same again.

I left Phyllis in London after the break appeared to grow wider, and I went back to Harton. There I found the county in a deplorable condition. Harton was still holding out, but it was soon apparent that it was teetering on the edge of defeat. So, too, were Marsden and Boldon. St Hilda had broken, and the men were struggling between the desire to work and the disinclination to act traitorously to their fellow miners. The argument in town was, to say the least, vociferous. It became even louder over the New Year holiday, and then the strike was called off. Meetings were held. Recriminations continued. The men staggered back to work and staggered home again, each carrying a lump of coal, a forbidden theft, in all conscience. No pen that I knew could, had it wished, declare the nature of the suffering that ensued. That they were almost insupportable must be presumed. The long lay-off had softened all the muscles of their bodies as well as the skins of their hands, which had been hardened and calloused over all the years of their working lives. Especially was it hurtful to the hands, but the agonies and pains of hewing had to be borne until the skins were re-calloused. Not only that, but their bodies had to relearn the constrictions of the spaces into which they were now again thrust. Even the eyes and the ears had to re-learn all that had been forgotten.

Despite all these physical exclusions and renewals, the mine itself had to be renewed, and in parts re-built, for the strike had wreaked its own vengeances upon the distant as well as the fragile structures of the haulage roads. No repairing had been attempted during the long lay-off, and so a freedom hitherto unexperienced had been granted to all the hidden and urgent pressures, and, accordingly, had accomplished their own devastations. The great timbers, untended over the long months, had broken and catastrophe had seized upon long tracts of important excavation. At many places, where the roof support had been calculated to hold immense forces in leash, the floor of the mine had risen up to kiss the roof above. Production could not take place until most of these depradations had been rectified, or nullified.

That was by no means all. In all mines the air is made to move into the furthest place along the decisive routes, mainly engine planes. To obstruct the intake is to defame the vent-ilation in its initial stage. All travelling by men and ponies to the places of work is restricted, so far as possible, to the return air-way. It was in these returns where the toll of the strikes could be seen at its most impressive condition. Structurally, the return is of lesser importance than other ways within the terms of mining engineering. Such repairing as is considered necessary is carried out by the old men who have passed beyond the toil of the coal face. The main duty is to keep the airway func-tioning. In Durham parlance the returns are called 'the waste', and the men are 'waste men'. It is comprehensible that the pressures exerted upon the barely furnished waste during the strike would wreak their immense toll, and that where this had been immense there would be a deep and dire effect upon the volume of air passing along the intakes.

Mining could not be presumed to be normal until the major happenings had been dealt with. When the hands and bodies of the men had become 'hardened', the work within the mine, as soon as the ventilatory tract was in some way functioning adequately, began to gather speed, and soon all the miners that were needed were able to return to their old ways of life below ground.

It was March, 1927 before I got permission to start again in the pit. The town of South Shields sits perennially in the track of the nor'easters. One was tearing viciously through the tree-less waste of low dwellings of all the town when I set off to walk the length of Stanhope Road to Harton Colliery. I walked alone right to the lamp cabin. Nothing had changed, not even the smell of the place. I was fulfilling my promise to return to the pit. Now I was back, right back in the world of hob-nailed boots, coarse yarn stockings, heavy flannel shirts, old cast-off clothing, a huge tin water-bottle slung on my shoulder and a packet of sandwiches in my pocket, wrapped in newspaper. During my two years in London I had had to have my eyes tested and my vision rectified, which was not fully stereoscopic. Now I was without my spectacles, and somehow naked. The further I trudged on my way the deeper became my reluctance to continue. My despair deepened. I swallowed it and went on.

I was given a lamp and passed into the waiting room. They had discontinued the testing of the lamps. I read the barometer and walked on to the pit head. I was desolated. The warmth and the stench and the foulness. It was like the stench of the abattoir. I took my bunch of tokens, hung them on my belt, and walked down to the bottom cage. I stood watching the process. The cage filled with humanity and the gates were closed upon it. The clanging of bells, a little upward lift and then the slithering of the monstrous thing into the darkness and vapours of the shaft. The other cage slid into view and I walked into it. Holding my lamp in one hand, my other hand sought and found the rail running along the roof of the cage. This I clenched and then I laid my head against my forearm. We left the cage and went into the narrow passage and made ourselves known to the overmen. I knew exactly where I was to go. The Second North.

I came upon the drift, running from the Bensham to the Hutton, I joined the group that was going the way I was going. When we had all foregathered we went on to the stables and took our ponies. We led the poor little beasts from the stables, across the engine plane and into the travelling way, and sent them on into the darkness unguided. Beyond the last trapdoor we discarded all our clothes except our short pants, boots and stockings, and waistcoats. Then we went on in the time honoured Indian file.

As we plunged along the travelling way I became instinctively aware that there was something wrong with the atmosphere. Nothing was happening to encourage my further speculation, but I grew alerted to some danger. The pit did not smell right. It did not feel right. The air was much too warm even for a return airway. The flow of air was distinctly loose. It was extraordinarily 'slack' – to use a miner's term. No movement was perceptible. Everything was still, uncomfortably suppressed, distinctively oppressive. I became uneasy.

Halfway to the district in which we were to work we took a rest. Further along into the darkness the ponies stood still. I noticed that none of my comrades sat down, instead, practically naked, they lay down in the thick dust and rested their heads in the cups of their open palms. None of them offered a remark, which was unusual. I cogitated the predicament I was in. I did not feel frightened, but I was disturbed, oppressed by the feeling that we were not safe. I made up my mind to expect a better flow of air when we got out of this return, for I knew that we would be working forward from the landing at the end of the engine plane.

After a while we got up and went on our journey, and in time we arrived at the deputy's kist, and there we squatted.

The air was almost as slack at the kist as it had been in the return. When the deputy came from his examination of the faces, he offered us lots for the 'goings' along which we would drag the filled coal tubs. This done, we took each an appropriate pony and went about our tasks. The shift of the men we had replaced went home. The lack of air was apparent at the kist. When I got to the face I found that there it was even worse. My pony was soon drenched with its own sweat. In the faces most of the hewers were naked to the tops of their stockings. All were drenched with a wet mucous of sweat and coal dust. A heavy inertia lay upon every one of us, man, youth, pony. As the shift wore on an agony lay upon all our flesh, sublimely, almost exquisitely.

By the end of the shift I was almost exhausted. I started out from the flat with my pony and my companions. I tried to walk manfully. I did try to keep in file, but soon there was no file for me to keep in. I was alone. They could not wait for me. I was sufficiently pit-wise to know my way out of the travelling way. The pony slackened his pace in order to share the light from my lamp, whose glass was almost smudged over with dust. He led me home unerringly. We came to the place where

I could pick up my clothes. I dressed slowly. My aching flesh almost rejected the coarse flannel of my shirt. Dressed at last I opened the trap door and passed into the fresher air of the drift bottom. We crossed the plane and I delivered the little thing to the horsekeeper. I walked up the incline of the drift.

I had not gone forty yards when I began to feel a strange discomfort. I sat down to endeavour to conjure some comfort in my strange physical condition. I put my lamp in a safe place, sat down, and began to fall into a swoon. How long my half awake condition lasted I cannot tell. Something had happened …but what? I had never felt like this before. I just had to sit and let happen just what had to happen. At last the pent up displeasure of my body found vent and I vomited as I had not vomited in all my life.

When I had regained composure of a sort, I drank the horribly warm water from my tin bottle. I forced myself to drink the torrid stuff. Afterwards I gained some slight renewal of my strength and I got to my feet to continue my climb of the drift. Slowly, painfully I plodded upwards. Before I reached the top of the drift my nausea returned and again I passed through the agonies of my body trying to expel that which was not there. After vomiting, I took a long rest before essaying the rest of my slow climb. The electric bulbs at the top glared a bluish-white pain right into my eyes.

Here the air was cold and I became somewhat refreshed. I knew that my sufferings were all on account of the bad ventilation. My lungs had breathed an atmosphere for nine hours that no Gissing had ever experienced and which no Gissing could describe. As I sat there, drinking in the cold, cold air I became aware of a sustained buzzing noise. To my astonishment, the noise became recognisable as that of a suction fan in full blast. A suction fan inside a coal mine! I was astounded, and yet I was much too discomposed to cogitate on so unusual a phenomenon. When I left the direct aircourse and re-entered the return which would take me to the shaft bottom I was again assailed by nausea, but this passed after a couple of vain retchings. I came at last to the shaft bottom where the 'waiter-on' recognised me.

'That you, Harold?' he asked.

'Aye. First shift,' I replied. 'Takes a bit getting used to after two years.'

'Your shift rode two hours ago,' he observed. He lurched a

bit on the top of his own kist. 'Couldn't you have found a better place than this to work in, in London?'

'Should I have done?' I countered.

'I should bloody well think so,' he cried, 'What made you think about coming to this place again after you'd got free?'

'I promised to come back, didn't I?' I said. 'I gave my promise to the lodge before I went to College.'

'That was long ago! Long ago!' he shouted. 'A long bloody time ago!'

'Do you think the Harton lodge would have given me a quid a week out of the funds if they'd thought for one moment I wouldn't come back?' I demanded.

'They gave you a quid a week?' He was surprised.

'They gave me a hundred and two quid for my own little promise,' I said. 'Wasn't it a bargain? A good bargain?'

'Pie crusts, lad!' he said loudly. 'Why yer bugger o'hell's flames! Do you think anybody've minded if you hadn't come back?'

'Well, I have come back,' I said, 'so let me get back to bank.'

I rode the shift alone.

By the fire I bathed myself in the time worn manner of the mining home. I ate nothing. I put out the gas light and went upstairs to bed.

When I awoke the buzzer had gone for the shift I should have joined. The shift after that I went back to the pit and once again I laboured in that airless district. All the time I pondered on that suction fan, but I did not express my fears to anybody. I was convinced that even with the aid of that fan the ventilatory tract was not functioning as it ought to function. I would have to make my mind up about it all later.

Chapter Fifteen

We furnished our little home with the fragile furniture of love and hope and poverty, and we shaped our lives within the conditions imposed by an urban assembly lingering on the edge of the collapse of a manually produced coal industry. It was difficult for us both as we struggled through those arduous days which added up to the year 1927. We were happy and alone in that north country setting which must have been torture for my wife, for she must have felt it more deeply than I did to be estranged from the immense social forest that was London and imprisoned in a down-at-heel borough like South Shields. We felt that there was no escape for either of us.

My father and his wife came to see us one beautiful Saturday afternoon in the summer of our year. They refreshed themselves at our table, and later we walked them to the edge of the cliffs at Marsden Rock and back to South Shields where they took the train to Newcastle. Neither of them entered my home again.

As I walked with my father behind my wife and my stepmother I told him of my fears for the colliery. This was the first time I had openly brooded on the subject. At that time I was working in a fresh cavil, but in the same Hutton seam. My father listened with his old avidity and enthusiasm to descriptions of the underworld.

'What's the height o' the seam?' he asked me.

I knew that he was somewhat impressed by my fears. 'It varies,' I said. 'It's anything from six or seven feet to fifteen.'

At that he stood in his tracks. 'Say that again,' he commanded. 'Thou's joking, surely!'

I repeated what I had told him.

'It's just not possible,' he breathed.

'But it is actual,' I cried. 'You should see it. It's marvellous.'

'Then just what are you worried about?' he asked me.

I could see that all his mining instincts were aroused. He did not press me. He just waited.

'The strike didn't do the industry much good,' I told him. 'And what is more it's done that pit of ours a great deal of

179

harm. It certainly has not improved conditions underground.'

He cracked out a sharp, seering guffaw which I might have taken for a laugh, but I knew it was not a laugh. 'You can say that again,' he said. He dropped into his native dialect. 'Thou abune all of us didn't need to be telt that,' he said, 'but it pleases me to hear thou say it. Thou dissent think that that fool A.J. Cook was sure he was ganna do the pits a lot o' good when he had y'all out on strike to starve.'

'I'm not interested in your side of the politics of the strike, Dad,' I told him.

'Then, just what is thou interested in?' he cried.

'The effects,' I said. But just then a large ship was edging its way out of the harbour between the two piers. We both stood and watched it. When it had got itself clear, I said to him, 'They've got a fan in the pit.'

'They have what?' he shouted.

Sarah, my step-mother heard and looked back somewhat anxiously. He waved her on. 'Gan on,' he shouted. 'We're only talking.'

I told him about the fan, and when I had finished he said to me, anxiously I thought: 'And is the district thou's in covered by this fan?'

I nodded.

'How far inbye?'

'Couple o' miles about.'

'What's the air like?'

'Slack,' I said. 'That's what worries me. I can get a fair sized gas cap anywhere in the flat where I'm working. I've never tested in the face. Better not to.'

I heard his sharp intake of breath. 'How much?' he demanded. 'More than two an' a half percent?'

'That and more,' I assured him. 'One has to be careful not to go too near to the roof, if one doesn't wish to lose his light.'

A soft whistle escaped his lips.

In those days gas was detected by pulling down the wick of an oil-burning safety lamp to its lowest permissible level. When this was done, even in the purest air, an oil-cap, hardly discernable from a gas cap, coned over the flame. In a *fiery* atmosphere the cone lengthened and took on a pale blue sheen. Where a higher amount of gas was present, that within the chamber created by the glass and the twin gauzes of the chimney would immediately ignite and extinguish itself. Five percent of gas in the atmosphere would not do this, but its lethal propensities would be recognised and the men working in the area would be withdrawn. All this recognition of lethal gas had to be reported.

I could see that my father had become alarmed. I watched him become the old mining inquisitor. 'Thou hasn't told anybody about this, hast thou?' he demanded in the old dialect.

I shook my head. 'Not yet,' I replied.

'An' I wouldn't if I was thou,' he said. 'Thou might be wrong.' Here he paused. 'An' thou might be right,' he conceded. 'Thou always had it in thyself to be a pitman. But what if she fires? Explodes. Has thou thought o' that my lad?'

'What would you advise me to do?' I cried out.

'Do?' He walked on. 'Only one thing thou can do, an' that's get out o' the place as quick as thou can.' He stopped to lean up against a stone wall to light his pipe. I could see that he was deeply worried.

'I've never known such a state'v affairs,' he said. 'They must be in a sorry state wi' their ventilation.' His eyes suddenly glinted. 'Hast thou had a squint at the deputies' reports?'

'They use only two words,' I replied. 'They write 'all right' every time.'

'There! See!' he shouted. 'Mebbies none o' them can test for gas?'

'I wouldn't say that,' I retorted. 'What would happen if they did report the presence of gas? What would you do if it was in your pit?'

He smiled somewhat sheepishly. 'Mebbies thou's right, lad!' he confessed. 'I'd want to know why they were jeopardising the pit.'

It was my turn to smile.

'The Mines Act's no better than all other acts,' he continued. 'There's a road through the lot.' And with that he paused on the top of the cliff which we were to descend in order to get on to the cement 'promenade' to survey the lovely beach that ran to the pier and then beyond to touch the waters of the Tyne. 'The trouble wi' most men,' he said, 'is that they take everything for granted. They never read. So, for them, hist'ry is only summat inside unread books. Did you ever hear of a man who lived in these parts, called James Mather?'

I shook my head.

'There! See!' His reverence changed swiftly into triumph. 'See yon pier. The near one. Whee do you think built that? It had to be built. It didn't just grow out o' the sands. It was James

Mather what did it.'

'Where did he come from?' I asked.

'Shields, o' course. My grandfather knew him. He told me about the man. But Mather did more'n that. He worked on ventilating the pits.'

I can see him now, a bright-eyed, woefully undersized man, a typical product of a civilisation taught how to hew coal. It is my fondest remembrance of him. In that lovely sunshine he stood revealed before me, not only as a man of the pits, but as my father.

'Remember that day I took thou into Bitchburn an' thou became interested in a roll o' brattice cloth thou was sitting on?' he asked, and when I had nodded, he went on. 'Brattice cloth was something added by men to help them overcome their own difficulties,' he informed me.

'How?' I asked.

'In the beginning, all the pits, if they were ventilated at all, were ventilated by a furnace, like the one we had at Bitchburn. But in them days there was only one way in to any mine. That being so, how does thou think fresh air got in and the bad air got out?' He did not wait. 'I'll tell thou. It was George Stephenson what discovered it. The rising warm air bratticed itself off *naturally* against the fresh air that had to fill the vacuum.' He grinned at me. 'George Stephenson was the man that defined the *natural brattice*,' he said.

I overcame my surprise. 'You mean the cold air came down one side of the shaft and the warm air went up the other side?' I cried incredulously.

'Zackly,' he said. 'George Stephenson, the man that gave us the railway, the man frae Wylam, was the man that discovered the 'natural brattice'.'

'I never knew that,' I said. 'But what about Mather? What did he discover?'

He shook his head. 'Thou hasn't changed a bit since thou was a bairn,' he said to me. 'Thou's more an unbeliever than thou is an empiricist,' he went on. I smiled at his bit of *Hibbert Journal* witticism. 'James Mather made the next big discovery. Until he proved it, every mining engineer and scientist believed that the more you stoked the furnace at the bottom of the shaft, the hotter you got it, the greater would be the flow of the rising hot air in the shaft. Everybody believed that until Mather showed them they were wrong an' that there was a furnace limit. So everybody got shocked.'

I had no riposte to make, and so I waited.

'So they had to find a fresh way to take the air into and out of a pit,' he said. 'Mather was working with a chap called Goldsworthy Gurney, and between them they tried to introduce a steam-jet method. This,' he went on, 'was overtaken by the rotary fan, and here we are. It's ta'en us ower a hundred years to get to the simple rotating fan, and it would appear that it is not as good as it was.'

I had nothing to offer to his off-the-pulpit discourse.

'But all that's just as maybe,' he said. 'We need not discuss that this fine day. It's Harton I want to talk about. It's that fan in the pit that interests me. Up to now we've all believed that the more powerful the fan the greater must be the volume and speed of the air that it draws. But, surely, thou can see that the assumption is made to rest on the fan and not on the air course. Everybody knows that air passing through a continously confined space experiences drag as is made by its passing against the sides especially in a pit. Surely, increased power increases the drag. You canna widen a shaft to increase the area of the draught, now can you? Surely there is a limit to a draught even when it's drawn mechanically. Take your pit. That fan installed downstairs can only steal from the existing air current. It canna bring any air down from above, now can it? If it increases the pull down the shaft it canna boost the push up the upcast. All yon fan is doing is robbing poor auld Peter to pay poor auld Paul.'

'Then there is a limit to the ventilatory force?' I asked.

'There's a limit to everything, isn't there?' He laughed suddenly. 'Go on, say it, lad. Say, so what? The limit is set upon the fan which is determined mechanically by the thrust of the rotator and the diameter of the passage for the flow. Efficiency is determined and limited by the tracks of intake and return of the wind, the column moving along the track. It is obvious, lad, that great violence has been done by untended nature to the ventilatory tract in that pit o' yours, an' that worries me.' He took his pipe out of his mouth and spat sharply, as of old. 'Knaa what?' he cried. 'I'll pray for thou when I get home.'

'Why?'

'I'll ask the Lord to deliver thou from that pit afore its too late,' he said, without offering a smile.

As we walked along the edge of the sea he returned to the subject of ventilation.

'The problem of the mining engineer isn't merely a matter

of getting the coals to bank,' he said. (He always spoke of coals as a given entity. 'Coal' was for him an abstraction.) 'The real problem is the flow of fresh air. Always fresh air. The power of the fan is retarded in many ways while it is hauling the air from bank to bank. Consequently, it is ever ready to steal.'

'Steal!' I echoed.

'Aye'. That is what always must be guarded against. The fan likes to steal as much air from the in-take as it can. It's a great thief of it's own property. Look!' He paused at that moment to watch a youth swimming powerfully. 'By sangs! Yon lad knaas how to swim!' he said.

We saw them to the train and waved them goodbye.

I need not have worried.

In order to save money the local lodges in the district combined in the matter of local inspection as was permitted by the Coal Mines Act. Instead of appointing two local coal-hewers to inspect the pits, they appointed a retired mining engineer to do it for them at a salary. After the passage of some weeks the inspector descended upon Harton Colliery. What he found there horrified him. He met the committee of the lodge and showed the members the report he was to give to the management. When this was done, the coal company had no option but to accept the findings of the local inspector and within two weeks the worst affected parts of the mine were closed and over one thousand of us were on the dole.

Phyllis and I were now face to face with crisis. I had to make application for unemployment benefit at the local exchange. As a result our income was sorely depleted. We hoped against hope that things might become brighter, but as the weeks glided by we came to the conclusion that it would be better if we went back to London.

I sent Phyllis to London while I stayed to see the packing and despatching of our furniture.

I spent the last Saturday night with Jos Mackey and Bill Blyton. We went to the Empire and watched a grossly short-ened version of Othello. We walked home, stricken to the soul by the great tragedy we had seen so mangled.

The next morning I left South Shields, only to return at rare intervals.

The last time Phyllis and I were to be together in the town of South Shields was to be on the day the National Coal Board closed Harton Colliery and rendered an entire tribe of miners redundant.

Chapter Sixteen

Thrust into the hopeless near-hunger of unemployment as we were, fate did not begin immediately to brood over our lives even though our waking hours were beginning to be haunted by impending disaster. It was obvious that we must do something, try to outwit the inevitable. Phyllis was most anxious to get back to London, where there might be some kind of a basis from which to build our joint lives. I had few objections to raise against her proposal. I indicated that I would agree to it if the manager refused to reinstate me at the colliery. I did obtain an interview. The manager was adamant. There was to be no place for me in the mine.

I have often wondered about just what might have happened had he given me back my employment. As it happened, he did me a great favour. At the time it appeared bleak and without hope. In London I would have only my unskilled labour to offer to any prospective employer. And so it proved. Having assented to my wife's proposal, we made the journey away from my native habitation wherein I had found it difficult to rehabilitate myself. I did not take wings away from the coal measures; I simply went by bus like a departing prodigal who had grown weary of scanty fare that was offered at the feast of dreadful toil.

There was only my own poor self to blame for this parlous condition. I had spoken and written rashly, sometimes boldly. The northerner treasures the bold son, but he disapproves of all rash behaviour. In addition to contesting the Shields Ward for a seat on the borough council and failing, I had moved enthusiastically within the Communist-controlled Minority Movement, a political departure that held the trade union movement captive for some time, but was now beginning to fade away. But, overall, I had become conscious of a deep aversion to the mines, and utterly out of commendation of the increasing intensity of the productive process. I could have gone to my father and asked him for a job, or to my brother, who was of some importance in another coal complex, but I did not for I knew that I would embarrass them.

It was painful to be lost and alone in the land that had fostered my being.

We came back to London.

Phyllis' mother had been alone with her two daughters for most of her married life. Consequently I was little more than an intruder in their little home in Princes Square, SE11.

One of the thirteen children of a farm labourer and his wife who fared ill on the fields that lie beautifully spread on the slopes of the Blackdown Hills, she had made her way to London and had 'gone into service'. She had married a Southwark cockney who had been in the same infantry platoon as her brother, and was present when the lad was killed somewhere in the South African War. After the birth of her third child – which died – the father had failed in his conjugal duties and the marriage had drifted into a slow dissolution. Undaunted, the stubborn lady had gone into the landlady business, and by the time I came on the scene she was possessed of the free-hold of the house in Princes Square.

Somehow we squeezed ourselves and our furniture into that little house. My first object was to get a job. I duly reported at the Employment Exchange in Walworth Road. Phyllis, too, looked out for a job, and was successful. I had some time to wait. It was not a happy employment which I secured. The work was in the smoked bacon department of David Greig and Co., near to the Old Vic. Into the yard each morning trundled two huge horse-drawn drays laden with newly cured sides of bacon packed in sacking, four sides to the pack. These we off-loaded and carried on our shoulders into the smoking chambers, huge affairs devoted to the hanging of the sides of bacon within a reek of smoke obtained by burning masses of sawdust on the floor below. My duty was to help lift each sack on to a table, cut away sacking, watch the foreman sprinkle the inner part of the flesh with some kind of meal, and help in the hoisting to the hanging rods some twelve feet above.

For the better part of the day we prepared the kiln, and at the end of the day we closed the great doors and left the smoke to do its own work. We had always plenty to do about the yard. The other kiln had to be emptied and the vans loaded for the drivers to take to the many shops scattered about London. The kiln which we had emptied had then to be made ready for the next day's smoking.

This job lasted until Whitsuntide. I suppose I was discharged because the cockney desire for commendable smoked ham and bacon had slackened off. I was not sorry to 'take my cards'. I was not unemployed for very long when I found employment in the engineering works of Messrs. Waygood-Otis Ltd, near the Elephant and Castle. The continously moving stairway had just arrived in the metropolis, and the American firm was by then fully organised to meet and supply the demand of the Underground and the large shops for this kind of simple transportation. As a result, work went on continuously round the clock.

It was the noisiest factory I ever experienced. Built over an area much larger than a football pitch, the organisation within was impressive. Down the centre of the main shop were the milling and drilling banks of machines, all devoted to the production of parts to decisive measurements. Here the raw castings were shaped and cozened into beautiful elements of the ultimate machinery. The idea of individual powering of the machines had not then been established, and, consequently, each machine was powered by a belt passsing over the machine and round the great wheels attached to the spindle that ran above along the entire length of the bank. The power was 'thrown off' when the mechanic switched a wooden lever which disengaged the belt, but left it spinning and flapping until it was re-engaged.

There was no pause, no curtailment of the whirling wheels. They spun. The belts flapped. The machines groaned and ground and screamed in all their own distinctive, irrepressible and distressful agonies. Noises thumped out a hellish drumming accompaniment to the screechings of the various mouldings as these were submitted to their incessant impalements. Strange noises from magnificent machines penetrated the roarings of that unholy ear-piercing clamour. There were machines which contributed their own specific screams which punctured the vast uproar with indescribable pain. Phosphor bronze castings were transformed into cogwheels that were a delight to the eye. Within that factory beauty was given birth amid a tumult that pursued peace to the end of imagination.

Men communicated with each other by signs and lip which would have put the best of racecourse tick-tack men to shame. When actual conversation became imperative, a pantomime of ear-to-mouth and an almost senile interchanging of nods ensued that was impressively funny to watch. Above the banks of machines hung a moving crane that was hardly ever at rest, hugging the great mouldings and lowering them down upon the beds of the appropriate machines, or carrying away the finished product. Beyond, on the gantry which ran round the four sides of the building, were machines, worked by men or boys, that contributed their own havocs of noise to the horrendous cacophony below. At times the entire building seemed to be ripped apart by a prolonged incandescence perpetrated in the welding department. Presses thumped out small pieces from sheets of tin plate continuously, while other machines thrust their own brands of noise into the unceasing clamour.

The vast place writhed and groaned throughout the twenty-four hours of the first five days of each week, and sometimes through the Saturday, in a paroxysm of production.

Mine was the job of the floor labourer. In addition to lending a hand at whatever task required it, I had to sweep and keep clean the gangways between the machines and pick up the millings and drillings, the swarth, and carry it to the dumps across the yard. As each machine ground or gouged out its own precise indentations over the faces of the wrought iron mouldings, its rejections were thrown upon the floor. The long twistings of steel, that were sculpted out of the important parts of the product, had to be gathered up separately. So, too, the phosphor bronze scratchings and scrapings. They were carried by me to their appropriate places in the scrap yard. To be engaged for any time helping the operator of the multiple driller meant that as soon as I was released I would have a long job sweeping up the shop. The trips outside, however, even in winter, were happy interludes of peace.

Despite it all, I was happy, for I was making a contribution to the peace of our family life. We had hours of great tranquillity. The stark gospel of political change was laid aside. We pursued the sunlight when we could. One of our favourite escapes was the trip from Epsom to Box Hill, which we made on foot. There were others, too, all made on foot, over the common and through Richmond Park, and the breathtaking view of the Thames from above the town.

The top floor flat of our little house in those days had quite a good rating as a home for any married, or unmarried couple. It overlooked what once had been a most pleasant square.

The small flat came to be occupied by a couple, Dick and Moira Beech. Dick, who bore a striking resemblance to Mr de Valera, was a Yorkshireman from Hull. He spoke the dialect without shame. Until he met Moira Connolly he had roamed the world. His purpose, politically, had long been squandered and now he was anxious to lead the proletariat to its 'last fight', which he was convinced it had to face. His travels had brought him to the lee of the home of James Connolly, from which hide-out he captured the ginger-haired Moira and carried her off to London as soon as she had passed through medical training. Before settling down to life with Moira he had broken the iron ring with which the allies had encircled the young Soviet state, and had made his way, almost on foot, from Murmansk to Petrograd, where he had made himself known to Lenin and to Trotsky. He became a founder member of the Communist International, and he carried the medalion, that was struck to commemorate its inauguration, on his watch chain, very proudly. When I first made his acquaintance he was in the employ of Russian Oil Products. Later he was transferred to the offices of Anglo-Shipping, in Bush House. When the Soviet gentlemen who employed him insisted upon the loading of the SS Karl Marx by blackleg labour at a wharf in Port of London, and succeeded, his protests were so vociferous that they gave him the ukase: shut up or get out! Unfortunately for Dick there came a time when the clerks in Anglo-Shipping walked out in protest against something in the office. Dick was not affected, but he did become affected when the said gentlemen requested him to work in the 'black' office.

I can hear him now, telling me his story. 'What? You are asking me to blackleg! Me! You mean me!' he said between his teeth. 'But you can't blackleg when you work for the Soviet Union, Mr Beech,' one of them informed him. And Dick simply said, 'Go to hell!'

Before that happened, Moria became pregnant. Being the daughter of James Connolly, this was some event. Being a medical practitioner, she marched through her dolorous nine months without fear. Her return to the square with her babe was another thing. She must have help from her sister Fiona. And, as Fiona was afraid to travel alone, Mrs Connolly had to convoy her from Dublin to Kennington.

Phyllis' mother and Mrs Connolly joined together to administer to the needs of Moira and her daughter, as women have done throughout time 'who have been through it'. Over the days the two women became confidants, as women do, of those intimate things that are not secrets among women. They were akin in soul, proletarian kin. Before each other they opened all the packages that contained all their great sorrows. They talked about the infidelity of Mum's husband and they talked about the death of James Connolly.

'I wouldn't say that Jim was wrong when he went to lead the rebellion,' Mrs Connolly told her new friend. 'No, I wouldn't say that at all. Jim groaned so deeply over the disgraceful oppression of Ireland…an' you know what it' like when a man gets politics real bad, Mrs Varndell.'

I can see Mum nod. She could listen better than any woman I ever met. When you told her a story which held her interest she not only listened, but she repeated every word with her soundless lips.

'The doctor was kind to him in prison,' she went on. 'When I got to know his name I went to see him. I asked him if he thought they would execute him, an' he said he didn't think so, for, as he said, Jim was too bad wounded as it was. 'No, they won't do that, Mrs Connolly,' he said to me. 'The man's too wounded as it is. Why! I'm not at all sure that he will pull through all the trouble he's in now.' He smiled when he said it. He patted me hands, both of them.' She held her hands on her lap, patting each one in turn by the other, just as the man had done. 'He comforted me, he did. "You believe me, Mrs Connolly;" he said to me. "They never execute a wounded man. Before they do they must get him better so they can do it proper. Jim has a good chance. It's probably better he is wounded, for by the time he's recovered the anguish will've passed from the souls of the English."'

There was a long silence before she spoke again.

'And with that comfort in me heart I went back home to attend to the wants of the childer,' she said. 'They were all helpless in their own anxieties for their father, you see. An' I was a bit encouraged, even though I knew that Jim had done a great wrong in the eyes of the English.' She paused, as if she was trying to break through the barrier of her own grief. 'But none of us need to have been,' she said. 'Ye see, they didn't let him get better at all. They took my Jim an' fastened him in a sitting position, and they carried him out an' put him, ill as he was, afore the firing squad, and they shot him. They shot him...my Jim...'

There was yet another pause and then she spoke. 'You see, I just didn't take it all in,' she said. 'The doctor came to see me. I never saw a man so angry. He told me what they had done. He told me that they never consulted him about what they were going to do. They did it all in secret. He said that he would have done all he could to stop it.' She shook her head, her beautiful old head. Her face became wrinkled with the savage pain all over again. 'But it would not have happened to matter,' she said. 'They would have shot him later. In their cruelty they saved my Jim a deal o' pain.'

A few days later she was gone back to Dublin.

Dick and Moira found a larger flat in the Brixton Road and went there to follow the tracks of their own lives.

They had four children. Their one boy they called Dick. They prospered after Dick took the plunge to found a paper which he called, *The Small Trader*. He held on to his membership of the Communist Party until the 'King Street bunch', as Bob Ellis always designated them, expelled him.

Bob was the greatest friend I ever had. His family originated in Pembrokeshire. He died in that county. We first met at college functions. He had been to the college with the group which held Aneurin Bevan. When Bob was a child his father migrated to the Rhondda, and there worked as a miner. Bob grew up in the great militant period of the South Wales miners, the period when Noah Ablett was the John the Baptist of the left wing, and Dai Lloyd Jones was the flame triumphant over all the Rhondda Valley. Those must have been boisterous times. The mining clan in South Wales still drinks the mead of those trenchant years. Poor Dai! The orator in both the languages! When poverty and unemployment swept him out of the coalfield he came to rest in Brixton, as a milkman. When Dai Lloyd and Tom Mann met there was no place in the enjoyment for any smaller man in the communist movement.

When I renewed Bob's acquaintance he was living in Camden Town. He was editing the Minority Movement weekly journal, *The Worker* from a little office in one of the buildings on the projection of the two streets that conjoin at King's Cross. During any of the periods of my unemployment, holidays, and free weekends I went there to lend him a hand with the paper. I did book reviews and wrote articles on the mining scene, and some times a short story. I enjoyed going to the office and helping to sub-edit the paper. Bob always brought a large parcel of brown bread, butter and cheese sandwiches. He was an enthusiastic drinker of tea. We made gallons of the stuff. We were often joined in our feasts by Krishna Menon. How we ate. How we talked.

Krishna Menon in those days was a lonely Indian who existed in the most meagre circumstances. He always came to the office in the hopes of refreshing himself. How he existed he did not trouble to tell us, and we did not ask. We took him for granted, a charming, harmless Indian. He did not trade textiles like many of his compatriots. If he did, he did not tell us. He wore quite threadbare clothes and down at heel shoes. He carried a torn satchel. Where he went to when he left the office was his own business.

Bob and I were both delighted when we learned that he had gained his own rightful place as India's representative at the League of Nations, for we knew that he would be an acquisition to the gentlemen who foregathered there. There came the day when he became a cabinet minister. I grieved when I learned of his fall from grace.

It was while I was working at Waygood's that Harold Shaylor, who at that time was London editor and manager for Brentano's Ltd, offered to publish a novel which I had asked Phyllis to take to his office on her way to work. I became wildly excited at the prospect of publication. I had worked a long time on the story. Shaylor thought the title, *The Gate of a Strange Field*, which I had given it eminently suitable. It was while I was writing the novel that I read H.G. Wells' novel, *Meanwhile*, and came across the sentence in which he catechised the General Council of the Trade Union Congress, as being 'like sheep at the gate of a strange field.'

Publication, I anticipated, might be a breakthrough for me. Shaylor held out high hopes of success, and these were enhanced when Appleton's took it for publication in New York. Unfortunately for me, the novel fell with an enormous, but silent thud, in both countries. I had anticipated the applause and I was rewarded with silence, a silence that reminded me of most of the places in a mine.

To my surprise, Shaylor was by no means discomfited by the failure of my novel, and asked me to get on with another one. I offered him the manuscript of the novel which had been published in Russia, but he rejected the idea, preferring, as he said, one written outside and away from the mines. One could not make one's fortune writing about coal pits, he told me. I had already cogitated a novel, and I set out to write it. Before Shaylor could publish the new novel, *Journey Beyond*, Brentano's liquidated all their commitments in London, and Harold Shayler Ltd took on from there. Although the novel received a sympathetic review on the BBC book programme, by Duff Cooper, it has sunk without trace.

In Helsinki, Maisky was quite excited and sent for both novels. On his recommendation the Moscow house, Zemlya i Fabrika (Fields and Factories) undertook the translations and published both novels. Both were quite widely discussed and caused much interest in Russia, as I found out when I got there.

What did interest me, even if it did distress me considerably, was the angry note of interrogation and criticism which my poor little efforts stirred in the workers' press. Bob did touch the novel in *The Worker* more candidly than kindly. The first review of any consequence came in the *Workers' Weekly*, and it proved to be a slating, incoherent at times, which hurt me deeply. But I had to wait until T.A. Jackson got down to reviewing it in *The Sunday Worker* before I got what might be termed a real dressing down. This did surprise me, for while the novel was 'going the rounds of the papers' I chanced to meet Jackson in Grays Inn Road. As he approached me he held out his hand in greeting, shook it heartily, and burst into a laugh. There was a scene, he told me, that made him laugh. He thought it was immensely funny. I thought he appreciated my novel, but his subsequent reviews proved to be the opposite of his approval. In the sunday paper he made an astonishing attack, and not content with that he came up with an ever more bitter review in *Labour Monthly*. I have a feeling that Palme Dutt, the editor, must have been ill or abroad when the review was fitted into the magazine, for shortly after it appeared he wrote to me and offered his apologies for Jackson's outrageous attack. He even went on to urge me to join the Party.

The strange thing was that Jackson and I had been friends from the days when he ran in double harness with Bonar Thompson in the north east. He was then the organiser of the NCLC in that area. Needless to say our friendship went cold after his second savage slash at the book. He must have meant all he said, and did not have any reason to change his views upon it. Why? I do not know. He could not forget either the book or its author. When Alick West published his little book, *Crisis and Criticism*, he actually devoted a whole chapter to a consideration of *The Gate of a Strange Field*, which followed his analysis of James Joyce's *Ulysses*! That chapter Jackson seized upon in order to pour a further stream of vituperation upon my defenceless head. And in the pages of *Labour Monthly*, then edited by Palme Dutt.

I have often wondered why this should have happened. Jackson was by no means a formidable man. He was too dishevelled a personality ever to be a cut-throat. I felt profoundly sorry for him, for he deserved a better fate than the one King Street handed out to him. His immense intellectual ability was recognised throughout the world. He even debated with George Lucaks on the subject of Walter Scott, and won the argument. He was kept away from all the flesh pots that were boiling in King Street. When Trotsky thrust out his tongue and called the burgeoning Stalin brigade 'a host of Thermidorians' it was left to poor Tommy Jackson to tell the communist world who the Thermidorians were. He was the spiritual father of all the hippies of a later day and generation, but he trundled his lean frame and flew his long hair over the communist field. His virile pen was always at the ready. Ribaldry of the most hilarious clung to his tongue. Oratory that was almost as magnificent as that of Edmund Burke was his for the speaking. And yet he was left to hunger for the bread he could not earn, and to thirst for the admiration that was rarely granted. He strode all the pavements of London with the intentness of George Gissing, often unwashed, always undignified, curiously unaware of his forlorn appearance. His was a brilliant mind. Perhaps I ought not to mind because it was my fate to be so often castigated by him.

Before any reviews of *Journey Beyond* could come to hand, Bob Ellis and I were on our way to Leningrad.

Chapter Seventeen

I met Nikolai Minsky in New Oxford Street and I told him that I was soon to go to Russia. He did not appear to be excited, but he did wish me well. A few posts later I received a card from Zina Vengerova suggesting that we should meet at some restaurant near where she worked. When we did meet I found her to be quite excited at the prospect of my visit to her native land. She presumed that I would be going by boat to Leningrad, and when I confirmed this she told me that there were two or three things she would like me to do when I landed there.

'You must visit Lydia Slonimsky, who is now translating your novel,' she said. 'She lives in Leningrad. You must meet her,' she went on. 'She is my nephew Sasha's wife. I have not met her at all, but I believe that she is a delightful person. As a matter of fact I would like you to take to her a parcel of gifts. Will you take them, please?'

I assured her that I would be delighted to do so.

'She is experiencing some difficulty with your novel,' she told me. 'If you can arrange a meeting when you get there you might help her.'

I need not have worried on that score, for though Maisky had suggested to Zemlya i Fabrika that it should publish the novel, it did not. The opposition of RAPP – the Russian Association of Proletarian Writers – had been too much for it to overcome.

'And there is another thing,' she said after we had disposed of Lydia. 'I want you to get into touch with Eugen Zamyatin. You must meet him, for he is a great personage in our literature. You need not say anything to anybody about this. You will find him on the telephone. All you have got to do is ring him up and ask to meet him.'

'Then what do I do?' I asked.

'First, you must get hold of a copy of our novel,' she told me. She always called her translation 'our novel'. 'It will be on the stalls. Take it to Zamyatin and tell him that I would like him to read it, and then see about giving it a good push. He will do it. We have always been the greatest of friends.'

Before I left her, when we were in the street, she told me that under no circumstance whatever must I write to her in the usual way. 'All you will do is send what you have to tell me on a picture post card. No other way is permissible,' she informed me.

On the day prior to my departure on the Sibier, the parcel arrived at Princes Square, and this I stowed away in my luggage.

Bob was aboard the vessel when I arrived at Hays Wharf. She lay close up to London Bridge. A Polish boat was at the quay unloading a cargo of butter and cheese. There was the usual clatter of cranes and a great deal of shouting. The purser received me and showed me to a second class cabin. He then conducted me to the dining room and handed me over to the immigration officials. I handed over my passport, answered their questions and went back to the cabin.

Bob was lying, fully dressed, on his bunk. There were four in the cabin.

'Got here, then,' he said. 'Take that bunk. We might get full up before we sail.'

The night became dark.

The next morning we went up on deck for a breath of air and found that we were at sea. The pilot had been dropped at the Sunk Lightship. It was quite dull. A scudding rain swept over the vessel. We went down for breakfast, where we found two other passengers, both American engineers. We made friends. From that moment we settled down to boredom. Luckily I had Eckermann's book on Goethe.

The unsettled weather continued until we got through the Heligoland Bight, when it changed and we had glorious autumnal weather all the way to Leningrad. We became mildly excited once we had passed through what appeared to me to be a most primitive sluice and into the Kiel Canal. We made a slow journey through the canal in beautiful sunshine. From the top deck there was much to see that was interesting. The immense length of the waterway, its comparative narrowness, and the flat, wet green of the level countryside added up to something that was most impressive. A prudent husbandry tended all that we could see. The rainproofs covering the browsing cattle intimated a care for animals that was foreign to British farming practices. The bridges that spanned the canal above the masts of the ships fitted into a scene that never forgot to charm. The population must have been otherwise engaged when we passed through, for we rarely saw a human figure. Sometimes a cowbell jangled oddly and a dog barked somewhere in the distance. One felt that one was intruding upon a scene sacred to Wordsworth.

Out in the Baltic the world with its sea and its sky offered us an unforgetable journey. The very waters appeared to be under duress, and so, unmindful of ship and men. The sun held aloft its light all day. The waters glistened their tears in rare beauty. Throughout the night the sea sank into dreams and gave grant to loneliness to eavesdrop on the souls of sleeping men. All things, even the ship, were enveloped in the soft foldings of a deep silence, a deep abounding stillness which absorbed and rendered mute the swishings of the ship's stern. The tremendous stillness and the beauty of the moonless heavens in their embroidery of stars hovered over the ship, as if to comfort it as it transgressed the peace of a sleeping world. Were I to forget all things that have come to delight me except one I would be content to hold on to the memory of that voyage from Kiel to Leningrad. Summer was drifting into the past experience of the earth and was whispering to the snows and the winds. One could almost feel the pulse of time as one leaned over the ship's rail and drank in the silence that attends the rest of the seasons.

After two or three days there came the excitement. Leningrad in the morning. A newer wind rose to brush its hand over the water that filled the delta upon which the city of Leningrad is built. As we approached, the city seemed to withdraw itself and become shy. Viewed from the top deck it appeared to be scattered over too much water. The distant buildings peeped shyly over the edges of the waters. It seemed to be a place of great peace.

We had picked up a few passengers at Kiel, and they must have been quite privileged persons, for Bob, the Americans and myself were the last to go through customs. The ship had drawn up by a landing stage that stood out stark from the waters, or so it appeared to us, and upon this we had to stay until called in to the office by a uniformed man. I was the last to be called in. The wind blew cold about me as I sat out in the open sky on an open boarded platform through which I could see the water. It was a most inhospitable place for anybody to lodge even for a few minutes.

There might have been some mistake in the shepherding process, for when I was brought in out of the cold I was greeted warmly. I heard one of the men mutter, 'Gislop. Pod Vlastyu Uglya.' They gave my baggage a quick glance and passed me into the care of an Intourist guide.

We arrived in Leningrad in September, 1930.

We were taken to the Hotel Europa and lodged in a vast room along with the two American engineers. We had breakfast with them on the following day, and we did not see them again. They must have been whisked off to some engineering project.

After a wash and a brush up we went down by the lift to the entrance hall, there to await the pleasure of our guide, who was to take us to dinner. While we stood I noted the bookstall, and there, sure enough, lay a copy of 'our book'. I bought it for something like two shillings and stuffed it into my pocket. It was while I was doing this that I heard a voice say:

'Bob! Why would you believe it? And Harold Heslop, too! What the hell are you both doing here?'

It was Arthur Horner, clad in one of those monstrous fur hats that the well-to-do Russians wear.

Arthur had come down by the stairs from his room. He had already dined. He was delighted to see us both, for we were old friends. The guide appeared and before following her to the dining room, we made arrangements to meet immediately after our meal. The guide sat with us at the table and when the first course arrived she got up and went away.

We ate a good meal. We were both anticipating a chat with Horner. After we had eaten, Bob suggested that we should go and get our overcoats. I demurred on account of the cold wind that was blowing outside, and also on account of the racket the radio was making from each tramway post. Bob simply led me to the lift and to our room.

'We've got to meet him outside,' he told me. 'There are things we cannot talk about in the hotel.'

'But why?' I demanded.

'Because he is not here on a holiday,' he explained. 'He's been here sometime, with his wife and his youngest daughter, in Moscow. I didn't expect to meet him in Leningrad. He said he had been over to the Putilov works.' He came closer to me. 'If you must know,' he said in a very low voice, 'he's here to be re-educated. Now can you grasp it, you blockhead?'

The light dawned. 'I could stay here,' I said.

'I don't want you to stay here,' he told me. 'I want the thing to look as casual as possible. Don't be a child, Harold!'

Bob Ellis had been far too long a technician in King Street not to know all the whys and wherefores of the party. He had been a member of the Political Bureau, for many years, and he had taken part in the debate on the suggestion that Arthur should go into voluntary exile in Russia for a specific period. Poor Arthur had been found guilty of a lapse in leadership. He had been reluctant to go, but had bowed to the pressures. His term was now almost ended and before returning to South Wales he was being given VIP treatment.

Looking back on that episode I can now afford to smile. We walked about Leningrad until we found out that Bob was thirsting for a cup of tea. We found a small cafe in some side street, and thither we went to slake Bob's aching thirst. The 'cafe' could not have been worse.

I paid scant attention to their undercover conversation. Inner party discussions were alien to me. What interested me was the manner in which they would speak to each other and then break off to drag me into a conversation about Arthur's domestic affairs. He told me that his wife preferred the Rhondda to Moscow, and had been on the point of packing up and going home when some friend suggested that she should take the little girl and teach her Russian. This she did, in three short weeks. We met the family when we got to Moscow. They inhabited a room in a tenement. Their largest piece of furniture was the bed. Poor Arthur! What he had to pay in order to become the elected secretary of the Miners' Federation of Great Britain!

Bob was quite indignant about the exile. He was deeply unhappy because he had been partly responsible for its execution upon the little man. He need not have worried, for the same sentence was passed upon him some years later.

It came about in a most curious way.

Arthur Cook was lying in the Manor House Hospital dying of cancer. We both went along to see him. When we got there we found that he had a visitor, none other than Sir Oswald Mosley, who was still a member of the Labour Party. We sat chatting the small afternoon away. Bob, aided by Cook, held deep argument with Mosley. Cook did most of the laughing at the sallies.

Bob must have impressed Mosley, for when he broke with the Labour Party and set out to plan his fascist movement, his first real job was to inaugurate a paper. With this in view, he approached Bob and offered him the editorship. What Bob ought to have done was obvious. He ought to have reported the offer to Harry Pollitt. This he failed to do. Some time later, some months later, in a heated discussion in King Street he told Pollitt about the offer he had received. The fact he had not reported the approach which had been made was regarded as being desperately serious. The fact that he had refused the offer did not in any way offset the heinous crime of his silence. The matter was reported to Moscow, and Bob was faced with a term of exile and re-education similar to that undergone by Horner.

Bob refused and was sacked from all the positions he held in the Party. Ultimately his membership lapsed. Some time later he joined the staff of the *Daily Express*. He resigned that lucrative job when he disapproved of the paper's attitude to Russia. In all things, Bob Ellis was a positive man. Politics as well as journalism were for him purposively educative attitudes and not an indiscriminate determination of evil.

After that night in Leningrad was spent, Arthur Horner drifted away into the anonymity of Soviet Russia. I was prepared for that because he and I were far separated on the philosophical front. He was a trade union activist, a simple politician who held a contemptuous disregard of capitalism. Marx and he were strangers, as unaware of each other as were Marx and the leading exponents of trade union leadership. Harry Pollitt was unaware of a Marxian attitude to life outside the pamphlet front that had been erected over the years by King Street under the facade of Martin Lawrence, publishers.

Bob became restless as soon as Horner had gone. He began to prepare for his journey to Moscow. He could see that I was interested in Leningrad. He laughed at a proposed visit to the Hermitage, and, without saying farewell he caught the train to Moscow. I could see he was perturbed about something, probably about Horner, and, as a member of the Party he was most anxious to get in touch with Losovsky.

As soon as he was gone I got in touch with Lydia Slonimsky. She came to the hotel for me immediately after receiving my telephone call. She insisted on talking to me in the public room. After enquiring about her husband's relations in London she went away, carrying the parcel I had brought away with her. It was agreed that after I had seen the Hermitage she would come for me and take me to her home.

Recalling her over the years, she was a young woman of average height, very good looking and slenderer than the ordinary Russian woman of her age. She was dark and cheerful. Her voice was gentle and cultured. She came for me in the afternoon. My morning had been swift. The Hermitage we went over, and then we made a viewing of the facade of the Winter Palace. On, then, to the statue of Peter the Great and a cold walk along the bank of the Neva, which was beginning to freeze on the surface.

We walked to Lydia's flat in a block of houses on Vasilievsky Island. I was surprised when she introduced me to her son, a boy nearing school age, which was seven, and I was pleased to meet her mother, who appeared to be part of the family. Sasha Slonimsky was not there when I arrived. He joined us at tea. He was some kind of executive in some shipyard.

'Did you like the parcel I brought you?' I asked her when we got into the house.

I thought she was going to cry. 'Why did she have to send me marmalade?' she asked me. 'It is horrible. Why did she not send me some stockings?'

It was when I suggested to her that she should ask Zamyatin to meet me that she became somewhat alarmed.

'Zamyatin! But why?' she cried. 'It may be impossible.'

The mother joined in her protest.

I stood firm on my request. I explained that all I was to do was to carry out Zina's request.

'But, surely, Aunt Zina must be aware of things!' Lydia expostulated.

'I don't understand,' I began, but she cut me short.

'It will not be possible to see him,' she said with assurance. 'He lives alone...I mean...nobody ever visits him...'

I suggested that if it was all that difficult for her we had better let the matter drop. I could, I said, easily arrange it when I got back to Intourist's office. At this, Lydia shook her head. 'The pity is that Aunt Zina does not quite understand,' she offered in excuse. 'It would be much better if you did not try to see him.'

On my exclamation she turned to her mother for help. They went into a heated discussion. The little boy squatted on the floor to play with a toy.

In the end Lydia did ring Zamyatin. Much to her surprise, her request for his number was granted, and a halting conversation in Russian followed, that is on Lydia's part. She did most of the listening. When she finally hung up the very old fashioned receiver on its hook she told me that Zamyatin would be pleased to see me the following day at three-thirty in the afternoon. Lydia was most curt when she gave me his message, and for some time thereafter acted like a maid who had made a mistake and was reluctant to confess. I can now feel sorry for her. At the time I did regard it as being amusing.

At the hotel every one of the Intourist staff became disconcerted when I asked for their help in guiding me to the venue of my meeting with the author. I could see that they were quite dubious, from the manager down to the latest recruit. I was taken aside and asked why I wished to see the man.

By this time I sensed more than an official reluctance to have anything to do with the writer. How had I got in touch with him? I pointed out that we in England had the telephone. All I wanted to do was to present him with a copy of my novel. Had I brought the novel with me from England? No, I bought it at the stall in the foyer. I produced the book. The girl who had sold it to me testified to the accuracy of my statement.

I was taken to one side by the manager and asked if Madame Vengerova-Minski had given me a letter, or any form of communication, a personal note, anything like that, to take to Zamyatin.

'She did not,' I replied. 'And if it is of any interest to you,' I added, 'it is my intention to communicate with the Minsky's by picture post card only.' And with that I produced a picture post card which showed a clear photograph of the statue of the Tsar and the clear wording on the pedestal that stood at that time near the railway station.

'You spoke to gospodin Zamyatin on the phone?' he asked.

'Oh, yes,' I replied, giving a bland smile. 'He speaks excellent English.'

'Very well, Mister Heslop,' he said. 'I will see if we can make arrangements to take you to the house. You will not mind if our guide remains with you throughout the meeting with Zamyatin?'

'She will be most kindly welcome,' I said.

I felt somewhat distressed. There was no one to whom I could confide. I had a feeling that I had not acted correctly, and that I might have transgressed the protocol.

Chapter Eighteen

Intourist assigned the same guide to accompany me to the home of Zamyatin. We went all the way by tram-car. Some of it we had to walk.

'We pass Smolny on our way,' she said to me. 'Would you like me to show you round? We have plenty of time.'

'I just wouldn't like to miss it,' I told her.

We left the tram-car and walked into Smolny, a great, lonely building that somehow reminded me of a vast nonconformist church. We passed into the great hall that has come down from 1917. A huge painting of Lenin gesticulating before an immense crowd stood far back of the platform, a picture of little artistic importance. My guide expressed some distaste of the picture and the artist. I was curiously impressed. I was glad to be there. For me it was a place that had held the sounds of vast periods of assertion and the loud murmurs of deep discussions by men who had achieved their victory. We went to a room which had been occupied by Trotsky. After glancing around the place we left it, and she closed the door almost reverently. Trotsky had yet to be impaled. We tramped along many passages until we came to the room which Lenin and Krupskaya had occupied. Here, reverence deepened into worship.

It was by no means a large room. It had been preserved in every detail as the couple had left it. There was a writing table, hard chairs and kitchen utensils. A screen concealed the two iron bedsteads upon which the couple had slept. There was nothing dignified about the place. As a matter of fact Smolny made but little appeal outside the physical act of revolution.

Outside, in the road, we waited for another tram-car which would carry us to our ultimate destination. When it came we boarded it and trundled along the streets. We passed the wall over which Peter Kropotkin had made his escape, but we did not get off the tram to inspect it. We came at last to the place where we had to disembark. We walked some distance until at last we came to a gate beyond which stood a rather large house. We walked up the short drive to the front door, which was reached by three or four steps. We stood there to await the answer to the knock delivered on the door by the guide. A woman opened the door, whom I took to be a newly-made widow. She bowed slightly and stood aside so that we could enter. She did not utter a word to either of us. Closing the front door, she moved on along the hall to another which she opened and went through the same pantomime. When we had entered the room she closed the door and went away.

A not too tall man rose from behind a writing table and offered us a gentle bow. 'Please be seated,' he said, indicating the two chairs which had been set for that purpose. He did not offer us a hand in greeting. He sat down in his revolving chair and pushed it on its casters against a bookcase. Nearby a roll-topped desk stood open, crammed with papers and files. The desk was over-laden with books and the paraphernalia of a business office. The piles on one side almost reached the ceiling. The writing table held the materials of his work in progress.

Eugen Zamyatin looked a well-fed, well-proportioned and healthy man. He was a shade above the average height. He wore no beard. His head was not cropped close to the skull after the prevailing fashion. The moustache was barbered after the once-prevailing English fashion, cropped to a bristle-like texture not permitted to roam from the upper lip. The cheek bones held the Slav elevation and prominence. The cheeks held the dark sheen of close shaving. The eyes were not deeply imprisoned beneath his darkly shaded brows, but they gleamed with humour, ironical humour perhaps. The overhang of his eyebrows complemented in some strangely defined way the stern, almost English bourgeois aspect. He was dressed in a dark suit of some not very elegant cut, but by no means Russian.

After a few soft sentences in Russian to the girl he turned to me. 'I am still at some loss,' he said, 'to understand just why you have made this call upon me, Mister Heslop. Perhaps you will explain after you have told me how my old friends, the Minskys, are. How is Vengerova, please?'

'She was quite well the last time I saw her,' I replied. 'That was the day before I sailed. A little bronchial, perhaps.'

He smiled. 'She always was,' he said. 'It is most pleasant to hear that she is still so vigorous…in literature.' Here he smiled again. 'And Kola? How is he? Very old and very well, eh?'

I nodded.

'It is grand to know about old friends,' he commented. 'Now, perhaps you will tell me why Vengerova asked you to call upon me?'

I handed him the copy of my novel. 'She wanted you to have this,' I said.

He thumbed the book. 'You wrote this in English?' he asked. 'And Zina Vengerova translated it?' He did not wait upon a reply. 'It ought to be a happy conjunction,' he went on to say. 'Just how many books has that indefatigable lady translated, I wonder. Oh! So Maisky introduces it. That is most interesting. You have met him, I presume?'

'Not recently,' I replied. 'I met him a few times when he was in London.'

'Ah yes! I forgot. He is in Finland now.' He reflected a moment. 'I will be pleased to read his preface.'

'Madame Vengerova thought that you might be interested enough to…to promote the book…'

'Do a bit of log-rolling. Is that it?'

I nodded to him on the other side of his smile.

'I do not think that Vengerova is fully aware…'

At that moment the silent, raven-black woman came into the room carrying a tray of glasses, each filled with tea. Silently she offered the tray to us, and then placed the tray on Zamyatin's table. When she had attended to our sugar requirements, she withdrew.

After sipping at his glass, Zamyatin set it down on a book lying on his table. He looked at me. 'I cannot quite place you,' he told me. 'Are you a 'Geordie', may I ask?'

I was so taken by surprise that I broke into a laugh. His question almost stunned me. A Geordie, indeed!

'I *was* born in south-west Durham,' I answered, 'at a place not far from a town called Bishop Auckland…'

'Near Darlington,' he interposed.

'That's right,' I said. 'Do you know it?'

'You left it and went south?'

'I've been away from the area five years thereabouts…'

'Quite long enough to corrupt your dialect,' he observed. 'But I catch the Tyneside dialect in your speech. Am I right?'

'I lived quite a long time in South Shields.'

He mused a while. 'South Shields,' he murmured. 'Yes, that is right.'

He smiled. 'And so you went to London and met Vengerova. Why are you visiting Russia?'

The guide intervened quietly. 'Mister Heslop is on his way to Kharkov…to the Conference,' she told him.

He barely acknowledged her intrusion. 'Is the British delegation large?' he asked.

'Only two.'

He glanced at the girl. 'You know the Ukraine?' he asked.

She nodded, and remained silent.

'I recall the first time I went there,' he said. 'I found the language quite different from Russian. It took me about four hours to get over the not inconsiderable differences.'

There was a pause. Then he took command. 'I happen to know the Tyneside very well,' he told me.' I liked the people very much. I also liked their strange, musical dialect. Often I found it most amusing. I was there during the war, in the shipyards. You know Newcastle?'

'I prefer Shields.'

'South Shields,' he whispered. 'Sooth Sheels! I never learned to sing the Tyneside speech.'

Thereupon he became brisk. 'You will see Vengerova when you get back to London,' he said to me. 'When you do meet her and Nikolai Maximovitch will you please offer them my kindest regards.' He waited for my nod of assent, the while putting his fingers to his lips, almost caressing his moustache. 'You must also inform them both that the opportunities I have to propagate …to encourage the sales of your novel are very limited. Very limited indeed. That I will do all in my power she can rest assured.' He smiled. 'I will read it with interest,' he added, and went on, 'I do not think that she is fully aware of the fact that I am no longer as deeply concerned these days as I used to be in publishing and journalism. Tell her, please, that I cannot promise much. I am sure that she will understand.'

And with that, he stood up. We both rose. He gave the girl a grave bow. His hand sought mine and I felt his strong grip. He walked to the door and held it open. We uttered our 'good byes' and we followed him to the front door, which he opened. Again we exchanged bows. At the bottom of the steps I looked back. He was closing the door.

As we walked out of the gate, the girl said to me: 'Did you like him?'

'I thought he was quite charming,' I replied.

She shrugged expressively. 'I think he was neither nice nor charming,' she observed. 'He was courteous. Like all Russians, of course.'

Chapter Nineteen

There is not the slightest doubt that Leningrad is one of the most beautiful cities on this planet. Everything must have conspired to make it so as soon as Peter the Great conceived it. How it may have fared over the years since I was there I cannot imagine. Much that I saw and admired may now be no more. So intense and so long a bombardment to which it was subjected would remove a great many things and places from the consciousness of the people who dwell there. It is sad to reflect on the fact that many of those buildings which caused me to catch my breath by their sheer loveliness may no longer exist. But this is no time to grieve, even over the things of the imagination.

No matter how one viewed the city, and from whatever vantage point, the city as it then was felt its way into the human emotions with almost the tenderness of the new lover. The manner in which it is disposed over its land mass – mass forever grudged by the waters of the four rivers – and the way in which each is joined by superb bridges, and the manner in which the islands are subdivided by canals are remarkable beyond estimation. The bridges are ever a wonder as well as a revelation. The approach to the city from the sea is breathtaking. It appears to loom up almost reluctantly out of the immense expanse of water, and then, as one gets nearer, to encourage its most majestic buildings to stand up on tip toe to view the stranger. There is a loneliness of exquisite beauty hovering over the city that almost hushes one to reverence. The spires and towers reach up out of the waters in quiet worship of sea and sun, almost supplicating reverence and worship from the stranger, touching all to tearful gladness.

There is a bridge that carries the Nevsky Prospekt over a fairly wide canal to allow it to pierce straight into the heart of the city. It is the Anichkov Bridge. At each end of each parapet there is the sculpted figure of a man and a horse in different phases of tense struggle with each other. Both are naked. The impact upon the passer-by is so powerful and so total as to bring him to a halt and an admiration. Such a bridge stands upon one's memory for a long time. It is a great experience.

I recall the moment of my discovery.

I was with my guide, a charming girl.

'The bridge!' I gasped.

'We cross it,' she said gaily. 'That is why it was put there.'

I stood in mute wonder.

'Shall we go on now?' she asked, somewhat perplexed by my adoration.

'How much have you to show me after that?' I demanded.

She offered me anger. 'But this is outrageous,' she told me. 'Leningrad has more than a bridge to show you, you know!'

'Was that bridge here when Dostoevsky was alive?' I enquired.

'I do not know. Why do you ask?'

'I do not recall his ever describing it,' I said to her. 'Not even when he took that demented woman and the children begging.'

'Who went begging?' It was her turn to make a demand.

'Marmeladov's wife,' I said. 'In *Crime and Punishment*. You know?'

She smiled that supercilious smile a woman offers to a child whom she would dearly love to punish for some misdemeanour. And then she shook her head. I *knew* at that moment that she was unaware of Dostoevsky's novel. I glanced at her in amazement.

'In the Soviet Union we do not concern ourselves with Feodor Dostoevsky,' she said loftily.

I took the rebuke in silence. 'He's buried hereabouts, isn't he?' I asked quite humbly.

'Hereabouts! What is 'hereabouts'?' she cried. 'I do not know the word.'

She listened to my explanation of the term. 'No,' she said. 'Not hereabouts. Somewhere else. What a strange word.'

My guide was conducting me to a church which had been erected on the spot where a Tsar was assassinated. It was called 'the Church on the Blood'. That deed of murder and the erecting of the monstrously unbeautiful memorial church had occurred long after Dostoevsky was dead. And yet, I could not escape the feeling that I was walking with him.

As we approached the church we had to pass through two lines of mendicants, mostly women, who asked alms in a low sing-song. This astonished me. How often had the Russian novelist described this scene. Did the old Russia still exist, for heaven's sake?

It was a dumbfounding experience. This Soviet Union, which had so kindly received me, was now almost thirteen years gone from the revolution. The Bolsheviks, the successors and continuators – as they styled themselves – of Marx and Lenin had held undisturbed power over all that long stretch of time. Yet here were the forlorn women and the age-laden men, beseeching alms, and moaning their poverty sing-song into the winds of their own change. Thirteen years! Back in England, all we had asked for had been five years of untrammelled power so that Ramsay MacDonald and Phillip Snowden could banish all poverty and woe from the land. And here, in Russia, after thirteen years…

My guide, nose high, led me through the lane made by supplicating, black shawled women, like any bourgeois lady passing into the foyer of a theatre on her way to watch a risqué play.

The church was vast and high, crowded with people, upon all of whom there had fallen the distressing mantle of poverty. I glanced about me, searching for a Mishkin or a Madame Epanchin, but I espied neither. It intrigued me to discover the body of a church so divided up. We stood on the outer edge of the ikonostasis, not touching the demonstration of head bashing and floor kissing. Beyond were the worshippers pressing against the low rail which held them from contact with the officiating priests.

I was impressed by the actions of the people before the ikons. I could appreciate Tolstoi's cynical utterance as I watched them at their antics of worship. 'Send a fool about his prayers, and he will smash his forehead.' The experience was fascinating beyond all belief. I had never before entered a place of worship where there were no seats. It is the row on row of pews that add some formality to a church service. Here there was nothing, and the consequence was that everybody was at liberty to express himself or herself in whatever manner was felt to be most suitable. The priest, a fat man with an extraordinarily long beard, stood on a platform, holding a wooden cross in his hand, bowing and smiling at those who were outside the ikonostasis. In actuality, the proceedings, when we arrived, were drawing to a close. A priest was at the lectern reading loudly from the gospels. While he did so, the choir somewhere in the background spilled out a glory of sound. One just had to close one's eyes to hear some smaller Chaliapin booming out parts of the strange litany of his church. Strangely enough, the deep, trenchant bass and the incredibly high tenor were members of this furtive congregation.

The church was incredibly bare. The architecture was almost modern, very florid, as befitted a memorial to a murdered monarch, whose remembrance was excluded from the Soviet mind. The floor lay unscored by the feet of the generations. From where we stood we could watch the men and women performing their purposeless genuflections. The ikons were secured to the columns supporting the dome of the church within the reach of the lips of even the young. Men and women jostled each other as they strove to kiss a selected ikon. Not one seemed to pause during the commissioning of adoration. I have been in places where I have witnessed the irrepressible impulses of men and women to commit their own raptures and vehemences of worship, but I had not seen anything to compare with this atonement. Women abased themselves as frenziedly as men. Some even thumped their foreheads against the tiled roof as loudly as the men. They moaned. They slobbered. They cried. Women held up their babes to the higher ikons, and the holier pictures, and, despite their cries, held them in an ecstasy of their own devotion. It was profound and disgusting.

The singing ended. The reading fell into a low monotone. The fat priest descended to the gate, leaned over it, and held out his small hand-cross for each worshipper to kiss as they passed him by. When a frenzied woman tried to take the cross in her own hand, he held it aloft and spoke to her.

The church emptied. My guide intimated to me in a loud voice that I had seen all the show. She made ready to depart, and this she did without any ceremony of her own. She asked no blessing. She permitted me to do without. When we reached the open air the line of beggars seemed to have lengthened. All were holding out their hands. All wailed their individual woes. I looked for Dostoevsky, but he had gone.

A woman approached me, her claw-like hands seeking to take hold of my coat. The guide spoke sharply, and the poor wretch sank back into the line.

'Professionals!' she snapped into my ear. 'There is work for them all, but they do not wish.'

Such an experience in the land of the Soviets I had not anticipated.

Chapter Twenty

I left Leningrad on the night train. I marvelled at the fact that there could be four classes on a Russian train, first and second class wagons-lits, soft class and hard class. I asked myself just what had happened over the thirteen years that had passed. The destitute I had already seen. Now I was come face to face with a four class status. Before the train moved off the remaining three berths in my compartment were claimed by three Russian men. They spoke to me in their own language, and I replied in my own. At that there was a joint cry of, 'Anglichanin.'

I had acquired a trashy novel in the hotel, and with this I intended to pass the time away until the compartment was turned into a four bed affair. After a while one of them offered me a few words in my own language.

'You read Galsvorty?' he asked.

I handed him my book. He examined it and spelled out the title on his lips. Then he handed it back to me. 'Not Galsvorty,' he said.

'You know John Galsworthy?' I asked.

He nodded and did his best with the pronunciation I had given of the novelist's name.

The three men fell to discussing some topic in their own language until it was time to arrange the compartment. The man who had spoken to me took the bunk opposite to me. The other two climbed up against the roof of the cabin.

We all fell asleep.

During the night the train came to a halt and there was a stampede of people to the kiosks on the platform. My friend returned carrying two glasses of tea, one of which he offered me, and which I most gratefully received.

Moscow came with the early morning.

There was a slight covering of snow. There was also a harsh nip in the air. I left the train and made my way along the platform. I had been informed in Leningrad that Intourist would meet me at the station. I went in search of such a guide. I discovered a girl, and I stopped in front of her. She asked my name.

'No,' she said, almost tartly, 'I have no knowledge of you. You must go to the entrance and wait. I am sure that someone will come for you. Goodbye.'

I did as I was bidden, feeling not a little discomfitted. I had not expected the carpet, but I had expected somebody.

A voice spoke my name.

I looked round and beheld a tall chap holding out his hand in greeting. 'Sasha, me,' he said. 'Sasha Bubnov. No speak English.'

Thereafter he remained Sasha, a charming, helpful, tolerant Russian gentleman. He led me out of the station and helped me into a droshky which he had waiting. We went jingling off to nowhere. Whenever we came to some point of interest he gave me a light nudge in the ribs. He spoke the name of the street or the building. His dig was pronounced when we came into the Red Square, and even more pronounced when we passed Lenin's tomb.

I was in Moscow after that. The dream had come true.

Moscow was rummaging all about me. I was staying in a hotel-cum-residence affair a furlong or so from St Basil's Cathedral, clinging through the ages to the height above the Moscow River at the end of the great square. Opposite the hotel was a boyar's house which was maintained as a museum which nobody even bothered to enter. From the door of the hotel, a walk to the right took one on to the square, while a walk to the left led one to the Chinese Market where nothing else but books appeared to be sold.

That vast rectangle, one side of which is the entire facing wall of the Kremlin is a fitting parade ground for any state. The Russians ignore it except on those state occasions. Most of the year it is just a vast square, unpeopled over its length and breadth, bearing witness to the gates of the Kremlin. The Lenin Mausoleum stands stark and huge away from those gates. A line of dark-clothed people stretches decorously from the entrance, moving slowly to the fulfilment of what might be a duty or the satisfying of a curiosity.

Bob and I took our places at the end of the queue shortly after we became reunited in the hotel. We moved slowly towards the entrance, and just as slowly down the steps and into the chamber. No pause was allowed to anybody. No time was offered any person to examine the beautiful marble of which the place was constructed. At the bottom of the steps a right turn brings one into the mausoleum which houses the honoured dead. The body lies in a glass case of considerable size. Three armed soldiers stand before it. The visitor must pass up the stairs, along the back of the case and down the stairs, then out to the day after climbing up the exit stairs. The viewing of the body is made as one moves around the three sides of the catafalque. For the westerner it was not a pretty sight. Death is not honoured by such a peepshow. It was not a sight to revisit.

In the hotel there was a gathering of the clans. The conference was organised by the Russian Association of Proletarian Writers, and was to take place in Kharkov from the 6th to the 15th of November 1930. It was to be known as the Second Plenum of the International Bureau of Revolutionary Literature. It was a magnificent presumption. And that was all. There were some days to go before we could entrain for the then capital of the Ukraine, and, fortunately for us our period of waiting held some joyous interludes. The leader of the Committee, so far as we could gather in Moscow, was a Hungarian exile called Bela Illes. He was a big, burly man who each time he met one seized one's hand, gave it a vigorous shake, and greeted one with the word, 'Drast!' He spoke no English. Ludwig Renn, then a prominent German novelist, who was a most competent linguist, told me that Illes spoke Russian like a German, and German like a Hungarian. 'I don't know Hungarian,' he confessed to me, 'so I cannot tell you how he speaks it.'

Bela Illes was never in the same office twice. He was as elusive as any fox. One simply took him when he appeared. Only once were we called to a joint pow-wow, and this was held in a room in a building opposite the gates of the Lubyanka. When a day or so later I made my way to that self same building and asked to see Illes I found that nobody in the place knew of him or could tell me where he might be found. I put it down to the Russian way, until I tried to find Sergei Dinamov, the then great panjandrum of literature in the Soviet Union.

I met him in Kharkov. In fact I spent the evening with him. I found him to be a most charming person. He gave me the address of his office and told me to call any time, when we would continue our discussion on English writers. When I got back to Moscow I set out to find him. I rang his office. The voice at the other end of the wire merely cracked a few jokes. I set out on foot to find the address he had given me. I found it. The place was full of clerks. Not one of them had even heard of such a person as Dinamov. I expostulated. Sergei Dinamov, I informed them, was the editor of the *Literatuna Gazette*. They merely shook their heads.

I never saw Sergei Dinamov again.

Bob was getting anxious about the conference. He paid repeated visits to the Cominform and the Trade Union Headquarters. He pleaded with Losovsky to get them to move. He threatened to return to London. He might just as well have saved himself the trouble for, one dark night we stumbled over the rails of a huge siding, clambered into the compartments of a train that, in some miraculous way, loomed up in the darkness.

It was the same old Russian train, soft travel for most, and wagons-lits for the top brass. Segregation of class remained adamant until we got back to Moscow. It was the usual Russian railway set-up, four beds to each compartment, so many compartments to the carriage, and an old man near the door to do the chores and keep the fire going.

The American delegation were in the same carriage. The remaining spaces were occupied by the clerks and stenographers attached to the conference. The Americans were the representatives of the John Reed Club, rather than of the proletarian writers. When we pointed this out to them we were assured that all the proletarian writers who counted in America were members of the John Reed Club. There we left it. Mike Gold, the doyen of the American Left, was not with the group. As a matter of fact, the conference was some days gone in its work before he put in an appearance. When he did arrive it was in the company of Leonid Leonov, a well-thought-of Russian writer.

What did impress us both was the resentment each American, except John Herman, felt for Mike Gold. There was A.B. Magil, a dedicated Jewish communist who was really born to be a rabbi, the cartoonists Bill Gropper and Fred Ellis, and Harry Alan Potemkin, a smart Jew who knew all there was to know about filming and the American film industry. John Herman and his wife, Josephine Herbst were also attached to the group. Herman was a great friend of Hemingway, and made no bones about the friendship, which was not reciprocated by the American delegation. He was also a sworn friend of

Michael Gold. Over all this delegation reigned the presiding genius, Joshua Kunitz, a Russian expatriate who carried an American passport.

On the train we were given a meal and after that we drifted off to our bunks. None of us resented the fact that the wagons-lits coaches at the front of the train were occupied by the leaders of the RAPP. In all probability it was accepted that such important people had need of such important ease. Let it be said in the honour of Ludwig Renn that he refused accommodation in the high class part of the train.

Control of our business had ascended from Illes to Leopold Averbach the moment we were entrained. This Averbach was a youngish man with a loud laugh and a head shorn to the bone and razored in that precise Russian manner prevalent at the time. He it was whose duty lay in giving the conference the precise proletarian tone. If the truth were to be known, he was the direct representative of the Kremlin at the conference. He it was who made the longest speech, one of Krushchev proportions, and the most sweeping reply to the discussion, at Kharkov. The poor man must have comitted certain errors when he spoke, or the truths he adumbrated may, by the time Stalin began purging, have become errors. Every speech delivered at the conference, my own included, was printed in the report and circulated world-wide, except that of Averbach and his reply. Poor man! The proletarian literary world was his oyster. His immediate cronies throughout the conference were Bela Illes and Sasha Fadayev. Fadayev was an accomplished man. He spoke perfect English. He was immensely tall, taller, maybe, than Henri Barbusse. He was as straight as a ramrod, ebullient, happy, determined.

It is sad to reflect on that trio even now. Illes returned to his own country; Averbach was executed; Fadayev, anticipating his own execution, blew his brains out in his home in Leningrad.

I felt an enormous affection for Fadayev. I can visualise his tall, slim figure even now. Always well dressed, always ready to laugh, clean shaven and handsome, full of fun, and happy as a cloud. I never saw a person who could eat so many sunflower seeds, and so quickly, as Sasha.

I recall that evening in Kharkov when we watched *Earth*, the most poignantly beautiful film it has been my privilege to see. It was the epitome of rural beauty. After the show the glasses of tea were served. Fadayev was in an uproarious mood. He called me over to where he sat with his friends. When I had joined them he took me a little aside to crack a rather risqué joke, to which I offered the Tyneside ejaculation, rather loudly of 'Wheee!' To my astonishment a silence fell, and men and women turned to look at me. Fadayev, taken by surprise, stamped his foot and then burst into a roar of laughter. The moment eventually lost itself in the ensuing talk. Quite recovered, Fadayev told me in a whisper that I had committed a most serious faux pas. The word I had uttered was the Russian for the female sexual organ. He counselled me to be careful in the use of my curious ejaculation. Curious, I asked him the Russian for the male organ, and, rather reluctantly he gave it to me. I must have repeated the word, 'pisdah' above a whisper, for he immediately stood up and left the room.

We were housed in a commodious hotel a mile or so from the conference hall, which stood at one end of a large square, around which the tram cars trundled.

There was no ceremony in the hall of Ukrainian writers, where the conference was to take place. The night previous there had been a concert given in our honour, and before the interval Renn announced the names of the members of the praesidium in five or six languages. Bob was to represent the English writers, which, to say the least, was a bit of a joke. The hall in which the conference was to be held was not vast. It stood cheek-by-jowl against the ruins of a church which had been demolished by explosives some time before. All during our stay in the town, the cupola of the church sat upon the top of ruins like some forlorn ghost escaped from some forgotten religion.

The entrance lobbies as well as the hall itself were plastered with quotations from the works of Stalin in all the languages of the members. The conference was timed to commence at 11 a.m., and to our surprise it did. To the English speaking group a young Jew possessed of a fearsome command of English had been assigned as our interpreter, but before the conference opened he was sent back to Moscow in disgrace, for what we never knew. The Kharkov people supplied us with an alternative, but his command of English, to say the very least, was less than elementary. Bob and I made no fuss. As to the Americans, they attached themselves to the German groups where they could get along with their own Yiddish-German.

Chapter Twenty-One

Bela Illes opened the debate on the morning of the conference. He offered up to discussion the RAPP view of world literature. It was usual for the main speaker in a Russian-sponsored conference or plenum to speak at enormous length. Illes was no exception to this rule. He went on and on interminably. At the end of his report he was granted a rapturous ovation. Thereafter, and for some days, the delegates climbed to the rostrum and there disported themselves courageously. They all criticised the leading writers of their day in their own country. Even Henri Barbusse was not exempt from French stricture. Nor did he escape a lot of other criticism. I asked Louis Aragon why they were all so critical of the great French writer. Had they all forgotten, I asked, that he had impressed Lenin with his novel *Under Fire*?

Louis Aragon was one of the nicest men any man or woman could know. 'Even Barbusse must be called to account when he strays off the line,' he told me. 'Do you know that he intends to write a life of Christ? Can you beat it! The absurdity!'

It was indeed the initiation of the world organisation for all the proletarian writers. The hall swarmed with them. They came from all the republics in the Soviet Union. You could identify them the moment they opened their mouths. The Russian speaking Russian addressed the 'proletarii pisaitelli' while the Ukrainian addressed the 'proletary pismeniki'. Other patois were distinguishable. The talk went on. None of these speeches were translated, not even the important ones.

The American boys managed to get themselves into some sort of trouble. They excoriated Mike Gold for not turning up on time, the world's worst conference procrastinator. When he did arrive they soon grew jealous. They talked among themselves in the lobby. I offered my own advice to them when I came across them fulminating excessively. 'If you have got all that against him,' I said, 'Why don't you go on the platform and get it off your chests?' They requested me to mind my own business. The world since then has learned to let the American mind his own business to the great cost of the rest of the world.

Shortly after that the delegation was called to account. An old lady, large of abdomen and immense of bosom bore down upon the conference. In the morning of her coming she made a long speech wherein she defined the policy of the Soviet Government to RAPP. She was not so rapturously applauded. After lunch she took the American delegation aside and when she allowed them to go free each member was suitably and most beautifully cowed. Criticism of Mike Gold subsided after that, but it simmered again when a place in the wagons-lits was given to Mike.

We had a good time in Kharkov. In the first place, the weather, still warm, behaved itself magnificently. Winter, so far as the southern Ukraine was concerned was still some distance away. One wondered just how the people got through the Russian winter when it was full blast over the wide steppes.

The Ukrainian government did the conference proud. They sent Skrypnik to address the conference. Poor Skrypnik. Stalin saw to his demise. They also sent the Prime Minister Chubar to distribute a few medals at a great open meeting. Poor Chubar. They put a symphony concert on in the great theatre. It was a marvellous show. All noise and tympany work. A badly dressed orchestra, if ever I saw one. They played Borodin until our ears rang. They gave a performance of Mossolov's *Song of the Machines* that was as startling as it was magnificent, impressively short. As I sat I was for the moment back in the Waygood Otis shop in Southwark. When the rapturous acclamation ended the conductor led a woman on to the stage who was huge enough to mate with a giant. I have never viewed the outline of so vast a bosom. She sang. And how she did sing! I thought the audience would never regain a rational repose.

It was a proletarian evening, to be sure. The orchestra was mounted and clad in the poverty of the Soviet Union as it then existed. The leader was not a little ashamed of his well-worn dress suit, yet indifferent to the fact that he was not possessed of a pair of black shoes. His were dark tan. They were all magnificent players, every one of them. They did the huge lady proud. Two or three days later they put on *Prince Igor*, in the same theatre, with the same orchestra, and with the same

huge lady in the soprano role. I had not seen the opera before.
We saw Igor bid his wife farewell. The stage revolved and
we found ourselves in the presence of the same lady and a
multitude of females who attended her court. When the scene
was completely changed we passed into and through, and out
of one of the longest bouts of soprano singing I have ever heard.
Bob was sitting beside me. He had missed the previous concert.
I saw that he was massively impressed by the lady. About the
singing he held his own peace. Welshmen have their own ideas
about singing, soprano singing included.

'Now we'll get the ballet,' he told me.

I wondered how he knew that, for he was no opera lover,
but I soon found out when the curtain rose and revealed all
the cast, Igor included, standing beside the great dame, and
all the chorus and ballet girls, clustered about Ludwig Renn.
He showed no embarrassment. He showed no fear. He did not
appreciate how ludicrous it all was. He came to the edge of
the stage, glanced down at the upturned faces of the orchestra,
smiled at the conductor, who lay back negligently, opened his
mouth and made an announcement to do with the conference
in Russian. He repeated his speech in Ukrainian, then German,
then French and finally in English. It was a marvellous exercise,
one which sent all his hearers into ecstasies. The stage people
pressed closer upon him. One of the dancing girls reached
up and kissed him. In the end, the under-dressed girls escorted
him from the stage. The great curtains fell. The conductor
sprang forth from his indolent posture and brought the
orchestra to order. I must say that the Polovstian Dance was
wildly acclaimed.

The final act was more than a tour-de-force. It was a revelation. A lot of bell ropes dangled from the flies, and upon
these two clownish creatures disported themselves, and in
the end sent the bells clanging. The stage setting showed the
ramparts and a slope leading up to them. And on to the stage
strode the great lady clad in a magnificent Ukrainian costume.
Here she paused to toy magnificently with all the notes Borodin
had written into the part, except those which she reached
after great effort, until the escaped Igor appeared upon the
ramparts. Carrying herself and her song up the slope, she
gathered the long moustachioed Igor into her vast embrace,
and there she held him. From where I sat I could see the beads
of sweat oozing out of the unfortunate man's brow. He was

under a double strain, that of singing his own part and that of supporting the woman, and especially when she had to tense herself in order to produce her highest notes. I felt sorry for the singer. He possessed a magnificent voice, and he knew how to use it. I groaned with him as he brought her to stage level, for he was almost on the point of actual physical collapse.

In time there came the great choir from Kiev to that same stage. I can recall over the decades the sheer beauty of their singing. Bob surprised me when he said that they were a disappointment, for they had no 'bwll'. He did forget about their shortcomings as singers when he became aware of the singular beauty of some of the ladies of the choir. They were young, and many of them were beautiful. Bob reached his own haven of delight when he discovered that the ladies were to be lodged that night in our hotel.

The big night for me was when the bandura players came and offered us their own particular programme. There were, if I remember correctly, nine men in that party. Their instruments were of ascending sizes, from one as small as a violin to one almost as large as a cello. The concert was given in the conference hall, and was mainly for the delegates. They were performers who sat still upon their chairs, nursing their instruments, caring for the fragance of those instruments with their own deep concern. They took their playing and their singing as the gift they had to offer. They sang from a castrata height down to Chaliapin depths. I do not recall a concert which touched me so deeply. I remember a trio sung by those simply clad Ukrainians against the continuous background of plucking by their six colleagues that was so touching, so elevating, and so deeply burdened with the powerful transports of the human voice, that I took it upon myself to ask for an encore. It not only affected those nine men deeply, it embarrassed them. Before accepting my invitation, they rose slowly to their feet, came forward, and bowed directly to me in gratitude. Where are those men and women today? Kiev and Kharkov stood in the track of the Nazi storm. I often cogitate their fates. We were all contemporaries, and barring untoward accident they must have all lived to the day of horror when total war fell upon those wide, flat, open steppes.

Memories of that black, flat country crowd upon me as I write. There was that hazardous ride I had in a two-seater plane, and skimming over that flat strange countryside. The horizon fled before me as we rose over the field just outside Kharkov. The great, black river, flowing vastly over the terrain, seemed to gather the vast space into its own embrace. What a steadily flowing river is the Dnieper, and how slow and gracious. Not like any river I had so far known. A river in tune with infinitude. The mountains, if there were any, were hidden beyond the rim of the world. The most wondrous things were the great, broad river, the vastly continuing earth, black, unfenced, much of it already under the plough, land made ready to receive the snows of winter, and the strange lack of wooded land. What a country in which to deploy tanks against the flesh of men and women and children.

What happened to it all? The tiresome construction sites here and there? The pretty girls from Kiev? The bandura singers. The quiet, unimpressive and ill-clad folks of Kharkov? Their unimaginable fates force me to lay down my book and glance back over the aeons that now stretch over the bodies of forgotten men. How did they all fare? Kharkov was almost totally destroyed. Is its market place still there? Life does bear on its breath great evils as well as great joys. Poor Kharkov.

During the sitting of the conference the November Celebrations were observed in Kharkov. It was only a provincial parade, with all the shouting that could be mustered, but none of the emotion of Moscow. The soldiers marched and the bands played. There was a tribune upon which the leading citizens foregathered to take all the salutes that might be offered. There were cheer leaders and slogan shouters. If Krushchev was there, he did not reveal himself.

When the conference ended there was a massive demonstration in the great Berzil Theatre. Chubar occupied the chair. Bob and I sat in a side box along with the Americans. There had been no preparation, no rehearsal. Chubar opened the proceedings with a thunderous speech, which elicited a thunderous ovation. He then called upon Ludwig Renn to address the meeting. Three speakers later he called me to the podium. I was never so surprised in all my life. A Red Army man escorted me from the side box, across the stage, and set me down in front of the great man. He gave me a smile and left me to face that immense throng of people, without a note, without the remotest idea on what to say. I stood there gasping in a thunder of applause. Chubar stayed the tumult. He announced my name with some difficulty. I recognised the three words, *'Pod Vlastu Uglya.'* But that was not all. He described me as an Angliski Proletarski Pismeniki. The resulting ovation was quelled by the band in attendance. It played the first two lines of the *Internationale.*

I am not a nervous public speaker. I raised my voice and thanked them all for their kind ovation. I spoke of the mines and the miners, subjects that were drifting out of my experience. I spoke also of the great strike of 1926. I told them of my pleasure in coming to their country. I shut up, and I stepped down. I received two rounds of the first two lines of the *Internationale.* I stood aside while a translation was given of my speech. I stood through a full rendering of the *Internationale.*

The next day we were taken on an interminable motor bus ride through the surrounding country. The road over which we travelled was unmade and uneven. From being tiresome it became agonising. We left the buses and walked down a lane leading into a copse. Into this birch grove we all walked. There we refreshed ourselves with Kvass, which had been brought in large containers. Then, under the leadership of Fadayev, we, or they, sang some of those languorous Russian songs so dear to the native heart. Any pause during which the individuals sought their memories for other songs was taken up with eating sunflower seeds. The trick is to select your seed, place it between the front teeth, crack the husk, hold the kernel and spit out the two halves of the seed, chew, swallow, and repeat time after time. The knack is to place the seed between the teeth. All Russians are adept at the art. Fadayev was more adept than most Russians.

After such an unappetising meal and more sad songs we got back into the buses and finished up at a large construction site. There were scores of men working under a heavy guard of armed soldiers. As soon as we got down from our conveyances the men came forward to offer us greetings. Fadayev became leader of ceremony. He insisted upon my sitting on a log of wood with him and talking to a group of these strange men. We had our photographs taken. This done, he selected about a dozen of the prisoners and set me in their midst. Our photographs were taken.

'Do you like these men?' Fadayev asked me. 'you should, you know,' he assured me. 'All of them are serving long sentences for murder. Every mother son of them.'

The next evening, rather late, we boarded the same train as

that which had brought us from Moscow. We slept through the night. In the morning we came to a halt at a wayside station. The platform was lined with troops. The officer in charge stood at attention in a continuous rigid salute as we detrained. He called for cheers as we passed off the platform. Outside the station were buses waiting to take us to the township in the distance. We were eventually decanted outside a stark cement building which was to be a hotel when it was completed. Breakfast was laid for us. We ate a simple meal and washed it down with kvass. While we did so a tenor regaled us with arias from operas. The pianist was quite capable, and where and when he was incapable he left the songster to do his own job.

We boarded the buses again. At the station we took another salute from the troops. Then we climbed on to the train and some hours later we arrived at the Dnieprostroi construction.

There was no accommodation for us at the dam and so we ate and slept on the train. We were all fully aware that Russia, in those now distant days, was a severely rationed country, and this we accepted implicitly. It would be impolitic to share the food in the canteens and so consume the rations of the workers, and we felt that it would be wrong to eat much better meals anywhere else than on the train. So we ate and slept in tolerable railway coach conditions, but I cannot say that it was home-from-home living in a stationary soft-class compartment for a whole week. Very soon the sanitary conditions became somewhat distressing. When this happened the train was simply shunted a little further along the line. We soon found out that sanitary arrangements were more on the take than on the give, especially in rural Russia. Under imaginable circumstances we lived through each day and slept through each night.

When we arrived, towards afternoon, we discovered that we had forsaken the snows and were once again resting on the back of a late summer. It was really beautiful weather, soft and cool, almost like that of a late English spring. Left alone, set apart from the leaders of the conference, we conducted all our forages into the area overtaken by this tremendous construction. Quite early we made our way down to the edge of the river Dnieper. The tumult was deafening. From where we stood we were able to appreciate to the full the mammoth proportions of the immense project. It was much bigger than any I had as yet seen. Work was being carried out on both banks, the intention being to mesh later. In the meantime the throttled water of the river roared into the aperture with stupendous force. The construction was shaping itself under the impulse of a gigantic labour force, and was slowly arriving at the point when the gap would be closed and the massive torrent held back and harnessed. The black water leaped to its own freedom with a shout of noise that almost impaled the ear drum. Here we beheld an unimaginable force resisting obstruction and imprisonment.

The railway along which we had come crossed the river a great distance from the site. We decided to cross it after breakfast the next day. By the time we set out the day had become torrid with heat, and our journey proved to be a long one. Our suggestion had been agreed, but we were warned not to loiter on the bridge. 'Nobody dares to loiter on any railway bridge in Russia,' we were told.

Our road led through a village which seemed to be half submerged. It was like any village described by Gogol, a street of half-buried dwellings. Each of the roofs could be reached by hand. As we saw, the dwellings were deeper in the earth than they were built up in the open. There was little else but dust. The foot sank into the fine stuff more freely than it sinks into the accumulated dust in a coal-mine. A policeman emerged from somewhere to have a look at us, and in doing so stumbled over a half grown pig lying smothered in the middle of the roadway. He gave it a savage kick and sent it squealing along the street.

We climbed the embankment to the railway, saluted the armed guard, and set off to walk across the bridge. We were now offered a magnificent view of the act of construction. We would have preferred to pause, but we knew that we must not do so. We greeted the armed sentry at the other end. He smiled. He did not speak. As we descended the embankment we could visualise the plan of building. Beyond was the concrete mixing complex, a huge place, where the trucks were filled with the prepared cement and organised into trains and drawn to the top of the dam. Arrived there, no time was lost in slinging the entire ten ton truck with its load into the air and over the finished side of the dam and dropping it exactly where the labour force could receive it. When the entire mass was disposed of in this way, the trucks were reformed into a train and taken back to the cement works for refilling.

We explored the construction from the far side of the dam.

The topmost height had been reached on both sides. At set distances all over the top of the cement plateau were set up boring machines, each tended by an old man or an oldish woman, who crouched over the borehole, seated upon an up-turned box, and watching the plunging of the drill. The hole was not of a large diameter. We were told that the hole would be driven right through the concrete massif and far into the earth to solid rock. When each hole was completed a very fine concrete mix would be forced into it under tremendous force, and by this means the structure would be rivetted to its base.

Having exhausted the sights on the top of the dam we were conducted to the base where we could see the work that was going on there. There, near the outward sloping foot of the dam we were placed in a most uneasy conjunction with the roaring river, the anger of which became more impressive the nearer one got to it.

That portion of the dam base upon which we stood was by then sufficiently tensile to accept the buttressing of the main wall. A huge area had been enclosed within vast concrete pallisadings and this was now in process of being filled with concrete. Scores of men, women, youths and maidens, all shod in thick leather boots were engaged stamping down the vicious mass. A whistle was blown and all at work in the enclosure moved out of it. Then a truck was lowered to a point above the stamping ground and its contents emptied. Another whistle was blown when the truck was out of the way and the workers leaped down upon the stuff and began trampling into the mass upon which it had been spilled. There were no shovels. These men and these women were actually building that colossal dam with their feet. They stamped and they prodded in an abandonment of labour I had not hitherto comprehended. It was almost pitiable. I stared at them as they laboured in their ant-like confusion and I wondered. I lingered to watch, fascinated, astounded. Here were men and women working to the command of a whistle, leaping in when it blew and dragging their cement clodded feet out when it blew again. And so it went on. They repeated the process with an exaggerated intensity of action. I felt sad and confused.

I quit the scene humbly. It was as if I had been passed over the centuries and shown the people of the Pharoahs building their pyramids. Why did they do it? Were they so young and so eager as to believe that with this slavery they were building socialism? Was socialism worth so much agony of energy? I spoke to Egon Erwin Kisch, a Czech journalist, and I asked him what he thought of it all. Did he not think it was a most strange expenditure of human labour power? Poor Egon! He died in the Spanish Civil War.

'You read Marx?' he asked me.

I told him that I studied Marx.

'I'd like to,' he said. 'I haven't the time these days. There is too much going on.'

We were approaching our train, and instead of going into his first class cabin, he took me by the arm and escorted me into the evening.

'Those cement tramplers you saw,' he said, 'have their feet examined every day. The doubtful twice a day. The wellingtons are also examined. I don't think you should worry.'

I could see that he was excited by what he had seen that day. He began to expatiate on the importance of such constructions as this for the building of socialism. I just listened to him. He had an enormous command of my own language and was never at a loss for a word. I did not tell him that Dnieprostroi had shed much of its romance for me.

'There is no such thing as romance in labour,' I said to him.

'That isn't Marxism,' he snapped, 'and you know it,' He walked on and turned to go back to the train. 'Didn't you expect this kind of thing when you came to Russia?' he went on, half angrily. 'These things are necessary, are they not?'

I told him that I could appreciate the need for the Bolsheviks to build the means for the construction of socialism, and he cut into my speech with 'Well, what more do you want?'

We reached the train and bade each other 'Good night'.

Bob and I were not brought into conversational relationship with the workers on the dam at any time, nor were we taken to their canteens or their sleeping quarters. Like all true Russians they were all irrevocably attached to the task of fulfilling the plan. The Five Year Plan in Four was their slogan. We had to take it on trust.

As I strode along the railtrack with Bob the night prior to our departure we met Kisch again, coming up from the site.

'You should have been with me,' he exclaimed, 'I gave a lecture to a good crowd.'

'In Russian?' I asked.

'Of course,' he replied. 'I speak seven languages. The questions they asked! You should have been there to hear them.' He pointed to where the illuminated tower glowed in the sky above the site. 'See that light?' he cried.

'What is it for?' I asked. 'Nobody ever tells Bob and me anything.'

He brushed aside my reproof. 'That light rules the site,' he said. 'It goes out whenever they fall behind the production norm. They have to work like they do in order to keep the light glowing.' He clapped his hands. 'That's building communism, my boy!' he called out over the still night air.

'Not Taylorism?' I conjectured.

'Come, come, Heslop!' he said. 'And you told me you studied Marx. You know as well as I do that nobody makes a profit in the Soviet Union. Nobody works for any person or thing but the state.'

He left Bob and me, and we continued our work. Bob was angry. He told me that I ought to guard my tongue.

During the night the train set off to jog its way back to Moscow. The day became fine. After breakfast the two occupants of the other two bunks in our compartment went off to gossip the morning over with their own nationals. Bob and I were alone and growing somewhat bored. I could see that Bob was growing anxious about his wife and children back in Tufnell Park. Luckily, Ludwig Renn tapped on the glass door of the compartment. We made him gladly welcome. He sat down and stretched his long legs across the chasm.

'I think that it is time we discussed politics, Bob,' he suggested. 'Do you mind?'

Bob, at no time averse to discussing such a subject, smiled and began to roll one of his thin, almost tobacco-less cigarettes. 'I've had that idea since we left Moscow,' he said. 'What's on your mind?' He saw Renn glance at me. 'Don't mind him,' he said. 'He's one of us.'

Renn nodded and began to outline the situation in his own country as he understood it. Things, he told us, were growing intolerable. The proletariat was recovering from its dismay and was thinking in terms of revolution. It was seeing through Hitler. He told us of a considerable accretion to the membership of the Communist Party, and he grew eloquent in a quiet way. Renn was a man who impressed his fellows by his singular charm and disarming simplicity.

'It is a pity that you feel so much out of countenance with the Party, Bob,' he said. 'I suppose it is because everything in your country is so...so...blank.' He waited until Bob's smile had drifted from his deep, sensual eyes. 'You see, in Germany, things are different. When I get back there we, the Party leadership has got to decide on the moment of the act of revolution.'

'You mean that?' I interposed, excitedly.

Renn put his feet up on the opposite seat and regarded them for some time. 'There is one thing to which we must pay deep regard,' he said.

Bob leaned forward. 'And that is the Five Year Plan?' he suggested.

'You are quite right,' said Renn. 'In Germany we are ready for the revolutionary act,' he went on after a pause. 'We are not sure whether to lead the revolution this year or postpone it to the next. All will depend on whether we can or can not employ suitable tactics. The party will consider the matter seriously.'

'And you think you will make it the year after?' Bob suggested.

Renn nodded. 'Yes,' he said. 'But no further. The German revolution will not wait after that.'

'In my opinion,' said Bob quietly, 'revolution can only be timed within the given set of circumstances. You will be unwise to consider any other conditions.' He shook his head. 'A revolution planned ahead like a trip to the seaside is as daft and as futile as a revolution postponed. Your German revolution will not wait for you and the Party.'

Writing all this down in full retrospect, it does not strike me as being at all fantastic. The year was 1930. The German revolution stood upon some order of some day. And Renn was not romancing.

Later, when I was working at my task in Bush House in the statistical department of the Trade Delegation, my colleague was late in getting back from lunch. I realised that something might have prevented her coming back when I recalled that all the Russian employees had been asked to stay at their tables in the dining room in the basement. That meant a private announcement.

When she came in she was somewhat excited.

I awaited her announcement.

'It has been decided in Moscow,' she said. 'The German revolution has been postponed indefinitely. It is good for our Plan.'

I bent my head and smiled. Poor Renn, I thought.

I was glad when I learned that he had been able to escape from Nazi Germany.

Chapter Twenty-Two

Johannes Becher was a typical German, huge, fat, almost ponderous, florid, good-tempered and deeply serious. I still think that he was in love with Anna Seghers, and she with him. Wherever and whenever one saw the one the other one was not far off. Anna was young and slim, and had made a name for herself in the German literary world as a novelist. I was surprised when I discovered that Becher was a great poet and writer of some repute. That he was a considerable figure in those pre-Nazi years there can be no doubt. He led the German delegation from behind the back of Ludwig Renn. His was one of the longest speeches made at the conference. He was a pronounced man of his own period. I lost trace of him after Hitler came to power, and I was most surprised when he emerged as one of the big men in the German Democratic Republic.

There was one moment in Moscow when he prevented me from drinking water from a carafe which was standing on a nearby table. 'Nein!' he called out. 'Nein trinken, genosse! Moscau wasser ist nein gut!' I smiled at the difficulty he experienced in trying to communicate.

I smiled my thanks, and reached for a bottle of Nazan.

When we got back to Moscow, Becher and all the members of the German delegation, except Renn, faded into the background after the banquet.

The day of the great bean-feast began with a privilege. We were each given a pass which admitted us to an off-ration store, where we could buy what we required and with no questions asked. It was camouflaged under the trading mark of 'Foreign Technicians' Store'. I went out of interest, but there was little I wished to buy. Zemlya i Fabrika had paid me a vast sum of roubles which I carried about with me in a brief case I had been compelled to buy for just that one purpose. It was most interesting to find one's self a man of considerable substance, and at the same time a strange experience to find that it was nearly impossible to buy anything. In the store I handed out quite a sum to those resident in the country who were eager to buy and had no money.

I did discover a shop which sold brooches and the like made from Ural stone, topaz, and that kind of thing, and I was able to buy a few things for Phyllis. I bought a coat made up of Siberian fox skin, and this I delighted to carry home. Phyllis was by no means impressed. She wore it once to Paris to the Persian Art Exhibition, and after that, when our daughter came, she whittled the poor thing into things for the cot and the pram.

At seven o'clock on the night of the banquet the taxicabs ranked outside the hotel to bear us off to the place where it was to be held. It was not in the Kremlin, for the journey was considerable and took us to the other side of the city. The night was bitterly cold. The building into which we were ushered was warm and brightly lit. In the hall there was a loud shedding of outer garments and galoshes.

The presiding officer at the banquet was old Felix Kohn, a tall, thin, well-coiffered Pole. His beard was barbered to a fine point. An old colleague of Lenin, he was held in great reverence by the crowd. Every Russian present who could communicate with us was eager to tell us the story of Kohn's escape from the death cell of some Tsarist prison. In Leningrad I had gone with Lydia Slonimsky to see a film which depicted the episode. My interest had been captured by the leading actress in that film, the widow of Anton Chekhov, Olga Knipper-Chekhova.

Felix Kohn was well-beloved of the Bolsheviks and could afford to be good-humoured as well as humorous. He greeted us all most gravely as we passed before him. He took no offence when the puppet-master reproduced him, whiskers and all, at the show after we had been replenished.

We took our appointed places at the tables, which were laden with food.

Particularisation was absent from the ceremony – and, indeed, it was a ceremony of guzzling – but there was the top table at which were gathered the most important stomachs. We all sat down before the vast collation, of what I took to be all the food we would get but which proved to be the merest of *hors d'oeuvres* of the banquet, in deep wonderment. It was spread over the tables and piled high above us on huge contraptions which held three tiers each of appetising tittivations. One wondered just what those men and women we had seen on the construction sites would have said had they been able to witness such an abandon of abundance.

I leaned over to Bob. 'Is this possible?' I asked him. 'What must we do?'

'Just eat and be thankful,' he replied, and added: 'It's more than I expected.'

'What did you expect?'

He shrugged. 'We're in Russia,' he said.

'But what about all the folk outside?' I cried. 'Aren't they constructing this Russia? What about all those people stamping down the cement at the dam?'

He took food on to his plate. 'Eat and be merry,' he said. 'Why worry? Eat so that tomorrow we can both have diarrhoea.'

Thus comforted, I ate.

When all the magnificent things that were preliminary to the actual feast were partially consumed, the decks were cleared for the actual meal. Jacketed waiters dashed about, and the banquet began. The waiters brought new crockery and real food. Real soup. Normality had come to the dining hall. Fish, white and tasty fish. Fowl. By that time I had had enough.

The waiter brought the head waiter, a stern, commanding man. 'Why do you not eat?' he demanded of me in Russian.

I understood what he said, for I had been in Russia long enough to understand short, simple sentences. I put my hand on my stomach and grimaced.

There was a short conversation above my head and the man departed.

The gargantuan meal wandered through its courses to the very end. The belchings and the teeth pickings followed while the waiters scampered off with the crockery and cutlery. The entertainers moved in. A soprano, vast of bust, and good in voice, came out of the Bolshoi to regale us with song. One song was a translation of a poem by Burns. I recognised neither song nor poem, but I acknowledged the tribute to the poet. And, accordingly, all about me smiled. Most of them took me to be a Scotsman.

The tenor sang well, but the base over-topped him as an executant. He, too, was from the Bolshoi. He had a pronounced limp, poor man. Something gained in the war. Then came the puppet man, and joy was complete.

Heavy snow had covered Moscow by the time we left the banqueting hall. The driver of our cab often found himself in grave difficulty. We skidded a little more than somewhat, so to speak. The extremely cold air sought its own sanctuary in our cab. Winter was moving towards the city on swift wings. We were glad to escape to the warmth of the hotel.

I expected to receive my tickets for my journey back to England the day after the banquet, and so I felt eager to visit the great cathedral on the other side of the river Moskva. After breakfast I walked to St Basil and from there went down to the river side to walk the great length of the Kremlin Wall. I paused often in my journey to regard the lovely buildings that peeped over the wall, as well as that of St Basil, to see how they were greeting yet another winter. St Basil always looks strangely beautiful, no matter what point of vantage one views it from. How it must have clung to its own exquisite existence without a shade of its own from all the rigours of Russia's weather. Walking had to be done slowly, for there had been a considerable fall of new snow. It interested me to note that most of the wheels of carts, droshkies and perambulators had been exchanged for runners. It was somewhat unfortunate for the horses when they had to cross a bare patch of roadway. The women merely carried the pram!

I crossed the river and found the cathedral, but I might have saved myself the trouble of the journey, for it was undergoing either a major repair or a preparation for destruction. All the ikons had been removed and a great tumult filled the vast sanctorum. I would have liked to have searched the place, for I found that it possessed a second floor. Men were working there quite noisily. I went out into the cold and made my way back to the hotel.

Arrived there I was informed that I was to stay in Moscow for the 'protcess' that was to take place. I was not asked to stay; I was simply told to stay. I was to report the proceedings.

When I told Bob he merely smiled. 'It's you who are staying and it is me who is going home,' he said.

The state trial of the members of the Industrial Party was held in the vast Hall of Columns in Dom Soyuzov, the great building near the Bolshoi Theatre wherein the Soviet government exposes its great dead. There the body of Lenin had lain.

The presiding judge was the hitherto unknown Bolshevik called Vyshinsky. He had for his assessors a Red Army officer and an ordinary working man who, throughout the entire proceedings, paid no attention to his dreadful beard. The prisoners, Ramzin, Karpov, Professor Fedotov, Kallinikov, Tcharnovsky, Larichev, Kondratov and Tchaigmov, were to be prosecuted by the Krylenko who had been close to Lenin during the 1917 revolution.

It was not suggested that I should report the trial, for I was not connected with any English newspaper. When I got to the meeting of the correspondents, which was chaired by none other than Bela Kun, I found that the *Daily Worker* was fully represented. I felt that somehow I was being asked to attend the trial in order to carry out some duty, but to this day I have not learned even the truth of that suggestion. Personally, I could not see any point in my staying throughout the long process of judgment, but I made no objection. If I went home I would have to start looking for a job, and I did not relish signing on at the Employment Exchange in Walworth Road. I wrote to my wife and explained what I proposed to do. There was much to interest me in watching from so secure a vantage point how the Soviet system of justice really worked, and I felt that would be much more to my advantage than being at home and watching the MacDonald Labour Government fading into shame.

All the American delegates except John Herman and his wife were given *mandats* to enter the Hall of Commons, and I took comfort from that because I knew that they were all as remote from newspapers in America as I was from those in England. We were housed in the same hotel. I shared a room with Michael Gold. I found him to be an easily tetchy man, most difficult to get on with. I was glad when he started a liaison with the daughter of a German technician, and moved down the corridor into a room of their own. The inevitable happened and the father was most cross, for she was a fine girl.

Gold was the veritable hero of the Russians. He was a dark, slim, medium-sized Jew. He could have been taken for anything except a prominent proletarian writer. There was always acid in his pen. He was quick and clever, one of America's great journalists. I read his novel, *Jews Without Money* while I was in Moscow. I found it telling of a life far away, aeons distant, from the life I had lived. It seemed to me to be an epic of the ghetto where only the women slaved, where the male halted outside the entrance to the factory and slunk back amongst the malefactors.

The trial opened in the House of the Soviets. The weather had turned bleak and raw. I was given a place at the reporters' table that ran below the entire length of the stage upon which Justice sat enthroned in red. A translator was assigned to each national group. Ours was one of Russia's top *perovochiks*, Joe Fineberg, a man who must have lost count of the volumes of Lenin and the Russian intelligentsia he has translated. Those who spoke Russian sat almost underneath the chair upon which Krylenko sat, and from which he sprang to toy with his victims with that lack of mercy which would have ashamed Judge Jeffries.

It was a vast hall which seated a vast audience. The places in the galleries were occupied by the diplomats and their wives. The stage held and housed the main features of the trial. In the centre, enthroned in an elaborate high chair, sat Vyshinsky. On lesser chairs, one on each side of him, sat his assessors. Before them a fine table. In front of the judges sat the clerical officers of the court. There was no clerk such as is found in an English court of law. There were many stenographers. To the left of the judge, near the edge of the stage, sat Krylenko and his assistant attorney. On the opposite side, as a counter-balance to the decor, sat the two counsellors acting for the accused. Along the wall, behind these defence counsel – though what they defended has never been made plain to me – was the dock, under guards with fixed bayonets.

The three judges did not appear until the prisoners were safely housed in their dock, poor, bewildered, unhappy men. The court rose when the well-dressed, well-groomed Vyshinsky took his seat. All three lit their cigarettes when the reading of the charge was begun. Three clerks undertook this job in relays of ten or fifteen minutes' duration. They read on and on, and interminably on. They did not reach the end until the night had almost worn to its close and the crowd had grown miserable. Finished at long last, Vyshinsky asked each in turn how he pleaded, and each replied that he was not guilty. This over, the cigarettes were stubbed and the judges rose and departed. The prisoners were taken away under the same guard. The great hub-bub arose as the crowd streamed away.

The trial was conducted in two sessions each day. The first began at 10.30 and the second at 6 p.m.. The duration of each session was three hours.

There was a room beyond the court area where most of the reporting was finalised and passed to the censor, and where orders for the next day were laid down. Those reporters of known sympathy for the communist press, went regularly to that room to receive undercover information and direction. Everything written for the press had to be scrutinised. A host of typists was available to carry out the typing, always in five copies. Once typed the author did not see his script again. Beyond that room the fate of all copy was sealed or sanctioned. The presiding genius was Bela Kun, a formidable figure who rested sumptuously in Moscow on the proud remembrance of an abortive revolution in Hungary. He was a middle-sized man, officious, brisk of decision, imperative. He it was who gave impressive orders whenever any damaging piece of evidence came out in the trial that implicated any person anywhere within the borders of the Soviet Union. Men and women literally fled from his presence once given their instructions.

In due time he received me into his presence. He spoke in German. Robin Page Arnot accompanied me and did the translating. I suggested a descriptive article for the *New Leader*, then under the editorship of Henry Noel Brailsford and to this he agreed. He told me to write the script under the tutelage of Page Arnot and indicated to me the girl who would prepare it for despatch – to the censor. The article was front paged in the *New Leader*, possibly because I had secured the services of the American cartoonist to do a drawing of Ramzin, the leader of the conspiracy. Maisky read it in Helsinki and wrote me, stating his surprise at my being in the Soviet Union. He said he would have wished me to postpone my visit there.

I attended the trial sedulously. The trial wound on and on. The morning session was generally humdrum, as if the big things were reserved for the night session when the workers could sit back and listen in their homes. The audience was changed at every session. Tickets of admission were obtained through the channels of the Party or the trade union. It was not until the buzz of excitement and comment had died down resulting from the identifications of the prisoners, that the court room came to orderly auditory conditions.

Soviet trials were carried on by confrontation. Should a prisoner implicate or even mention a fellow prisoner under cross examination, that prisoner was immediately brought forward and made to affirm, or reject, or dispute the tendered evidence. Should he, in his defence, and quite unhelped by his counsel, implicate another prisoner, he, too, was brought to stand and submit himself to the same process. I saw four, sometimes five miserable prisoners arguing and gesticulating at the stand, and always much to the sardonic amusement of Krylenko.

It was indeed a most strange affair. All through its long process, which spilled over into the second week, not one interjection was made by either of the two defending counsel. All they did was to sit down at their table and remain as immobile as stuffed dolls. Not once did they offer any protest, or intervene to help or instruct their clients; nor did they go to the dock in order to give guidance or hold any conversation with the prisoners. It was an affair in which no one addressed the accused men except Krylenko or his assistant. Throughout the process Vyshinsky maintained an abstracted stance, spruce and upright, unmindful of the men who lingered before him on their lives. Never was judgment more foregone, more fugitive and inevitable, and more pitiless.

There was that moment when an officer led into the court a witness, one of the few brought in from outside. We had been apprised of the fact that he was to appear, and that he would come from a distant prison camp to which he had been condemned some years previously. He proved to be a little man, tired, worn and naked to the further condemnation of his peers for his acts, unkempt, doing his best to savour his own moment of freedom. He was brought into court through the centre of the packed assembly. I think that he savoured their hostility. As he passed down the gangway he broke into a trot in his eagerness to get to the witness stand, almost stumbling against Krylenko.

He waited almost breathlessly for Krylenko's first question. He was not sworn. He was addressed by his name. He spoke garrulously in answer to each question that was put to him. In the end Krylenko spoke to the officer in a tone of awful contempt. 'Take the fool away,' he said.

The day eventually arrived when Krylenko was called upon to make his summation of the evidence and utter his demands. It was anticipated that it would be a tour-de-force, and so it proved. It was one such as the Soviet courts had not known. The spirit of Dostoevsky's magistrate did not hover over that court. That Krylenko had some pity in his make-up could be assumed whenever he took apart the evidence of the old, almost blind, tottering Fedotov. Perhaps he had the idea that the old man would not bow to the sentence he would be given.

There had been that moment when he rasped out at the poor old man: 'Tell us. Tell us, please. Did you believe that the interventionists would help you to overthrow the Soviet power merely out of their charity? That they would have no motive other than that?' In his speech he recalled that dreadful moment, when the poor old man shaded his eyes against the arc light and said, 'Such was my belief at first.'

I can still hear his shriek. 'At first! At first! But after?'

And then that fateful confession: 'Subsequently I realised that either Karpov, with whom I had a conversation in Berlin, had deceived me in telling me that the interventionists did not want anything for themselves, or that Ramzin had also deceived me when he told me the same...' He became confused.'...or perhaps Ramzin and Karpov had themselves been deceived...or that,...later...they had both been deceived by the interventionists...'

And that bitter smile that spread across the prosecutor's face when he said, rather gently: 'Very well, accused Fedotov. Very well. Let us dismiss the question of who deceived whom, shall we? Or whether you were deceived by Karpov and Ramzin, or they by the interventionists. Let us dismiss it as irrelevant, shall we?' And that sneering leaning forward towards the old man and the quiet assertion: 'And shall we just say that you were a fool, shall we?'

And then the silence during which the old fellow bowed to his interlocuter and to his own soul.

There was nothing impressive about Krylenko. He was always clad in khaki, more like a British infantryman of the first world war. Sometimes he wore puttees, and sometimes worsted stockings. The belt of his khaki coat was always untied, and the ends flapped against his hips. He looked a most vicious man. But was he? He took his duties seriously and he carried them out to the moment when Stalin dismissed him and, later, sent him along the same short *via dolorosa* that he had sent so many of his compatriots. Was he without mercy? Most undoubtedly. Was he an orator? Yes, a Russian orator, lacking all the verve and reserve of an Edmund Burke. He did not rant. Was he a showman? He was, precisely. That day on which he delivered his speech and demanded the death penalty for all the prisoners, he was the attorney supreme.

He did not address the court, but his audience, and he made it the instrument upon which he played a fateful tune. He wheedled, he stormed, he made his audience laugh like any politician on the hustings, and he forced them to ejaculate their rage. He swayed his willing host as a wind sways a bed of rushes. They leaned forward, intent upon hearing every word, fearful of missing any of the flavour of the least important sentence. His voice rose almost to a scream when he uttered the names of the chief of the accused, especially Ramzin. It was always a little softer when he mentioned Fedotov, for the old man was pitiful in his own dire distress.

My mind often returns to that trial to recall Fedotov. He sat next to Ramzin, the youngish Ramzin. He was a man who owned his own great span of years as well as a considerable bulk of flesh. He had grown old after a gentle ageing, white of hair, deficient of sight, pitiful beyond degree in his appointment with his shame. He never recovered from the shock of his sentence. I was glad for him when Kola Minski told me that he had committed suicide. How that poor, deluded old man cowered under the blistering indictment which Krylenko hurled at him through a willing audience.

Krylenko reminded me most forcibly of a salesman in the Bigg Market in Newcastle, only he was selling the death he purloined from his own hatred, not a cure for baldness or rheumatism. Poor, strange, deluded Krylenko, the man who loved to climb mountains. Elbrus was his playground until the state he had served so laboriously snatched it away from him…a whole mountain.

'It has been most truly stated by Lenin,' he thundered, 'that our state is already no state, that it has not and cannot have anything in common with the old bourgeois state, that our state is already the transitional form from the State to the Non-State, to the broadest democratic self-government of the toiling masses. And our method of checking up from below constitutes the practical method whereby we shall most speedily and most assuredly frustrate all the wrecking plots of our enemies.'

No, there was no stopping this Krylenko, for he was in full flood. Sitting there and listening, did Vyshinsky catch the ideas streaming from the lips of the public prosecutor which he would later publish as his own? Krylenko demanded the death penalty for all his prisoners. He did not exclude Fedotov. And he justified his demand with words which brought his audience, shrieking, applauding, to its feet.

'There is but one motive by which the Soviet authorities may and should be guided, and by which this proletarian court must be guided, and that is the motive of safety of the Soviet Union, and of rendering the enemies of our land innocuous.'

Towards the end of his speech he became prophetic, more prophetic than I ever thought he could be, more truly prophetic. Pausing as if to draw an immense breath, he rapped out:

'When a new tide is rising, yes, when new clouds are gathering on the horizon, when perhaps in the near future the masses of our people will have to stand up for the defence of our country. At such time it will be necessary to sweep away everything which aided the old order of things.'

I stood, shuddered to the core of my being, all through that ghastly pantomime until the little man resumed his seat, and then I went out of that court room deeply humiliated, leaving the crowd to roar its own approval.

During the last week of the trial there was a massive parade of people through the streets of Moscow demanding death for the traitors. The night on which the parade was held was cold and soggy. The snow was not fully hardened for the winter. All roads that were open led to and beyond the Dom Soyusov, the scene of the trial. I left my hotel intending, if possible, to make my way to the trial without joining the slow column of marchers. As I walked I heard a band approaching which was playing a slow march such as that which we miners had our colliery band play when we escorted the corpse of one of our comrades who had met his death in the pit, to the cemetery. I waited upon the approach of the marchers with some interest, although it was very cold.

Above the noise of the instruments I could hear, as they approached, the wailings of the mourners. I moved to a street lamp to find out as much as I could about this strange intrusion upon the vast march of protest that was invading the quiet night of the city.

The band preceded a contraption unlike any hearse I had ever seen. It had almost a fret work character. On the open platform lay the open coffin. The head of the corpse was raised so that all who cared could view it as it passed. It was the head of a young man. A screaming girl, roughly supported and escorted by two young men, was obviously the widow. I was torn between two impulses, whether to go on to the trial or follow the cortège. I still regret my choice, which was to attend at the court of Krylenko. I found my usual way blocked by soldiers. Beyond the street guard the horses stamped their disapprovals of the night. The officer asked me the reason for my wanting to walk along a street which had been closed for the purpose of controlling the parade. The officer had a smattering of English, and to him I showed my *mandat* for the trial.

'Anglichanin?' he asked as he handed me back my pass.

'Yes, I am,' I said.

'You speak the Russian?' he asked.

'Orchen ploxo,' I told him, at which he and his squad laughed as if they had heard a joke.

They passed me through the barrier.

I underwent the same pantomime some four times before I arrived at the venue of the trial.

Inside, the journalists were estimating the numbers of the marchers. When one suggested half a million there was a loud protest. Later, when the figure was given officially as three million not one of them demurred.

The trial did not end with the speech of the prosecutor.

The time had come at last to the two silent defence counsellors. I watched them with interest. They bowed to the court. They almost apologised to the court. They spoke at some length. Nobody troubled to translate their speeches. What did it matter, anyway?

Then came the turns of the prisoners to make their pleas for mercy. Ramzin spoke at some length. Others spoke quietly. Old man Fedotov stumbled in his speech over his tears and the officer of the guard led him back to his seat, gently, as one leads a child. All reflected on their misdeeds. Each man must have felt servile as he returned to the dock.

The prisoners were led away. The judges had to consider their verdict.

Next night the court gathered for the last time.

Joe Fineberg explained to me that the judgement would have to be given in accordance with the criminal code in every one of its appropriate details. It would be typed and Vyshinsky would read from that. He would not make any comment on the trial. He prophesied that we would have to wait a considerable time before sentences were declared.

Midnight boomed over the quiet city.

It was after one a.m. before the prisoners were brought into the court room. Krylenko and his comrade emerged, as did the two defence counsel. When all was set the court rose, and Vyshinsky and his two assessors took their places, but did not sit down.

When all was quiet Vyshinsky began to read from the papers he held in his hands. He read on and on, without pause. The court stood upright, and the second hour began to spill out its long minutes. On and on went the clipped, meticulous voice.

The audience gasped with relief when he intimated that he would now pronounce sentence in accordance with the decision of the court. He paused before he sentenced Ramzin to death.

We all stood while he sentenced the main figures to death. Compassion came to two, the compassion of long and servile hours.

A cheer broke out, only to be hushed.

The prisoners were guided away, stunned and affrighted, like all who have received the doom of death.

Outside the night was viciously cold. We walked into it and stumbled through it.

As I walked along the long road at the side of the Red Square my soul was as cold and as dense as the stones upon which I walked. I was alone. The Americans had gone on into their own silence. I stood opposite the Lenin Mausoleum and gazed upon the scene. The great red wall bounded up and about the sleeping Kremlin, comforting in its own stony silence the famous dead sleeping within it near its base. The mausoleum reflected the light that enveloped the tower above the gateway. All was red and dull. The five pointed star was almost pricked out in white light. Beyond, one of the churches raised itself almost on tip toe to look over the wall and upon the city now lying silent in its own agonies and its own slumbers. At the far end of the square St Basil loitered in its own incredible magnificence, unmindful of any terror of the human soul, unaware that it had witnessed over vast stretches of time the barbaric acts and scenes, and of the fact that it still heightened the beauty that somehow clad the whole city.

The cold was intense. The snow had fallen, and it was freezing. The air stung my face with the points of many needles. Unmindful, I stood and looked into my own being. I had passed through a tremendous experience. I wondered why fate, or luck, or fortune had lifted me out of the desecrated bowels of the old earth below far away Durham, and set me down in this unimaginable Moscow. Why? To Moscow, with its millions of faces, with its seeming contempt for the necessities of correct human judgment. I seemed to be transfixed, bewildered, thrust beyond astonishment. I had been now almost three months in Russia and I had been shown precisely nothing that could have liberated me from my own nagging doubts. Was it all real? Had we all acted like rational human beings when we had watched the agonies and the distraits of those now condemned men? I was a stranger in a world beyond my own belief. But where was I?

I felt terribly cold.

I walked past the cathedral of St Basil and left it standing on its own frozen site to dream on into the future.

I was still cold long after I got into my bed.

Chapter Twenty-Three

The man from Intourist brought me my tickets for the journey back to England, and these, I found, routed me through Warsaw, Berlin, Paris and Calais to London. I asked him why they had not included Rome in my itinerary, but he failed to appreciate my joke. I told him that I did not look forward to a long overland journey and if it were at all possible I would prefer to return the way I had come. He went away and came back with the information that the last ship which would depart from Leningrad would be leaving in three days' time, and that if I joined the ship, the SS Soviet, I would be able to travel supercargo. He gave me a soft class ticket from Moscow to Leningrad.

I spent my last evening in Moscow in the home of Mikhail Zenkevitch and all his family, which seemed to include a goodly amount of family relations who were sharing his space. The next evening Mark Vollosov escorted me to the station and saw me safely into a soft class cabin, which I had to share with an American engineer, his wife and his daughter, and a huge dog. It was an interesting journey, for the engineer had many caustic criticisms to make of his late employers. Passenger trains between the two capital cities in those days only ran at night. There was none of the romance of Anna Karenina on that train. We were all soon asleep, even the huge dog. Arrived in Leningrad I was met by my old guide, and she took me to the Hotel Europa, which had by then changed over to Winter accommodation.

The weather was extraordinarily cold. On the barometers outside the hotel the three types, Remur, Centigrade and Fahrenheit stood very low on each scale, and offered their own individual readings, which perplexed my guide. The entire city had taken on its initial coating of ice, and this was thick and slippery. Logistics were accordingly much disturbed. All things seemed to shiver.

The vessel would not be ready to sail for more than three days. I was not sorry, for this gave me a chance to see more of the city. Under instructions I set off to buy a fur hat, but I might as well have saved myself the task. There were no fur hats in Leningrad for sale. I took a chance to visit Detskoi Selo, the country palaces of the Tsars, but after that I refused further rubber-necking and stayed in the hotel. I shall never be so cold as I was on that day. We drove in a droshky many miles from some wayside station to the palaces and we drove the same number of miles back to the station in the same droshky. Since then I have always pitied the fictional characters in Russian literature who made droshky journeys in the depth of winter. The Russians must be superhuman to stand the rigours of such cold.

The great palace of the Empress Catherine was open and I was conducted over it in the conditions of deep freeze in a refrigeration plant. To say that it was bitterly cold is to praise the place. The old crone who let us in made us put on overshoes of felt. I blessed her for them. We saw all the rooms and all the expensive decor. It was coldest in the ballroom, for the place was vast. The ceiling was painted after the fashion of rooms with ceiling paintings. The passage along which we walked reached from end to end of the building, and each room led off to that passage. The dwellers in that place must have been of heroic mould.

The more modern establishment of the last Tsar was open, and, luckily heated. There was nothing one could wish to see other than the elaborate bath and the fly whisk of the empress which lay on her table. And yet I lingered, fearful of the ride back to the station. It proved to be the most wearisome and the coldest journey on earth. Sitting in that ambling droshky I felt that my ears might fall off. As for my toes…

I did not see Dostoevsky's grave. That is my one regret.

When we arrived on the frozen dock at night the ship was fully illuminated. The race was against the freeze-up. They appeared to be taking aboard a cargo of carpets and textiles. Why, I do not know. After a long wait inside the taxi and in the crushing cold I was taken aboard the little vessel. She was of a thousand tons burthen.

Inside the vessel it was warm. The sudden change in temperature made me feel a little unsure of myself. The immigration authorities, who appeared to be present in force, waited until I had thawed out. They were all excessively uniformed gentlemen. The one who searched my baggage did it with great care.

I have little recollection of the answers I gave to their questions. Their main concern was to know if I had any Russian money in my possession. They carefully counted the roubles which I exposed and filled in the requisite documents.

The chief officer handed me a receipt for the money. 'You must take this document to the Moscow Narodny Bank in Moorgate, London,' he told me, 'and you will be refunded in valuta.'

I sincerely believe that the man believed what he was saying. I need not have troubled even to make the journey from Kennington to Moorgate. The clerk to whom I spoke merely asked me if I was trying to perpetrate a joke.

I signed all their papers. I said good-bye to my guide. An old man came and escorted me to my cabin. Later he bought me an exquisite glass of tea and left me to get into bed. I found a copy of Dickens' *Pickwick Papers*. I enjoyed reading it again. I continued to read it at the height of the storm.

The steward took me under his care for the rest of the voyage. The next morning he brought me tea and told me that I would take my meals with the Kapitan. I went up to the saloon and breakfasted alone.

After breakfast the ship cast off and the engines began to throb. I went out on deck to see what was happening. The cold almost choked me. I stayed in the lee of some structure to watch the amazing sights. The harbour was one dense sheet of ice. It clung to the superstructures of the vessel in icicles reaching almost to the deck from a thickness of a man's body to a long point. The ropes were encased in ice. The deck was a sheet of thick ice. The vessel was held upon a great waste of ice. What interested me was that we were actually moving. I went forward and discovered that we were following an icebreaker. I lost all sense of cold as I watched that powerful vessel force a passage through that tranquil mass of white. There came movement forward, then a pause, a tremendous shuddering of the vessel and then a loud crack as the ice broke under the enormous force exerted upon it, which made the fractures speed ahead through the massed ice and peter out beyond the zone of the force. The powerful engines broke the track through the ice to the next point of force, and our little vessel followed as foal might her dam.

Progress was slow and deliberate. Our vessel kept close in the wake of the ice-breaker. As the morning wore on progress became easier, and there came a moment when the vessel sheared aside, gave a loud roar of farewell and left us to go our own way into the Gulf of Finland. Leningrad fell astern like a beautiful ghost that had strayed into a white sea.

Had I known what awaited me I would have taken the long journey across Europe to England. Here I was, supercargo on a small vessel which was moving into a fearful storm, which did not abate for almost three days. The waves tossed us about as easily as any piece of flotsam. We toiled over mountainous waves and tumbled into troughs of the most fearsome depths. The engines raced at speed until the propeller found the water again. The noise of the storm excluded all things. During that time I did not see the skipper, for he did not leave his bridge. There was one whole day when I did not leave my bunk, much to the distress of the old man who was mightily pleased when I accepted a glass of tea.

'Kooshite, tovarish?' he almost pleaded. When I shook my head he hung his and departed.

Eventually the storm abated, and there came a meal when I made the acquaintance of the captain. He looked utterly worn out, big and robust as he was. I still hold him in my memory and admire him.

During that meal he said to me. 'Crick-ett…kak etta?'

I was surprised.

He smiled and went on with his meal.

A little later he said another word which interested me. It was 'Douglass.'

I remained mystified until we got to Kiel. The man who hawked his dirty postcards through the passing ships told me that they had not expected a small vessel like the *Soviet* to get through the storm. 'The Finnish vessel sank with all hands,' he went on. 'There was an English cricketer aboard, called Douglass.'

'You mean J.W.H.T. Douglas?' I asked incredulously.

'Might be him,' said the man.

So that was it. Poor Johnny-Won't-Hit-today was drowned. What a fate! How often I had watched him play at the Oval.

The last of the ice disappeared from the superstructure of the vessel as we crossed the North Sea. We docked at Hull late on a Saturday evening. I left the vessel the next evening and caught the train to King's Cross.

It was bitterly cold.

Back in London, dreary, unfriendly London I emptied my pockets into the palm of a taximan, a few shillings and a few coppers. He reckoned it all up and took me to the Elephant and Castle, and dropped me. I had a suitcase and a folio of reproductions of some of the famous pictures in Russia which had been given to me by the manager of Moscow Kniga. I walked heavily along Newington Butts and up Kennington Park Road. I reached the square and came to my own door.

Phyl opened the door in response to my knock. She was half asleep. Tom, my brother, heard the commotion and joined us in the kitchen. We talked while the kettle came to the boil. We had a nice cup of tea and then went to bed.

The morning came. Phyl and Tom went off to work. And I was back.

There was nothing I could do but go down to Walworth Road Employment Exchange and make an application for unemployment benefit. Nothing had changed during my absence, except that the long snakes of men stretching from the usual parts of the counter had grown longer. Tired and bored clerks dealt with each man in turn. Insurance card in hand the clerk went to the files, withdrew my claim, and came back to me at the counter. Armed at last with my U.I. 40, my little yellow card, I made my way back home and sat down to think.

One particular morning I crossed Lambeth Bridge and went down the slope into the gardens, there to walk to my chosen point where I could gaze upon Rodin's *Six Burghers of Calais*, that most impressive, and at that time the worst-sited piece of sculpture in all England. My trance was broken when a voice spoke to me.

'Haven't I seen you in Princes Square?' I heard it say.

He was older and a little taller than myself, middle aged, a man without a troubled muscle, more like a bird than a man, flooded with the moods and the manners of a Glaswegian.

'You may have,' I returned. 'I live there.'

'That's why I asked,' he said. 'I've missed you. My name is Clark, John S. Clark. I'm a member of parliament. I have a couple of rooms in Princes Square. Why haven't I seen you all these weeks?'

'But isn't Parliament in recess?' I countered.

'It is,' he replied. 'But London is so full of opportunities to make money, I just couldn't tear myself away. I'll be up there for the New Year, of course. But you haven't answered my question?'

'As a matter of fact, I have just got back from Russia,' I said.

'You have! Now isn't that strange!' He almost pulled me to a nearby chair. 'Sit down,' he cried 'Sit down. Leningrad?'

I nodded. 'I went to Kharkov...'

'The Conference. Are you a writer?'

'Couple of novels,' I confessed.

'I write, too,' he said. He laughed swiftly. 'You'll be like us all,' he went on. 'You'll have to live a lot of your stuff down. Do you know that Ramsay MacDonald reviewed a book of poems I once put out...favourably? It took me some time to get over the shock. Know the book, a wee red one?'

'I treasure it,' I told him.

How we laughed. We became friends from that moment to that one when he left London to fight a Glasgow seat, and lost. I never met him again.

'I was in Russia shortly after the revolution,' he told me. 'I met Lenin often. I have quite a few of the notes he slipped over to me when he was listening to a debate and getting ready to reply. I was with Willie Gallagher. Now I am a member of parliament.' He stood up. 'Look at me,' he said, 'the permanent pair for Nancy Astor. I have to go and ask the whip if I am paired.'

The last I heard of John S. was on a much publicised fire in Glasgow when a lion was trapped. He went into the beast's cage and soothed it until the firemen helped him to get it out to safety. It made a big story in the press.

Life was a cheerless affair. I made my usual journeys to Bob's office and helped him to put *The Worker* to bed. It was interesting working on the stone, shaping the pages and presenting the paper to its rapidly diminishing readership. It was becoming obvious that the trade union movement was slipping beyond the aid of the Minority Movement. Energy went out of its bones when the electorate almost denuded the Labour Party of its membership in the House of Commons. In my own county Jack Lawson and Joe Batey were returned in the mining strongholds. Ben Spoor managed to keep his seat. Even Will Lawther was cast out of the Barnard Castle seat, and for the only time in his life found himself actually unemployed. Not that unemployment was unknown to him. He never did much work at all!

There was nothing for us to do but sit and wait for the end.

It was a sad experience for any person to undergo. There was that occasion when I revisted Hunwick. The contrast with the village I had always known was unbelievably striking. It was shattering. The chapel at which my forebears had worshipped during those long decades when coal was king, was now a rejected, unkempt, unminded thing. Many of the men I had known still survived. The once invincible members of the army of Christ were now desolate and threadbare specimens of mankind, condemned to live out their lives as human scare-crows in a rootless misery. Rough Lea Colliery had been closed for years. All the joys of their religious endeavours had been pared away and consumed at their firesides which lacked fuel. It was deeply pitiful to meet them and listen to the sad stories that accompanied their disillusionments. These men had exca-vated coal from its most pitifully circumscribed fastnesses in order to sustain themselves in order to experience all the pleasures of rendering their thanks to God for the privilege of being able to work.

It is excruciating for me to remember them in their power-drained flesh.

Chapter Twenty-Four

There were two reasons why I was able to join the staff of Arcos Ltd. In the first place I was invited to do so by a member of the Russian Trade Delegation, and in the second, because I had gone to Seaham Harbour to assist Harry Pollitt in his hopeless contest with Ramsay MacDonald in the 1930 general election. He it was who overrode all the objections to my being employed by the 'bunch in King Street' when they came, as was their right, to vet those who were to be employed in the Russian organisations.

When the election, which decimated the parliamentary Labour Party, took place, I was unemployed. The telegram from Pollitt came out of the blue, and I went North. I wanted to see the old county again. I deeply resented the betrayal of the party, and I was most anxious to find out how antagonised the mining proletariat could be. I soon found out. At the first meeting I addressed on some square in Seaham, I very soon realised that the name of Ramsay MacDonald was still held in reverence.

As we plunged into the constituency to Dawdon, Horden and the sites of the deep mines, it soon became clear that our quest was hopeless. Despite all the help which Tom Mann and the luminaries of Covent Garden lavished on the candidate, all the votes which Pollitt collected were not worth the counting. The political fraility of the Labour Party was fully exposed in that pre-Nazi period. It remains exposed.

In Arcos I worked with a couple of delightful Russians in the statistics department. All the figures of the trade between the United Kingdom and the USSR were there reduced to percentages and made into pretty little graphs for the edification of the heads of departments. There were many departments from timber and matches to shipping and oil. It was interesting work, the salary was good, and I was quite happy. The amenities of the offices were quite good. The cafe and the co-operative in the basement of the East Wing of Bush

House were at the disposal of all the staff. The hours, too, were reasonable. Overtime payment was a thing unknown.

About a year later I was called into some office in the Trade Delegation, and there I was introduced to a young Russian who had been transferred from Intourist, New York to the office of the firm in Bush House. His name was Gortchakoff. During our conversation he asked me if I had ever had any experience in advertising. I did my best to assure him that I had not had any such experience. For some reason, Gortchakoff required an affirmative answer to his question, which was: would I undertake the duties of advertisement manager for the London office? Under pressure, I acceded to his request, and in a couple of days I was installed in a small office in Intourist.

Luckily for me all the advertising done under auspices of the Trade Delegation had to pass through an advertising agency that was controlled by an Anglo-Russian, Dr Louis Segal. The ostensible purpose of the agency was to cream off the ten percent agency fees. The chief executant realised that I was quite raw in the business and was kind enough to instruct me in all the mechanics of advertising and shield me from the snares of the space-sellers. I still feel thankful to her shade, for without her guidance I would not have got into the run of things so easily. Within a short time I was able to deal with the bland representatives who crowded upon me as soon as it became known that I had money to buy space.

Gortchakoff was by no means a helpful man. He was withdrawn and unhappy. His marriage was not wrecked; it was abandoned. His glances were always cast over his shoulder. Suspicious, temperamental and sulky, he travelled his own way to the execution shed, poor fellow.

A decision had been made in Moscow to create a popular tour of the European part of Soviet Russia, starting and finishing at Hays Wharf, London Bridge. It was my business to 'put over' the project.

Up to the time of my arrival overland tours were arranged in conjunction with Thomas Cook and Sons Ltd, who had a branch office a few doors down the Aldwych. Six motor vessels had been put into service on the direct London/Leningrad run, with a fortnightly diversion to Hamburg. All the ships were of the same burthen and looked as if they had come out of the same mould. Three classes of travel were offered. A full load of passengers was a hundred and thirty, about eighty of which were tourist. Prior to this the business done by the office was confined to the passing of American technicians through London, and the arranging of comprehensive tours for the very important members of the Parliamentary Labour Party.

The plan was to offer cheap tours to the travelling public: a thirteen day trip to Leningrad and back with five days sight seeing in the city at £17 inclusive, a more popular tour of twenty-one days which extended the sight-seeing to Moscow, at £24, and a longer trip of three weeks in Russia which included a trip down the Volga and a rail itinerary through the Don country to Kiev, and back to Leningrad at £32.

Once I had organised a comprehensive advertisement scheme scattered over most of the English press which would accept my advertisement – there were many who would not – the popularity of these tours became manifest, and we began to do a large business with the travelling public. Every Saturday one or other of the six vessels left Hays Wharf with a full load of enthusiastic passengers. In addition, our overland business was increased when it became possible for tours to pass through Belo-Ostrov and over the Polish border. We did not worry about the financing of these extraordinarily cheap tours. All we had to worry about was to meet the insatiable demand of the Moscow office for valuta. We left it to the toiling Russians to share their food with the crowds which went holiday-making among the cement and derricks of socialist construction.

It interested me to come into such close contact with those ordinary people who could afford to pay so much for a holiday, young, eager people mostly, products of the inter-war years, who had not come into contact with the ravages made by economic depression, school teachers, men and women with excellently remunerative jobs, girls from desks which loaned the affluence, and folk with money to spend. All the while I kept in touch with Jos Mackey and Bill Blyton, who were hewing coal in Harton colliery, and glad to carry home something near to two pounds a week wages. I wondered often how and why it had all happened while it was my business to excite people about making holiday in Soviet Russia.

In the beginning of 1933 Gortchakoff was recalled to Moscow. Before he went away the man who was to supersede him took over his office. Poor Gortchakoff! He was a man who was always hedged about by enormous fears. He suspected all men while he cowered before all bureaucrats. I realised that something had gone wrong for him some weeks before he took me into his confidence and told me that he was returning to Moscow, and that a Mr Scheinmann was taking over. He warned me to be careful with the new man. He succeeded in making me somewhat apprehensive. I had reason to be anxious, for Phyllis had become pregnant.

It was obvious why Gortchakoff had lost his job. He had been unable to make contact with the big people in Westminster. He had shown himself to be a minnow in a big pool wherein swam many large fishes. He failed miserably with one of the leaders of the Labour Party, who had come to grief in the great election fiasco. That gentleman had been given a long, free trip to the Soviet Union. Gortchakoff made the mistake of informing the good socialist that the trip was for so many days, travel-free, at five pounds ten shillings per day. What happened in Russia we did not learn, but the great politician arrived back in London with five days of unexpired holiday-making. To add to his misdeeds, Gortchakoff was a little more than emphatic when stating his refusal to make a refund of twenty-seven pounds to the political gentleman. He might have been more diplomatic when he refused an application which ought not to have been made.

With the deepening of the depression, and especially after the Joynson-Hicks episode in high politics succeeded in damaging Anglo-Soviet trade, the tourist business began to fall off. Scheinmann, who had been inveigled into the organisation, took charge of the advertising fund. Very soon he was the office.

We were all interested in Aaron Scheinmann. He was a man about whom his compatriots whispered. When he did arrive he proved to be a very big man in all ways. He was tall and broad, a well-fed man, slow of movement and ponderous of decision. He was well-dressed after a German-Dutch style. His shoulders were broad and his belly copious. His head was massive. Every Monday morning he paid a visit to his barber and had his head completely shaved. Every hair of his head was removed. His excessive balding was uncompromisingly completed by the razor. His beard, eyebrows and all protruding hair were cut as close as the razor could take them. When he left the barber's shop he was always in danger of catching his death of cold. We got over the first shock, and every subsequent Monday morning was accepted with equanimity by all members of the staff.

What the barber really did was to sharpen the glitter of his eyes as well as to discover the track made by a bullet across the great dome of his head.

Aaron Sheinmann was one of the most remarkable men I have known. As a linguist he was superb. He seemed to be able to converse in most of the European languages. There was one occasion when I stood near him as he discussed a tour with a small group of Chinamen in their own language. He was informed on most topics of the day. He possessed a sense of humour that is rarely granted to ordinary Russians. He was always courteous, and almost generally happy. Whenever he was annoyed the staff knew how to leave him alone.

He was of the time and the order of the world of Lenin. He fought in Helsinki on the side of the Bolsheviks, and when that country dragged itself out of the orbit of the Soviets he crossed into Leningrad. He it was who took over the catastrophic rouble and shaped it into the chervonetz. The notes which he issued all bore for many years his own characteristic signature, which began with three or four legible Russian letters and ended with a finely drawn scribble. He piloted the finances of his country through the scissors crisis, leaving all the argument to the politicians. He often went abroad to do business with foreign governments. While he was in London his eldest son died. And there came a time when he did not return to Russia.

The Soviet authorities were at all times anxious to secure the services of Scheinmann. Years after his defection they discovered him carrying on his own business in Holland. As a first step in cajoling him back to Russia, they offered him the job in Intourist. This has always puzzled me. Why did he accept so menial a job? He knew, for he told me, that they were anxious that he should return to Moscow. He smiled when I once asked him if it was his intention to go back. 'No,' he said. 'I will let Prince Mirsky go and find out.'

In a less Stalinised Soviet Russia he might have gone back, and had he done so most certainly would have contrived to bring some kind of political sanity into that deprived world. He never hid his cynicism when he discussed his country. He was a strange man. The first thing he asked me to do was to find the grave of the boy they buried in Kensal Green cemetery. When it was located he took his wife and son to stand by the pitiful little mound, and to weep. Aaron Sheinmann was possessed of a deeply dug soul.

Under Scheinmann the office ran smoothly. For a Russian businessman he was unique. He was the most apt diplomat I ever met. During his early months in the office the Soviet government offered to provide passports to their nationals if they could persuade their relations abroad to meet the cost in the foreign currency. The scheme was advertised and some business was transacted. A deposit of £200 had first to be made and the matter was then referred to Moscow. If the passport was granted the rest of the money had to be paid before it could be issued. For a person who wished to leave the USSR permanently the cost of the passport was £500. The lesser figure of £250 had to be paid for a period of time up to six months. Should the passport be refused, the deposited sum was returned less ten percent.

Scheinmann dealt with all this business himself. The applications came in the main from Jewish persons. There was an old rabbi who paid his deposit on three occasions for his son who was living in Odessa. He gave up his quest in the end. I pitied the poor old man and I admired the manner in which Scheinmann dealt with him. When the poor old man took his leave on the last occasion, he and Scheinmann embraced each other as friends.

He left all the business of the office to his staff. He removed any member peremptorily when the occasion rose. He demanded fulfilment of all tasks. Within the terms of Arcos employment codes he was generous. He had more smiles than frowns in his general make-up. I still regard him as a man it was my privilege to know.

I was at the counter dealing with Dmitri Shostakovitch's brother, an engineer who was returning to his native land from Detroit, when Scheinmann came into the office. On seeing him, the young man said to me: 'Is that Scheinmann?' When I told him that it was he pondered for quite a while. Then he said to me: 'Now I *have* seen him.'

Coincidental with the shooting of Zinoviev and Kamenev there was a grave casting out of the unsecured personnel in the Russian offices. The OGPU moved relentlessly. All without clearance were sacked. Scheinmann was one of them. I lost sight of the great man. In all probability he and his family were snatched up by the Nazis and found their ways into Belsen. I know that after leaving Intourist he went back to the Low Countries.

Scheinmann did a splendid job for his erstwhile employers. He was able to meet all the great people of London and converse with them after their own fashion. In the capitalist world he could not have prevented himself becoming a millionaire. I have a feeling that Malcolm Muggeridge will forgive me when I say that Aaron Scheinmann held him in high esteem.

When Muggeridge first came into the office to discuss a trip to Moscow he was by no means the man who later strutted across the television screen. I recall him as a tall, well-groomed, good-looking and eager young man. I interviewed him. He told me that he was making the trip on his own and that when he got there he hoped to become the correspondent for the *Manchester Guardian*. In other words he was going to walk out on a limb. He waited while I went to see Scheinmann.

'Do you suggest that I should see him?' he asked me.

'Yes,' I replied. 'I think you should.'

'I'll go and see him myself,' he said.

Scheinmann laid his great body across the counter and gave the young man a solid stare. Then he raised himself up and opened the counter door. 'I think you had better come into my office,' he said.

When the young man came out of the office he nodded his thanks to me. 'Who is he?' he asked. I told him and he went away.

That was the first of the many visits he paid to Intourist.

Scheinmann received him with all his graciousness whenever the young man came in. He arranged the visit to Moscow and sent him on his way. From that moment he kept his eye on Malcolm Muggeridge. He made a point of buying all the books the young man published at that time, and, what is more, he thought highly of them. When he returned from Moscow he called upon the old man. Their joint happiness was obvious to us all.

Mr Muggeridge, the father of Malcolm, came into the office. I interviewed him. I forget the details of his visit. He was no longer a member of parliament. We talked about his son. I asked him if he thought that Malcolm would follow him into the Labour Party.

'Malcolm!' he said, smiling. 'How should I know what he will do? He will go his own way despite all the advice I might give him.'

So the days passed by.

For some time the staff in the office had dealt with Lord Passfield on the question of a deep incursion he and his wife wished to make into the Soviet Union. They told us that they were at work on a book, so we understood that some importance was attached to their proposal by the gentlemen in the Trade Delegation. The rotund little man of the gleaming spectacles and sharp-pointed beard became one of our constant callers. I had known Sidney Webb from the day when he took over the representation of Seaham. For often he came to South Shields to speak at our meetings at election times. Indeed, we never knew when he might pop in of a winter's night at the Marsden Miners' Hall, clad in his dark ulster. A splendid man to know among the great figures of his generation of politicians.

The old couple travelled on their last journey to the Soviet Union in one of the boats, probably for the pleasure of the trip, but more probably because it cut their expenses down.

It surprised us in the office when we found a postcard from Mr George Bernard Shaw among the morning mail, requesting a permit which would admit Mrs Shaw and himself to the boat so that they could see their friends, Lord Passfield and Mrs Sidney Webb, off on their journey. I posted the permit, which I concocted, to the old gentleman.

It happened that there were few tourists sailing on the boat that Saturday afternoon. It was a lovely day when the Shaws arrived on the wharf. The Webbs came down to the gangway to welcome their friends and took them up to their cabin. There was no one to welcome them. The captain remained in his own quarters. None of the Russian captains dined with the passengers as captains do on the great transoceanic liners. The Shaws passed through London and on to the Soviet ship without being noticed by one single journalist. I had informed Vladimir Krivopalov that Shaw was going to the wharf and he made it his business to be there with his camera. He found the quartet on the top deck and asked permission to photograph them. Shaw posed the group himself like the expert he was. I have looked everywhere for the copy Volodya gave me, but without success.

The old people basked in the warm sunshine. There was only a handful of American engineers travelling, none of whom was aware of the great man's identity. Beatrice was her own frail self, overshadowed by Mrs Shaw, a magnificently dressed lady. They sat together talking, woman wise, neither of them leaving their seats. The two men strolled the deck, talking, pointing at the buildings and vessels they saw. At times they laughed, at least Shaw did most of the laughing. Sidney Webb had grins to spare and nods in plenty. The chief steward brought them light refreshment and they sat at a table like ordinary people.

To my surprise, the captain came and paid them his respects, and left them to talk. It was the same captain who had brought every Russian soul aboard his vessel to rigid attention when Litvinoff and his wife came aboard one Saturday afternoon to join the vessel on its trip to Leningrad. What is more that captain kept them standing at attention until Litvinoff and Maisky, and their wives, had disappeared into the ship. Different men; different degrees. The famous four were left to do their own talking. At times, Shaw accepted his wife's reproof or expostulation when he was really witty and had made himself laugh uproariously. Once or twice she shoved his arm away, rather petulantly playful, as women do who are in love, and once or twice he bent over the table and touched her on the cheek, and once he did the same to Mrs Webb.

The pilot came aboard and the ship slipped away from her moorings. The Webbs saw their friends on to the quay and stood on the deck. Both men were bare headed. They waved farewell. Then Shaw took his wife by the arm and led her across the lines to the car.

Vladimir and I walked away together.

I still possess Ilya Ehrenburg's letter written in Russian to Scheinmann asking for a couple of first class to Leningrad. I was interested to meet the writer from Paris. He came on the ship with André Malraux. The photograph I have of them is one taken on the same ship and in the same place on the top deck which was occupied by Shaw and Webb. They came and they went. No one in London noticed them.

The man I remember most distinctly was Henri Barbusse.

It was dusking when the ship disembarked its passengers at Hay's Wharf. As the immigration officials were leaving the chief called me aside and told me he would be glad if I would give an eye to a French couple in the first class…chap called Barbusse. I told him I would be pleased to do so and he hurried away.

The chief steward showed me the cabin. The door was open. Inside an exceedingly tall man was standing watching a weary little woman trying to pack their bags which, apparently, had been searched most thoroughly. Barbusse was almost distraught.

They were transit passengers, and for some reason which I did not understand, they had received instructions to leave the country as soon as possible.

The lady travelling with the great author was not Russian. She spoke the language much better than I did, which was not saying very much. We made some kind of contact. I did all I could to help them repack and finally I saw them off the ship and away from the wharf. I saw them on to a bus which would get them to Westminster. I believe that they were without English or French money, a fault that was guaranteed to stir the ireful suspicions partaking in a disembarkation.

What astounded me was the height of the French author. He was thin and woefully haggard. He looked a man upon whom death was gazing closely. Each time he drew himself up to his full height he seemed to reduce the dimensions of the small cabin. He was formidably bent at the shoulders. All the time I was in his presence he did not speak. He left everything to the harassed little woman who was his companion. Despite all the confusion, anger and anxiety, I felt that I was in the presence of a great personage. He seemed immense in some undefinable way. That he could be kind and generous was obvious. That he had suffered some unreasonable exercise of authority was plain for any stranger to see.

I felt privileged to be in the man's presence, for I knew *Under Fire* backwards. That glorious moment in the trenches when his comrade-in-arms had called out the name, 'Liebknecht', and that lugubrious scene about the egg that so emblazons the novel with the man's huge pity seemed to come starkly into my memory. Barbusse did not know it, but his immediate novel of the war did rest somewhere between us, close enough to cause me to catch my breath. This was the Henri Barbusse that Louis Aragon had almost denounced, almost apostasised.

Not long afterwards Louis Aragon walked into the office. I recognised him before he recognised me. He was the same eager, well-dressed man. 'I never expected to meet you here,' he said to me. 'Where have you been hiding?'

I told him.

'And your books?' he cried. 'Your novels? Surely…'

I merely smiled.

I did not tell him about the publication of *Pod Vlastyu Uglya* in English under the title of *Goaf*, nor did I mention *The Crime of Peter Ropner*, for I was ashamed of the Fortune Press. Failure compels reticence. Perhaps all failure is deserved.

We disposed of the preliminaries. His wife was well. They were staying with her mother, whom I knew was working in the Trade Delegation, as was her sister. My wife, too, was well, and so was our baby daughter. Her name? I told him it was Maril. His eyebrows went up. I then told him that we had stuck the letter 'l' on the end of Mary.

'Magnificent!' he breathed, almost in ecstasy.

Then he flung his bomb. 'I'm out on bail,' he said. 'I am under interdiction all because of that poem I wrote, the one published in *International Literature*.'

I smiled. 'The one about the "fat arsed bottles"?' I interjected.

He nodded. 'That is the one,' he told me. 'It cannot possibly be called a misdemeanour, but I suppose they will get away with it and I will have to pay the penalty.'

'We do not imprison writers for their excesses in this country,' I pointed out.

'Mine was not an excess,' he said. 'It was real proletarian criticism. In this country perhaps your writers are not courageous enough.' He smiled. Aragon always had a lovely smile. 'You see, Harold,' he said, 'French law is more…more expansive. Sometimes it is so stupid that I am grieved…right down here.' He laid his hand on his stomach. 'No, no, I wouldn't try to explain. I haven't got the time.'

We went into a huddle over the table by the window, the huge one which had been the target of early morning raiders on two occasions. He explained to me that if he could get beyond extradition and stay thus over a given period the case against him would lapse, and that was his purpose in coming to London.

'Russia?' I suggested.

He nodded. 'But how can I get there?' he went on. 'If I contacted the Soviet consulate in Paris I would be apprehended immediately'. If he could get to Russia he would have no further problem. His wife, being Russian, would follow him there.

I could see no actual difficulty if he conducted his business in London. He could make an application for a visa in Rosary Gardens, Kensington. All he had to do was fill in a visa form and post it from here. After he had scrutinised the form I suggested he should have a chat with Scheinmann. I left him and went along to Scheinmann's office and asked him if we would care to see Louis Aragon. His face beamed all the way up to the back of his bald crown.

'Aragon!' he cried. 'The French author! Why, of course! Bring him here at once.'

I went back to Louis. 'Scheinmann wishes to see you,' I told him. 'You'd better come and keep me in the clear. Smuggling Frenchmen out of France!'

'Scheinmann,' he mused. 'Not Aaron Scheinmann surely!' He rose to his feet. 'But I thought he was dead,' he muttered.

Both men met in the centre of the office. I left them grasping each other's hands.

The great men of Russia passed through the office of Intourist. There was Pavlov, but he was merely rushed to the embassy. Rochelle Townsend told me that she did the translating when the great man met the scientists at the embassy. She also told me that in answer to a question about Freud and Jung he denounced both great men. And there was Mikhail Sholokhov.

Sholokhov came to London to meet his publishers, Putnam, and collect some of his royalties. Maisky put on an afternoon reception and asked me along, much to the annoyance of Scheinmann, who kept an exacting control over his staff.

'You can go,' he said to me, 'seeing that Maisky wishes you.'

I counted myself as being on the brink of redundancy from that moment, yet I went along to Kensington quite happily, for I wanted to meet the man who had scored so immense a success in the western literary world. I knew Garry Stevens, his translator, and I was glad because of the fame which had come to him, secondhand. Rochelle Townsend was present to act as interpreter. When I got there only a small gathering was present. Rose Macaulay came and had a chat with the Russian writer, and went away.

Sholokhov was not one of those huge Russian cossacks one meets in the presence of Gogol. They must breed small cossacks, too, on the Don country, for Sholokhov was one. He came and sat with Rochelle and myself and together we drank lemon tea. He asked me in Russian – he only spoke that language, I think – if I spoke Russian. I told him that I spoke it very badly, and he assured me that he would rather have me talk bad Russian than the most excellent English. And we all laughed.

When Montagu Slater breezed in upon the Left he was met with open arms, for it was rare for a man to come down from

Oxbridge and attach himself so courageously to what was known as 'the movement'. King Street was most anxious to tack on to the upsurging of popular revulsion which manifested itself when the danger of fascism was seen and recognised. Slater was encouraged to the extent of his being helped to put on a play one Sunday afternoon in a Westminster theatre.

I bought a ticket and found myself sitting next to Ernst Toller. I recall very little of Slater's play. It had a Welsh mining locale for its action, but it was a formless affair in all proletarian conscience. It did not herald the arrival of a librettist for Benjamin Britten. Toller was not impressed, and said so when he shook hands with me at the end of the show. The next time I met Toller was when he came into the Intourist office. He had been invited to Moscow, and he came in to buy a ticket to Leningrad. The fare as I remember it was just over six pounds. He did not recognise me as his companion at the play.

I asked him if he was serious in his intention to go by ship, and I pointed out to him that he would put his personal safety at hazard by boarding a ship which had to make the passage through the Kiel Canal. He could buy a ticket, but we could not guarantee a safe journey. He saw the force of my argument and decided to circumvent the Fatherland.

I did not see him again for some weeks, when he called at the office to inform us that he had left a satchel containing his most valuable papers on a train somewhere between Baku and Samarkand. He said that he did not notice his loss until he was going through the customs.

Scheinmann immediately instituted an enquiry and some two or three weeks later we received word that Toller would be able to recover his satchel from the captain of the m/v Smolny when it arrived at Hays Wharf two or three days later. I got into touch with the German author and arranged for him to meet me at Bush House when we could go to the ship and retrieve his property. He was in a happy mood when he came to the office. After he had had a chat with Scheinmann we set out by bus for London Bridge. It was a lovely, warm night. It was, indeed, an evening to accompany the joy of Ernst Toller, for not only was he going to recover his satchel, but H.G. Wells had actually written to the *New Statesman* and felicitated Toller on the observations he had offered to the paper a week before. As we sat on the crowded bus he insisted upon reading to me passages from Wells' letter, and offering me his opinion on the points which the great man had made. He was as happy as a child. He wanted to know if I had ever met the great man, and when I said that I had not he expressed his sorrow.

'But you know his writings, and appreciate his genius?' he cried out. 'You read him deeply, conclusively?' And then he sat a while. 'And to think that he could spare his time to reply to my observations in a paper like this!' he said. 'Oh! How happy I am!'

We got off the bus and went down under the bridge to Hays Wharf. The ship was tied up out of the way of a Baltic butter boat. Soviet vessels habitually sniffed when in the presence of those from Poland. Kapitan Suzenko, newly shaven as close as Scheinmann, came to the door of his cabin to receive us. The peasant visage of the man, dark, frowning, near pugnacious, made the German pause before taking the proferred hand. The door closed upon us. The valise lay upon a map spread over a table.

'Ah! It has come. Do let me thank you, captain, please,' said Toller.

'You recognise it as your property?' Suzenko asked in English.

'Yes, indeed,' said Toller.

'Then I will hand it to you after you sign this paper,' said the Captain.

Both men signed the paper, but not until the First Mate had been called. He and I witnessed the document. 'And now,' said Suzenko, 'we drink.'

I knew the captain and his drinks quite well. He compounded them himself during the night watch. He kept his current supply of the vile stuff in long bottles, from which he poured liberally. I always did suspect that the basis of the concoction was vodka and tar. One was requested to swallow it by the half pint. When we had torn ourselves free from the convivial company on the Smolny we passed on to the wharf. On the way, Toller remarked that he had not liked the drink very much, and asked me why I had not drunk. Was I one of those teetotallers?

I merely smiled, and I assured him that I had a warm respect for my own stomach.

Schienmann had gone when we got back to the office. As the office had closed, I walked with him to the Strand, where we shook hands and said our good-byes. He was, he said, going to America.

He went to America and to his suicide. Life was not gracious to the author of *Masses and Men*. I often ponder on his fate. There was much that was likeable about him. He was courteous in all his ways. And yet he was not a man to stir deep friendship at the first point of contact. He was lonely. He was outside his own world and embroiled in one which bewildered him and left him to grieve sacrificially for all his fellows. Peace lie upon his ashes.

Scheinmann had more interests in life than his worrying about the lost property of a German author. I do not think that he ever had even the remotest sympathy for any work by Marx. His life held two compartments. In the one he secreted his wife and his little son, and in the other he lived out the tasks of business with an assurance and an aplomb that were startling.

In London he had to build up Intourist and prove to his distant employers that he was still the same intrepid entrepreneur he had always been. He laid his finger unerringly upon every point and aspect of the business. He cracked immense jokes. He never grew angry, but one knew instinctively if anything displeased him. It was astounding that he should be managing an unadventurous travel agency when he had once been the leading banker during the founding and funding of a new civilisation. Why did he accept the post? I knew that he possessed as much sympathy for communism as he had for a dead cat lying in the roadway. Like all Jews he possessed an abundance of irony. At times he was humourously cynical. He rarely mentioned the Soviet government, and yet one could sense his objections to it when in conversation with him. But he would allow no one to speak disparagingly of that government. Once he loudly reproved an irate tourist who spoke offensively to him.

'I do not offer you congratulations, sir, when you praise my government,' he said sternly, 'and so I reprove you when you force me to speak in its defence...unnecessarily. I ask you not to abuse it any longer. Please have a care of my words, for I do not wish to grow angry with you. I request you to leave this office.'

What had the Soviets done to lose such a man? What did they lose when he defected? And why were they tempting him back? Throughout his employment in the office he played 'pussy' with Moscow. Reasons for this came when he spoke to me about Prince Mirsky going back. I recall his smile, that special one which appeared to make his eyes loft above his naked eyebrows.

'I think that he has made a bold mistake,' he said to me. 'Yes, a mistake from which he will not escape.'

Had he cared to do so he could have persuaded Mirsky to stay in England, but he chose to let the tall, proud man have his head.

It was different with Peter Kapitza. He just let that man go.

The office staff had no admiration for Kapitza. As far as we were concerned he was a scientist who worked with a man called Rutherford at the Cavendish and who was a Soviet citizen, and who lived with his wife in Cambridge.

It was his wife whom we heartily disliked. I will not say that we detested her. Whenever she was making her way to Russia the office staff had almost to stand to attention. She filled the place with orders and poisoned the atmosphere with complaints. We all dreaded to see her enter the office. None of us bowed when she took her leave. She was the epitome of the Soviet bourgeoisie, a creature high in the ranks, who trod the creatures of the lesser world under her feet. As for her husband, he was an aloof creature, who trod his own world with a crushing weight of superiority. Undoubtedly he was young; undoubtedly he was brilliant; undoubtedly he could peer down at all his lower contemporaries. He strode his own world like a colossus.

Both were going for a holiday to Russia, an important holiday. Their house in Cambridge had been hermetically sealed. All their immediate goods and chattels had been confined to the care of Anglo-Soviet Shipping, who ran the motor vessels. We all survived the visit of Madame Kapitza, and then we prepared for the advent of Peter.

He came. He admitted himself to the back of the counter and walked majestically to Scheinmann's office. There was no humility about Peter Kapitza. He stayed with Scheinmann, and then the old man accompanied him to the street door. As he came back into the office he bent over me and asked me to accompany him to his office. 'Shut the door,' he said when I had entered. Then he indicated a seat, which I took.

'What I want you to do,' he began, 'is to act implicitly with these instructions. You must stay with the boat until she sails. All the time you must stay near the professor, but without making a nuisance of yourself.' He smiled. When the boat has sailed you will ring me at my home and tell me. Is that all clear?' He waited until I had nodded. Then he went on. 'Mister Kapitza is a most important man, and Mrs Kapitza thinks she is a most important wife.' He paused. 'You have never met Molotov?' he asked me. When I had got over my surprise he said: 'He, too, has a wife. Such a wife!'

He lit a cigarette. He smoked them by the score.

'I want you to see that they both get all they want,' he went on to say. 'You had better consult the chief steward and explain to him that both must be kept happy all the time they are on the boat. After they get off they will not be so happy. The chief steward has his instructions, of course,' he went on, 'but it is better to...to emphasise this importance.' Again he smiled, but this time he leaned towards me. 'You see, he said to me in a low voice, 'they are not coming back.'

I sat, almost mesmerised. I picked up his voice later, which said: 'There is now much important work to do in Russia. When their holiday is over and they begin to make preparations to return to this country they will be told.' He talked softly. His face was lit with a grin. 'Then will come their surprise. They will become happy in time, when they discover that the home which has been prepared for them is an exact replica of the one they lived in in Cambridge...down to the last detail...'

We talked a little while longer, and then I went back to my desk. Later I made the short journey to the wharf and there I carried out my imposition. On the ship I did find myself somewhat compromised. It was publicly known at the time that Rutherford was doing something with the atom. In the interests of the Cavendish adventure, and the exploitation of the research I could have warned the man of his impending severance of his association with Professor Rutherford. But there were difficulties. Apart from the fact that it would have meant the loss of my job, there was the insuperable aloofness of the man as well as his vast assumption which could scarcely bend to acknowledge even a hard won doctorate had I possessed one! And there was his wife. So I held to my duty and stayed until the boat was taken into the stream by the tug.

I went to the telephone and rang Scheinmann. I told him that they had gone. He muttered his thanks and put the phone down.

I have often thought about that episode. If I had warned Kapitza I wonder if he would have left the boat. I am sure that if his wife had been told she would have taken the initiative, and would not have found the act of defection difficult to carry out. Kapitza was too important a figure in the world of emerging physics for anything to happen other than that which did happen. It was his misfortune when he was compelled to remain in his native land, and it was his misfortune when he went back to Russia. I doubt if he ever saw Lord Rutherford again.

It is now known that Rutherford insisted upon the Soviet Government being allowed to purchase all the equipment which Kapitza had designed and worked on in the Cavendish Laboratory, and that when the deal was made he insisted that Professor Cockcroft should supervise the packing of everything and the despatch to Russia. Had it been the fate of Peter Kapitza to remain in England he would have been enrolled in the team which left our shores when all the work at Cavendish was taken to America. Once there, he might have achieved the fame and distinction which was showered upon other scientists. But there is no reason to speculate.

Looking back on that episode I am fully aware of the fact that the part I played in it was small and circumstantial. The life history of the important Russian scientist was, perhaps, purified by what happened in London. It would make an absorbing story. He had to pass through the Lysenko period, which was almost as catastrophic as that of the Stalin madness. He could have perished in either episode. Kapitza is merely a figure of those awful years, years when my own generation was compelled to wait upon the most appalling events and confrontations conjured by men.

As I look back and try to recall those years I find myself trying to relive a social disaster; the induced cataclysm that comes to term within the disrupted strata above the floor of the mine. There was the same ebbing and flowing of the ultimate purpose that led to the culmination, the long roar of the destructive fracturing, the groanings of immense pain and the final devastation of terror which sinks into the deepest awareness of the watcher who is held in thrall until the crescendo has passed into implausible whimperings, dying away into softly gulping sobs like those of a thrashed child.

I did at times wonder if I would be alive when the silence descended upon the nations, just as it always came upon the mine, and if I would be able to watch the dust laying its thick carpet over the mangled earth as it covered up the shame of those who had, unknowingly, encouraged such horrors and intrepid hatreds out of the fastnesses of time beyond barbarity, leaving it all to go by unremembered.

Epilogue

My father died early in May, in the year 1935.

I made the journey by overnight train to Newcastle, and arrived in Ryton in good time to make the remainder of the journey to Blackhill, where he had died in the home of one of my step-sisters.

It was a most beautiful day.

The coffin lay in the front room of a little semi-detached, and about it were gathered some of my father's sisters, none of whom were at all distressed. I found it a distressing experience looking down upon him lying so still and white and clean. Some of our relations had made the journey from Hunwick, men and women I had known and had forgotten. Sarah, my step-mother, kept aloof from the gathering. When the Methodist ministers arrived she left all the obsequies to the family, emerging when it was time to take my brother George's arm and head the cortège.

They bore him into a huge Methodist chapel which was no different from any other chapel in the country, only it was vast and cold, and forbidding. The men from the old pit he had managed at Burnopfield set the coffin down alongside the penitent form, behind which the ministers took their places. We plodded through the ceremony and came to the moment when one of the minister's chose to speak a panegyric on 'our departed brother'. He was something of a psychologist, and I suspect that many of the sentences he uttered he had composed long ago when my father had contrived to create pandemonium at quarter day.

Sarah did not make my father's corpse the gift of one tear. Proudly she walked out of the cemetery. She walked as one might who has bestowed laurels and is to be in receipt of fresh gifts. She had buried two husbands, my father being the least and the kindest.

In the semi-detached we were given refreshment and then we began to depart. Before my brothers and I went to bid her goodbye she took me upstairs to her bedroom where she opened a drawer and took out of it the watch and albert that had been presented to my grandfather in the year 1905. 'Your father said that you were to have this,' she said to me. 'I have respected his wishes.'

I followed her downstairs.

We saw the Hunwick people off and then my brothers and their wives went on their several ways.

And so the chapter was closed.

My father's struggles under the earth were ended, all fifty three years of them. A life time under the lip of the rock, and not a useless lifetime. Coal is the only mineral mined in quantity that glitters with the lives of past ages. I believe that my father enjoyed every one of his struggles with coal, and that he accepted the profession of mining as the one great challenge to his being. He often spoke about 'bonnie coal', but then, coal is never dull, never without life, never without the life it has lived within its own ageless fastnesses. It is so alive that it gives its own voice to its own pains and its own raptures whenever it is dragged out of its own layered imprisonments. It is as if it remembers its forests. The earth weighs upon it with all the enormity of unchaptered time, and yet the earth is incapable of disturbing its impregnable aloofness even when it has re-buried it by forcing the floor of the mine to kiss its roof. It is all part of a monstrous world, and it has always felt the need for men who have dared to brave the monstrous.